Herbert A. Thelen received his undergraduate and masters degrees in chemistry from the University of California. He taught natural science for five years at the University's demonstration school, University High School. Professor Thelen served as an instructor at Oklahoma A & M and at the laboratory school of the University of Chicago. He received his doctoral degree from Chicago in 1944 and is now a professor of education there. During 1960-1961 Professor Thelen will be on a year's leave from Chicago and on the staff of the Center for Advanced Study in the Behavioral Sciences, Palo Alto, California. He is the author of *Dynamics of Groups at Work*.

Education

and the Human Quest

Education

and the
Human Quest

by HERBERT A. THELEN
Professor of Education
University of Chicago

HARPER & BROTHERS
Publishers New York

Contents:
The Course of Inquiry

	Prologue: *Intention*	1
1	Plan: *Predicament and Promise*	4
2	Man: *What Makes Johnny Tick?*	16
3	Knowledge: *The Instinct for the Jugular*	29
4	Society: *The House That Jack Lives In*	54
5	Suppositions: *Four Models for Education*	74
6	Model 1: *Personal Inquiry*	89
7	Social Order: *The Subterranean World of the Group*	113
8	Model 2: *Group Investigation*	138
9	Model 3: *Reflective Action*	160
10	Model 4: *Skill Development*	181
11	Do-It-Yourself: *The Greatest Project*	188
	Epilogue: *Destiny*	211
	Index	221

Education

and the Human Quest

Prologue:
Intention

As judged by our hopes for mental health, social stability, or scientific competition with Russia, our schools are good, indifferent, or bad, depending on how you define your terms. As judged by what could be done if we were to understand and apply modern knowledge to educational problems, all our schools are obsolescent. It is in the latter view that this book is written.

We know a great deal about the nature of man, knowledge, and society; about the dynamics of learning by individuals; about the factors affecting group performance; about intergroup relations and social action; about community improvement. But most of this knowledge has so far made almost no dent at all on educational practices, and, with the present tendency to think that educational problems can be solved with money and organizational changes, the likelihood of any significant improvement is discouragingly slight.

This state of affairs is downright maddening. I don't know whether this book will make a dent either, but one does what one can. What I have done is to essay a nontechnical formulation of Education as an applied branch of social science; this "branch" actually overlaps and draws on parts of most of the social sciences. For such a formulation to pay off in the practical enterprise of guiding educational experiences, it must be interpreted: its practical implications have to be stated. So I have done that, too.

In general, this book only puts in words notions that I have been seeking, gleaning from my betters, and trying out on teachers, social scientists and phenomena for the last fifteen years. Many of the ideas have been put into practice in various community and University of Chicago Projects. The Hyde Park–Kenwood program of citizen action demonstrated the inseparability of education and thoughtful action (1949-   ); the development of the Intensive program for the Preparation of Elementary School teachers (1954-1956) was also a conscious exploration of the principles of Group Investigation; the Workshops in Community Human Relations (1952-1955) contributed ideas about the citizen-participant role of the student in the classroom and school; the Sophomore Project (1957-1958) attempted to find out what would happen if teachers acted as if they believed in inquiry; our present research with the U.S. Office of Education (1958-1960) has turned up a highly practical solution to the problem of selecting students into "teachable" classes. Many of the ideas have appeared in print in various guises, although their present appearance may be somewhat altered by virtue of the overarching pattern and context of my present intentions.

I think our present situation is grave; more, it is immoral. For to act ignorantly when knowledge is available, to deny realities that patently exist and make a genuine difference is the worst crime of civilized man. I am optimistic in the belief that men of good will can move toward a state of grace through hard work, persistence, and study. I hope that this formulation will be stimulating and intriguing to citizens and that it will be suggestive and encouraging to teachers, whether they be old hands or fledglings.

The extent to which this book contributes to the realization of these hopes will be largely due to the spirit of tough-minded inquiry which is the proudest possession of the University of Chicago; to the stimulation and challenge of my colleagues in the Department of Education who are continuously engaged in the great dialogue between the world of constructive imagination and the world of things as they are; to Chairman Francis S. Chase, who has set the tone for this dialogue and made sure that means could always be found for the exploration of its more promising themes; to Professors Roald Campbell, Jacob Getzels, Harold Dunkel, Bob Gowin, John Goodlad, Francis Chase, and Oscar Oeser (on leave from the University of Melbourne) whose conscientious and wholehearted efforts have led to rewriting many sections of the manuscript; to Dr. Donald Nylen, Seattle Public Schools, and Professor Ronald Lippitt, Research Center for Group Dynamics, University of Michigan, who offered abundant encouragement from the beginning; and to Alexander Morin, editor of my first book and now directing Quadrangle Press, who is largely responsible for such niceties of organization and style as cannot "be attributed to the linotype operator."

Herbert A. Thelen

University of Chicago
June, 1960

1

Plan:
Predicament and Promise

In which we distinguish among four ways to go about making the school educative, note that much of our difficulty in improving schools arises from the nature of the society in which they are embedded, and finally conclude that we shall have to think our way through to better concepts of education. We suggest what this will involve and lay out the plan of inquiry for the rest of the book.

Let's begin with the School Burning Theory of Education. The 'thirties were a period of much experimentation in schools, and, after reading a number of accounts of the most significant experiments, I formulated this theory, which I now gladly present to the world.

Imagine a perfectly terrible school. The morale of the faculty is scraping bottom; the students are cliquish and many of them don't even speak to each other; the building is an old barn in a muddy field—an affront to any self-respecting white horse; the citizens are apathetic, depressed, and bored. Now comes Rudolph the Brand-new Schoolman with an Idea: school is part of life, and life just doesn't have to be that way.

So, over a period of years, things happen. Somehow time is found in the biology course to plan and plant a garden and lawn; in English and social studies, to survey and report the school's plight in an exciting skit to the townsfolk; in homeroom to clean up the classrooms and make plans for their rehabilitation. Parents are invited to help, and work weekends are inaugurated. The men citizens and high school

4

students work side by side on Saturday morning, doing carpentry and landscaping, painting and construction. The town ladies provide the lunch, and, in the afternoon, the Men's League plays baseball with (or is it against?) the Boy's League. The teachers join in adult activities in town, and lose no opportunity to "involve" citizens. Several committees of students, teachers, and citizens are formed: for developing and equipping the library, modernizing the science laboratories, getting audio-visual equipment, organizing car pools to bring students from outlying districts in to school.

The students, with so many activities to challenge them, develop a club program and an active social life. The student's theater group becomes the talk of the state, and goes on tours. The budding scientists participate in science fairs, and bring home prizes. A student government is formed, and its officers sit on various boards and committees with the townspeople. Election to office in the government is a prize much sought after. The student government quickly converts bullies and terrors from the grammar school into true believers. Through the student government, an employment service helps students into part-time jobs set up by the delighted merchants, farmers, and businessmen. "Give a boy a job" becomes a slogan (the girls learn tatting, I guesss). By the end of seven years, juvenile delinquency has all but disappeared.

The parents, infected by the clear-cut purposive ambition of their children, draft some of the teachers to put on courses for adults in the evenings. The beauty of the refurbished school, and its charming auditorium make the town a stopping place for dramatic and musical artists on tour. The town swells with pride, Rudolph the Brand-new Schoolman develops a most distinguished fringe of gray around the temples. And nobody can think of anything further to want.

Many of the original teachers have now left, regretfully, to take important jobs in which they can spread the gospel further. Brilliant new teachers, the pick of their graduating classes, are easy to recruit. They come into a handsome building full of well-mannered students, and these teachers happily re-introduce the old talk-type social studies, the descriptive classification-type biology, the formalized abstract algebra (with workbook), and the grammatically precise book reports on foreign authors—read in translation, of course. The specter of academic achievement rides high in the saddle. The faculty meetings begin to peter out because nobody seems to have anything to talk about. The student clubs lose their zip as the need for their productions disappears. The honor roll is introduced, and a sizable number of flunking students is discovered. The school board budgets $3,825.63 cents each year to cover windows broken during the summer. Vandalism begins to appear in nasty little ways around the school. The students form secret organizations to exclude each other. A tough police captain is elected on his promise to "really lay down the law." The students no longer linger after school; they disperse silently with the last bell at 3 o'clock. Attendance in the adult courses dwindles, and it has been several years since a new course was introduced. Somehow it seems to Rudolph the Brand-new Schoolman—who has developed a paunch—that the "good" families have moved away; and the students in school now certainly aren't up to those he used to get.

The golden age has passed.

The only thing to do now is set fire to the school, plow up the gardens, retire Rudolph, and start over. Except that this should have been done right after "And nobody can think of anything further to want."

The difference between Rudolph's school before and after its golden period is the institutionalization (ossification) of attitudes, procedures, and status hierarchies that will be very difficult to change. Hence the Persian wisdom of shattering to bits and remolding nearer to the heart's desire.

But we are not Persians.* I am not sure that even if we were we would burn down our schools. Assuming that we wish to improve them, it seems to me that there are four approaches available. One approach is to bear down more heavily: to make stronger demands and enforce them by means of drastic threats and punishments. This approach in effect argues that when bureaucracy fails the solution is more bureaucracy. In line with this approach is the across-the-board demand that all high school graduates must take an additional year

---

* Frankly, I cannot find fault with the logic of the School Burning Theory. If the farseeing school board were to allow the fire insurance to lapse I do not see how a charge of arson could be sustained. Money for rebuilding, raised a little at a time, would still come to less than the cost of delinquency and corrective action. The salvaged earning power and ambition of the students, while hard to translate into dollars and cents, should add great wealth to the community. Recapture of the town's spirit, cohesion, and sense of purpose would be reflected in savings from all the city services, in its ability to attract and hold industries, and in its desirability as a place for new families to raise their children.

of math, English or science; that achievement will be defined by performance on tests constructed by anonymous experts who do not know the students, do not know what was taught in their class, and do not know the aspects of education valued by the community; that government money will be used to develop counseling for talented children but may not be spent on other children; that all high school physics teachers should teach the same specific materials in the same sequence and with the same activities. All these efforts are potentially valuable, but when they are applied without taking into account the pertinent facts about the students, teachers, and community, they amount in fact to direct impositions "justified" only by the pressure behind their enforcement.

The second approach is tinkering. This can be distinguished from experimentation by the absence of any thought-out theory. This approach assumes that if we are dissatisfied with what we are doing then we should try anything else that sounds plausible and that does not require any significant change in attitude, insight, or administrative arrangements. In line with this approach are most present experiments with ability grouping, closed-circuit TV, team teaching, and "group dynamics" techniques. All these innovations would be valuable if useful things were learned from them, such as how to define "ability" so that better ways can be developed to teach different kinds of students; what sorts of visual and auditory communications are most effective for defined communication requirements; what ways can be employed by teachers working with the same students to complement each other's resources; how to divide responsibility for learning activities among adults and children; what particular emotional and social conditions lead to interactions among students that stimulate different sorts of learning or readiness to learn.

The third approach is experimentation, which is tinkering with something in mind beyond "let's see what will happen." In line with this approach are the very good efforts one finds occasionally to set up a special class for students who are not getting much out of other classes; to make use of new technical aids in the "language laboratory"; to study the use of role-playing as an aid to emergent awareness of attitudes in social studies; to develop better ways of reporting grades to parents. On a larger scale there was the eight-year study of thirty progressive high schools, most of whose major findings have been ignored (e.g., that success in college depends on quality of high school experience *regardless* of the particular subject matter in courses the students took); and the New York activity study, which demonstrated the superiority of teacher-class planning and cooperative determination of goals. The U.S. Office of Education began in 1956 a highly commendable program for research. During its first three years, 234 projects were approved from universities and state educational agencies. Of these, 61 deal with mentally retarded children; 29 with special abilities of students, 26 with staffing problems, 15 with retention of students in school; 14 with school organization and administration. The remaining 89 cover the widest possible range. Most of these studies involve thought-out experiments, and should contribute to the body of educational knowledge.

The fourth approach is through education of everyone concerned (whether they know it or like it) with the enterprise of education. It would involve teachers studying and formulating the basic discipline of the field of knowledge they teach; administrators and counselors studying the bases for deciding which particular children should be assigned to which teachers; community agencies studying the over-all range of education-relevant experiences of students in the community and then trying to decide which kinds of experiences could best be supervised in schools, in families, in clubs, and in work situations.

This fourth approach is the concern of this book, and we shall see that it is not so much an "approach" as a part of the way of life that must be developed in the school and community. In the remainder of this chapter I shall consider in general terms some of the obstacles to making education a significant part of the human quest; some issues that we shall have to come to terms with; the nature of the ideas we seek; and finally, the design for the inquiry undertaken in this book.

OBSTACLES

Υ The greatest obstacle to improvement of education is the nature of modern society itself. A great many changes, beginning roughly with World War I, have occurred in our way of life and I think that to understand the problem of improving education we had better be aware of some of these changes. What I am about to say applies not only to schools but to churches, universities, labor unions, governments, industries, and school boards.

Ever since World War I, which ushered in the present era of industrial and technological expansion, we have become increasingly fascinated with our new and useful machines, gadgets, and toys. The Protestant ethic has always approved of enhancement of the standard of living, and the dazzling success of technology has taught us increasingly to ask how to do it rather than why to do it. The great debate about national purposes and policies has ground to a halt, shot down in part by such slogans as "maintain the American way of life." Life has become engineering: engineering of more goods, greater wealth, more power—yes, by heaven, even "better" human relations. We have assumed, when we thought about it at all, that these changes could be justified by good reasons and what we and Rudolph the Brand-new Schoolman did not allow ourselves to realize was that technological procedures, like the Sorcerer's Apprentice, had taken over and *that their own activities had become their own justification.* Now that other nations are able to compete with us on our own grounds of technological know-how we have become fearful; our dependency on procedures is no longer safe. We tell ourselves that their technology is in the service of bad ends (ideology). But this raises the uncomfortable question of what are our ends, then, that are so much better? And it is as we and Rudolph pose this question that we become aware of the fact we are no longer sure, and that we have substituted the organization and the procedures for the Human Quest after the "cultivation of the mind, feelings, and manners."

But in the meanwhile, what has been going on in education?

In one sense, the progressive movement in education began at the same time and for some of the same reasons as the explosion of industrialization during the 'twenties, for both were reactions against the formalism of the 'nineties, and both found their chance to grow during the chaos following World War I. Progressivism, as practiced, tended to be a reaction against stifling traditional procedures in schools; and it also, I suspect, nourished itself on the post-World War I social attitudes of "teacher has gone, let's kick the house down." (It also brought in some good things, too, which have caught hold in the primary grades, safely remote from adult life.) The difference between the new industrial and educational movements, however, was the difference between the lion and the ant. The industrial lion changed the world and most of its way of life, whereas the ant barely kicked up a local fuss. By the mid-forties the good ideas about building education on the child's own efforts to make choices and test their consequences were clearly on the way out, partly because they had not been understood well enough to attain validity, and partly because of a curious alliance between two oddly mated bedfellows: academic tradition and industrial bureaucracy. The common attitude and value that allied these two powerful forces was the assumption that their procedures were their own justification. At the present time, these strange partners have snuggled together most cozily because each has invented for itself a rationale which, like some exotic perfume, increases the desire of the other. The industrialists are trying to show that industrial expansion is the way to free the human spirit, develop universal democracy, and make peace permanent; whereas the educators are beating the drums for bright creative people with sound scientific training and minds disciplined for industry. Industry looks to liberal education to give substance to its rationalizations, and education looks to industry for its goals.

ISSUES

We must seek a different kind of education: an education that takes persons into account, that seeks, fosters, and builds on the universal human quest; an education that believes man should be master, not slave, to his own inventions; an education guided by unattainable values, creating its own procedures from insights which reflect detailed knowledge of boys and girls, communities, and worlds without number. In short—an education.

No one decision will be important in this reconstruction, but the cumulative force of many, many decisions, guided by a consistent point of view about education will, in the long run, add up.

By "consistent point of view" I mean a thought-out and intelligent position with respect to a number of basic issues. Four of these issues, with which we in our own times must come to terms, are:

Issue I. The education of a child is contributed to by the school, the family, the peer group, his contacts with events and people in the community. Should we not know or care what the contribution is to a child's education of various types of experiences, in and out of school? Is the net result of conflicting values and assumptions of the different parts of the community breeding confusion and doubt, or furthering self-mastery and wisdom in the child? And what part of the educational job belongs to the school (and why do you think so) and what part to other agencies? And who is to help the "other agencies" do their part properly?—or do they need help? Is education the responsibility of the total community or only of the school and possibly the family?

Issue II. Most statements of objectives of education reduce to two goals, which reflect the biological and the social nature of man. Thus a typical statement is that we want maximum self-realization of human, individual potentialities and we want the development of an enlightened citizenry capable of maintaining a society adapted to its times. Are these two separate objectives, as implied in the hog-wild "child-centered" school of the early 'thirties on the one hand and the talent-oriented "manpower technician" schools of the late 'fifties and early 'sixties on the other hand? If both these objectives have to be listed because gaining one does not insure gaining the other—a position I find most distasteful—then how is the balance to be found? And by what means can the two concerns be integrated within one individual? While we are on this issue, we may also ask: What balance do we seek between individuality and conformity?—and between intellectual and social-emotional development as the aims of education?

Issue III. How are we to regard the "funded capital of human experience," the accumulated knowledge of mankind? Is there a permanent core of true knowledge that must be passed on to each generation or is there only a body of provisional truth whose meaning must be rediscovered and re-interpreted by every learner for himself? Or, as the philosopher would put it, is truth absolute or is it relative to situations? The first position led to the "transmission belt" system of education: lecture, recitation, examination; the second position led to the "activity" plan in education: teacher-pupil planning, action, and evaluation. Are either or both right? Is there some third possibility that makes better sense? If so, what?

Issue IV. The imagination of the civilized world has been captured by the concept, pioneered but not perfected in America, of "equal educational opportunity for all." What does this mean? Does it mean, for example, equal opportunity to learn a particular body of knowledge set by the school—regardless of its meaningfulness to students having different capabilities and need? Or does it mean opportunity to learn whatever each child needs to learn in order to profit from his particular capabilities? Does it mean that every child in every state should have the same amount of money spent on him? Assuming that some teachers are better than others, who should get the best ones—the child who learns most readily or the one who learns least readily? What about the "culturally deprived" child, whose "background" has built-in resistance to learning; or the emotionally disturbed child, whose preoccupations keep him from listening; or the physiologically precocious or immature child, whose biological needs are out of step with the social possibilities for those of his age— what does equal opportunity mean here?

DESIGN FOR INQUIRY

I do not believe that any amount of tinkering will give us the solution we so desperately need to the four philosophical issues described above. And what we need is in any case not just tinkering but a drastic overhauling. Our present limited research-based theories, blooming so profusely in college textbooks, are useful, but we need something in addition: namely, broad general theories and propositions that tell us what the human being is like, why knowledge developed and what it is for, how the school and community influence each other, and so on. The sort of general theory we need takes in a lot of territory; it makes sense for all educational situations. It is also believable; it snuggles down where we live and resonates with our reflected-upon experience. It makes sense even though it cannot be demonstrated by scientific data alone, though neither will it be disproved. Believable general, useful, and handy theories and suppositions serve their purpose like generals and then gradually fade away through incorporation in more general, believable and useful theories.

To invest any general theory with belief is to take a risk; to believe a theory hard enough to act on its suppositions calls for commitments to ideas—not to the idea of an idea but to ideas as representations, inadequate though they may be, of the real world. It is out of such beliefs and commitments that this book is written.

So what do we want to know?

Item. We want to know in the most fundamental terms we can what a living, breathing, feeling, and thinking human being is about. We especially want to know what happens when he is confronted with stress, for education is supposed to change people, and to do this it makes demands on them. Moreover if any learning is to result, the demands have to be ones to which the human being does not know for sure how to respond; and hence the stress. We want to know what tendencies in the human being we can count on to help us educate him and we want to see if we can use this knowledge the better to capitalize on these tendencies. We want to know whether inquiry and critical thinking serve a useful purpose for human beings; if so, where did they come from and how can they be strengthened?

Item. We also want to know about knowledge. Educators place great store by knowledge; It is obviously a Good Thing. Is it like money in the bank? Is it power? a bag of tools? a key? a set of filled pigeonholes? an end in itself (like ice cream)? insurance? Is it something to use to distinguish between the educated (good guys) and the uneducated (bad guys)? We also want to know two further things about knowledge: What light does the way knowledge was gained in the first place throw on how it can be learned by others later? And, in view of the arguments between "science" and the "humanities" we want to know what sort of importance each kind of knowledge has.

Item. We want to know what education has to do with society. What does the educational system have to do with the system of government, of economics, of politics? It is all very well to say that education is for the purpose of maintaining our nation or developing a world order, but what does that mean? Does it mean that every individual must be made literate, wise, loyal and conforming? What are the facts about the age-old conflict between the "individual" and "society" or between the adolescent surrounded by social and emotional pressures and the demands of the school that he learn to think?

We want to know what the talk about community-school relationships means. Is a school a cultural island, separated from the community mainland by the same kind of thing that separates fantasy from real life? Does the school lead or follow the community or both? We hear a lot about the need to "involve" citizens in school problems. Who, how, why? Is it just to keep them quiet? or to manipulate them into contributing more money? Is school supposed to "induct youth into the community"? What does that mean? In primitive tribes this is done with teaching by the wise men followed by the celebration of the rites of puberty; how do we do it? What would it mean to have an educative community, with educational responsibilities divided up? Can the school do the job alone? Or is the school only one part of a community-wide educational system which exists in fact whether the school board knows it or not? Can you distinguish education from welfare? And the kind of welfare that goes on in schools from the presumed other kinds that go on elsewhere?

Our inquiry into these matters will begin with a look at Man, Knowledge, and Society simply to understand the nature of the materials education deals with. This examination should reveal to us "factors," processes, and tendencies that represent the realities most pertinent for education; and the values which these tendencies imply as the actual purposes of human effort. These kinds of ideas together set limits and suggest opportunities for educational activity. Our too brief excursion among the social sciences will occupy Chapters 2, 3, and 4.

Our next step, overviewed in Chapter 5, is to construct the basic suppositions of an educational theory. Such ideas lie in the field where scientific theory and philosophy interpenetrate. They will identify generalized and significant tendencies which we believe do exist in America today. We shall consider how each of these tendencies might be harnessed to the job of educating children, and we shall proceed rather speculatively (and certainly tentatively) to spell out in some detail exactly how this harnessing might be done in the school.

The first general tendency we shall propose is the quest for autonomy and captaincy of self, and we shall show how this provides the basis for a type of learning experience which we shall call "Personal Inquiry" (Chapter 6). Personal inquiry is driven by strong needs of individuals, and the educational requirement is to place the learner in a carefully chosen environment in which he can discover the insights he needs to behave more "intelligently."

The next general tendency we shall propose is the development of the social order, and we shall show how this tendency in groups can be used to develop motivation for all sorts of learning. The type of learning experience based on this tendency is labeled Group Investigation" (Chapters 7, 8). Group investigation capitalizes on the fact that when people are confined in a room they begin to interact, and the group that emerges must develop a system of controls and supporting attitudes and values of such a kind that the interactions maintain rather than destroy the group. The educational requirement is to guide the group in such a way that its culture and values are oriented to inquiry and to learning appropriate to the school subject or field of knowledge.

The third general tendency is to take action in order to improve the relationships between persons and groups on the one hand and their social and natural environments on the other. The type of learning experience based on this tendency has been dubbed "Reflective Action (Chapter 9). With reference to children and youth, reflective action capitalizes on the very strong need, presently thwarted, for an adult-recognized "place" in the functioning of the community. The educational requirement is to help youth become educated through their own voluntary efforts to assume responsible roles in the school and larger community.

I shall try to show how these various tendencies toward the values of autonomy, predictability, and two-way adaptation—scrambled, mixed up, and mutually interfering in today's classrooms—can be used to educate the child. They will, however, not accomplish the whole job of education, and the missing part has to do with those learnings that call for repetition and practice rather than insight. However much we may succeed in making education an experience of inquiry, there will always be an irreducible core of learnings that cannot be developed simply through insight. Some part of the three R's, for instance, must be learned through drill because there is no way in which intelligence can produce the right answer. In Chapter 10, on "Skill Development" I shall consider how these learnings may be developed.

Finally, in the last chapter, I will tackle the question of how the sort of schools I have been pointing to can be developed, and here we shall try to apply our own principles to the action strategy so sorely needed right now in many communities. Chapter 11 is entitled "Do-it-Yourself: the greatest project."

2

Man:
What Makes Johnny Tick?

In which we let Johnny show us the richness and the complexity of human behavior; note the fundamental conflict between our animal and our social nature; and propose that life is a continual natural inquiry into ways of resolving the conflict in each of its confrontations; we suggest that the task of education is to supervise this natural inquiry and make it educative; and we identify as most crucial a phase of the learning process that is generally ignored or seriously bungled in schools.

All sorts of peeople go to school: toddlers, tomboys, thirsters; squirmers, dreamers, thinkers; men and women; widows, adolescents, housewives, teachers; and persons who just want to learn to tie flies for the fun of it. Teachers are of all sorts, too: they range from nimble piccolos to thumping basses, from mellow horns to clashing cymbals; from sparkling champagne to flat beer; from lovable lizzies to champing Cadillacs. And lessons are learned in all sorts of places. Formal education goes on in bungalow-type schools, in glass and steel factory-type buildings, in rustic redwood and vine-covered retreats and in penitentiary Gothic monuments. Informal schooling goes on on street corners and in streetcars; in churches and carrousels; playgrounds and police stations; museums and mausoleums. Need I continue?

I have named only a few of the countless influences that help explain what happens in a particular educational situation. To a wide

16

assortment of pupils, teachers, and settings, we could add a wide assortment of subject matter, resources, groups, and community attitudes. The variety of educational situations is endless. If you combine only the categories of pupils, teachers, and settings listed more or less facetiously in the opening paragraph, you get 416 combinations, and each of these will have its own distinctive flavor.

In short, every educational situation is unique. Every classroom group writes its own history, has its own failures and successes, its own mélange of the animal, the vegetable, and the spiritual. To compound the complexity, the experience of each pupil in the classroom is in some ways different from that of every other pupil. The same classroom may, for different pupils, be deadly, exciting, boring, challenging, important, stupid, fearful, ego-building.

To discover the basic nature of the educative process, we must dig beneath all these complexities. But even this resounding topic can be broken down into three kinds of ideas—ideas about the nature of man, the nature of knowledge, and the nature of society. For it is the interaction among these natures in each educational situation that constitutes the educative process.

To think about anything as grand and gaudy as human nature requires a plan. How shall we inquire into human nature? How shall we identify those aspects of human nature that will lead us most directly to an understanding of the processes of education?

Generally speaking, four approaches are open to us. First, we can ask experts—sociologists, psychologists, anthropologists, theologians, lawyers, and others who are concerned with the nature of human beings. Certaintly the ideas of specialists would be useful—if we could see their relevance to questions in education. Second, we can observe the behavior of human beings engaged in learning and try to come up with insights that directly expose the educative process. Third, we can visit a great many classrooms and try to synthesize or select a model of education that we think would be most valid and most useful for the creation of other educational experiences. Fourth, we can harken to our own intuitive feelings about our own educational experiences, for we all have more wisdom than we are aware of.

Each of these approaches is useful: the scientists can sharpen our sensitivities and help us formulate significant questions; observation of human learning is necessary to link behavior to principles; class-

room models represent practical wisdom expressed in the vocabulary
of action; and our intuitive feelings of what is important and what
makes sense will help guide any approach we take.

Having paid my respects to the available fountains of wisdom, I
shall proceed to get a slice of behavior before us so we will have
something to talk about. I shall try to choose an incident that has
universality, an incident that could be part of anyone's life. I also
want as little interference as possible from such artifacts as laws,
deadlines, or other imposed requirements. In short, we seek a slice
of natural behavior—a slice in which we can see inherent tendencies
of human beings.

A SLICE OF "NATURAL" BEHAVIOR

Consider a child. Let's make him a four-year-old and have him
take a walk in the park. On the way he sees a building, and he says:
"What's that?" We say, "That's a garage." And he says, "What's
it doing?" We see that the four-year-old already has a well-developed
system of word logic which tells him that an object must have a
function, must be able to do something. When you name something,
he wants to know what it is doing: "Is the clock going?" "Yes."
"Where?"

He starts down the sidewalk, and we notice that he walks slowly,
stops, then walks fast; and he also weaves from side to side. What accounts for this odd locomotion? We notice that when he stops, his
eyes focus on something: he gives his attention to something. Now he
picks up a rock and drifts off into what seems to be a bit of a day-
dream; he seems oblivious to his surroundings; he mutters to himself.
Then he puts the rock into his pocket and moves on. He seems
to forget the rock: he is looking at other things. But pretty soon
he takes the rock out of his pocket and drops it on the ground; a
look of annoyance or frustration crosses his face; and shortly afterward he kicks a tin can.

Let's try to see what is going on in this situation. First of all,
Johnny goes into the park, not as a blank slate, not as a vacuum;
he goes in with certain anticipations that he probably cannot put into
words. He may be expecting adventure or challenge. And he has
feelings about his anticipations—feelings of eagerness, of delight,

of—well, heaven knows what. Relief at getting away from Mother? At getting out of the house?

He wanders back and forth, and he runs and he walks. Why? Because he is a human organism and eats food. There are only three things you can do with food. You can build body structure with it, a step often followed by buying scales for the bathroom; you can translate it into motion; or you can get rid of it, as being of no bodily use. This boy has a need for activity; he cannot help it; he simply has to be in motion.

The process of giving attention is an interaction between the child and the objects he looks at. The stone he picked up must have a good deal of meaning for him—or at least more meaning than other objects he might have picked up and been attentive to. This attention is probably accompanied by a procession of thoughts, though it is possible that he cannot put the thoughts into words. Let's consider what the stone might mean to Johnny, what might have caused him to give it attention.

First, he might see it as a weapon. He might have seen a rock thrown through a window recently. He might have heard the story about David and Goliath. Or was the weapon in that story a pea-shooter? Johnny might have a slingshot of his own—or he might wish he had one. If these are Johnny's thoughts, the rock is linked with aggressive impulses; one of his feelings at a subliminal level may be that the rock might make a good weapon.

A secondly possibility is that the rock is pretty. Because it is pretty, he thinks that somebody might covet it. He could hide it in the gold-fish bowl. His fish might like to have it there. Or he could use it for barter.

Another possibility—and who knows what goes on in the mind of a child—is that the rock is a talisman; all he has to do is to rub it in the right way, and he can float off into space. That would be an escape reaction.

Still another possibility is that somehow this stone is connected with Mother. I don't know how, but with little kids sooner or later almost everything gets connected with Mother. Maybe Mother has a rock collection, or maybe she hates rock collections. It doesn't really matter. In either case, some of his emotional investment would come from his perception of Mother's attitude toward rocks.

These are some of the thoughts that may flow through Johnny's mind as he picks up the rock. Johnny is under no great pressure to put his thoughts into words; but as the thoughts come, he savors them and the new patterns they form. The ideas make the stone meaningful to him; it is thus invested with positive value, and he puts the treasured object into his pocket.

Now he becomes uneasy. He is ambivalent. He becomes aware of his feelings about the whole situation—a situation that became real the moment he decided to keep the rock. Maybe he shouldn't put it in his pocket and take it home.

Let's assume that Johnny's mother is getting awfully tired of sweeping trash out of the house. After taking six lizards, three old playing cards, and a bottle cap (rusty) out of Johnny's pocket, she probably said something about not bringing trash home. Johnny becomes aware that his first impulse to take the stone home—because it has value to him—is being tempered by recollections of other people who will be involved. That is, he is becoming aware of a larger social context of his act. Interpersonal feelings are mixed into the situation. You'd think that picking up a rock and taking it home wouldn't be an interpersonal situation, but it certainly is if you have a mother like Johnny's.

He becomes aware in some vague way that all is not well. If he takes the rock home, he may suffer deprivation of his mother's love —or whatever loss he feels in Mother's anger at having trash around. If he is a fortunate child, he is able to interpret Mother's anger as anger at trash. But if he is like the typical child of many homes, he interprets Mother's anger at trash as being directed at him in some subtle way. He must make a choice now, to keep the stone or to throw it away. But this is not just a choice about a stone; to him it is a choice about a kind of belongingness. How important is the stone compared to Mother's love?

He decides to throw away the stone—something that for the brief space of a few minutes was meaningful to him, something that in his fantasy was a jewel. He has flung away this precious bit and his daydreams with it. So he feels deprived. He has to do something with his feelings, which have translated themselves into anger. So he kicks the can.

"NATURAL" BEHAVIOR AS INQUIRY

With Johnny's help I have tried to show the richness and the fullness of individual behavior. My account goes far beyond simple objective description. I have speculated freely. Many of my speculations would be difficult to prove. I hold no brief for the accuracy of any details of my story. But I do allege that the sorts of processes I described do go on.

Human beings do act; they have ideas and feelings; their memories are jogged by cues in the environment; they do make decisions—or appear to make decisions; they change their minds on the basis of second thoughts; they react to their own ideas and feelings, and to their reactions to their ideas and feelings; they do have awareness of past experiences and of future consequences; they do have relationships to other people and feelings about these relationship; they live in their own worlds which, while close to objective reality in some ways, also contain distortions, dreams, hopes, and expectations; their desires are influenced by wants from within and fears or demands they perceive from without; they are aware of some of their behavior and may even consciously hold theories about it; at the same time they are unaware of much other behavior; and everything they do has a lifetime of history behind it.

These statements are glib textbook generalizations. They are useful to sensitize us to what to look for, to call attention to possible motives and meanings of behavior. The generalizations mean nothing of themselves; but they mean a great deal when we use them to help answer the questions: How does Johnny behave? Why does he behave as he does? But note what we assume in these questions: that Johnny's behavior is purposeful, that the whole sequence of behavior we watched has unity or coherence; and that this unity cannot be understood apart from Johnny's own needs, interests, experiences, ideas, and feelings.

A great deal becomes clear when we note that Johnny acts as if he were caught in a tug of war between his spontaneous desires and his mother's anticipated displeasure. Such a notion might help explain Johnny's behavior in many other situations as well, for it suggests a conflict embedded in a long-standing and continuing relationship between Johnny and his mother.

Diagnosing the theme, however, is but half the task of understanding Johnny. The other half is empathizing with Johnny's feelings or mood. How does he react to the conflict within himself? Does he become angry, bored, delighted, apprehensive, affectionate, or withdrawn? The expression of a mood involves all of Johnny. It is not merely Johnny's brain that gets angry: his fists clench, his neck flushes, his speech becomes incoherent, his features contort, his feet twitch. A dog would detect that Johnny even smells different when he is angry.

✗ Thus to understand behavior we must be able to answer two questions. First, what is its theme, its purpose, its problem-to-be-solved? Second, how does the individual respond to this theme emotionally?

Our lives represent the interplay of themes that come out into the open in certain situations and then, like a spent melody, retreat into the background as other figures achieve prominence. In each reappearance, a theme has a new configuration, a new flavor, a new way of functioning. It may find direct expression in conscious seeking; it may be projected as if it belonged to someone else; it may provide an undercurrent of almost-felt meaning; it may suddenly unleash a new insight or discovery.

At root, human experience is dramatic. The basic themes are themes of conflict—conflict between our wishes and the wishes of others, between our present needs and our future capabilities, between our animal nature and our social ethics, between what we are and what we want to be, between our easy habits and our creative urges.

It is unfortunate that the word *conflict* has become a dirty word, for our emotional reactions to the term blind us to the fact that without conflict neither growth nor education would be possible. In our Organization Man society we tend to assume that conflict is all bad and destructive, not realizing that it is ridiculous to think of a universal fact as anything but a universal fact. It is true that we may deal with conflict in ways that are stultifying and destructive; but we may also deal with conflict in ways that lead to individual enlightenment and social cohesion. Man has both capabilities, and the task of education is to enable man to develop the constructive capability to the full.

Human nature contains a basic conflict between two ways of dealing with stresses inevitable to life. The first way of dealing with stress can be traced to our animal origins. According to La Barre[1] this way is automatic and reflexive. Sensing danger (if one is an animal), one attacks, runs, or freezes. Given powerful claws, fleet feet, or protective coloration, one can survive. But man does not have these special bodily features, so for him outright attack or flight is mostly futile. His reflexive behaviors are muted; he lashes out with biting words, changes the subject, or daydreams, or merely flushes beet red.

The development of families added another reflex to fight, flight, and immobilization. This way is through dependency, and it has its clearest appropriateness for the survival of the young: sensing danger, one runs to Mother (and the family as a whole turns to Father). In adult human beings we see this reflex in irrational impulses to look up the record, to get the boss to repeat the instructions, to find out what "they" want to do.

With the development of society and the requirement that the young adult go outside the family to find his mate, still another kind of reflex developed: seeking intimacy with another, as, for example, in gossip sessions.

None of these impulses is bad unless it is simply acted out without any understanding of what one is doing. In this case one acts without responsibility: one surrenders the ego functions, which make man free, to the conditioned or inherited animal reflex.

The second way of dealing with stress, or conflict, is through inquiry. This is the way of insight, of learning, of consciousness of methods, of diagnosis, speculation, hypothesis testing. This capability probably began with the use of tools, which required the ability to distinguish between self and object, organism and environment, cause and effect. Such distinctions require consciousness, language, and the ability to learn from one's own and others' experiences. This way tries to deal with stress through reflection on the situation, which includes oneself as actor. It involves discipline and the ability to curb tendencies to "act out," the ability to live with tension and challenge long enough to formulate a plan.

The method of inquiry is learned, and the long period of human infantilism and family protection—as well as formal education provided by the community—is designed to develop Johnny's natural quest into an educated inquiry. Educated inquiry is a social development stimulated by the interaction of man with man. It is the central capability of man is a member of society. [2, 3]

Both the animal and the societal capabilities exist and blend in human nature. If either takes over too strongly, we get into trouble. Acting out does not change a situation for the better, nor does one learn anything from acting out. Yet the spontaneous expression of impulse, which is the beginning of acting out, is required to enable us to diagnose a situation. For we understand situations by seeing not only what thoughts we have but also what feelings and inclinations we have. The awareness of anger tells me something, not about me alone or the situation alone, but about the interaction between me and the situation. This awareness yields important information to be interpreted through inquiry. The destructive possibilities of acting out should not be confused with the constructive need to obtain knowledge about our involvements, conflicts, and commitments. To subdue the beast within, we must learn to accept the fact that we have a wide array of impulses of all sorts. We must learn nondestructive ways of expressing our impulses sufficiently that we can become aware of them. And we must learn to interpret their existence as the source of nonrational intelligence about ourselves and the world.

But inquiry, too, can be distorted and become an end in itself rather than part of a constructive way of life. When we limit the data of inquiry to objective facts, denying the existence of individual meanings and reactions, and when we confine the process of inquiry to the solution of puzzles already put into words by someone else, then we are being rational but not intelligent. When rationality runs amok without continuing or at least frequent contact with mood and feeling, it leads to fantasies. Some of these fantasies, like the Nazi plan for a totalitarian state, are highly rational; but they also flay human nature and carry within them the seeds of their own *Gotterdämmerung*. Inquiry is meaningful and constructive only when it takes individual intuitions and emotional responses into account; and emotional expression (except in such consummatory expressions as music and dancing) is constructively creative only when it provides data for inquiry.[4]

As we again look at Johnny we begin to see part of the educational task; for we realize that his experience in the park is not, by itself, educative. I have great sympathy for Johnny, but I would like to be aware of his thoughts and feelings. I am sorry he solved his problem by throwing away the rock, just as I am sorry whenever anyone deprives himself of something of value to himself without testing to see whether the deprivation is necessary. I would like Johnny to have taken the rock home and shown it to his mother; and I would like her to have responded with interest—not in the rock perhaps, but certainly in Johnny's ideas about the rock. After that, there would be plenty of time for the two of them to decide together what to do with the rock.

I would also like Johnny to be able to laugh at the spectacle of himself kicking the tin can, to accept the fact that he feels better for having done so, but also to know that he was angry, that it is all right to be angry, and that while he has, perhaps, gotten rid of some of his anger he has in no way changed the situation or bettered the relationship which he thinks exists between himself and his mother. I would like Johnny to know—through discussion now and through reading when he is older—that other people get angry too and that there are many different ways of dealing with anger. And, further, that a rock collection can pose many intriguing questions that open doors to the big wide world. In short, I would like Johnny to have the equipment and the guidance he needs for finding some of the many meanings the experience had for him and might have for others in similar situations. Such learnings as these distinguish between natural and educative experience.

THE CRUCIAL FAILURE OF EDUCATION

Consider the old chestnut: Johnny can shell 18 walnuts in three minutes, and Harry can shell 42 walnuts in four minutes. How long would it take the two of them to lay bare the meat of 101 walnuts? This is a problem.

Or take all the thousands of problems at the back of all the millions of algebra books; take all the tons of workbooks that keep the more docile children quiet while the teacher works with a committee; or take all the clever "aids" designed to make education a lockstep through a prepackaged curriculum (in the name of "democracy" or, possibly, of bad economics). All these exercises provide opportunity for the child to be reasonable, to apply information in the way any reasonable child would. In all these exercises, the number of answers possible is implied in the way the problem is stated—and this is true even for intelligence tests. After all, there are only a limited number of ways you can go wrong in applying logical processes to a word problem. While some children are more ingenious than others in finding wrong ways, the possibilities are strongly limited by the way the problem is stated. When we are confronted with a serious perplexity, our problem is 90 per cent solved when we hit on the "right" or key question. The right question is the question that makes available to us a large amount of explicit information and judgment.

It is in the formulation of the problem that individuality is expressed, that creativity is stimulated, and that nuances and subtleties are discovered. It is these aspects of inquiry that give birth to new social movements and political orientations, and that are central in the emergence of insight. Yet it is precisely these aspects of inquiry that schools ignore, for they collapse inquiry to mere problem-solving, and they keep the student busy finding "solutions" to "problems" that are already formulated, externalized, depersonalized, and emotionally fumigated. The school is concerned with the student who formulates his own problems only when he is so creative with school property that he perforce enters a "counseling" relationship (on pain of dismissal). But as far as the academic work of the school goes, personal stirrings and strivings and self-discoveries have no place. In effect, what is missing is the investment of learning with personal emotion and meaning.

The part of inquiry that gives birth to creative awareness of problems is closely linked to character; to personal commitments, causes, and goals; to temperament; to basic orientation to the world. These aspects of personality comprise the individual's fundamental psychic equipment, and this psychic equipment largely determines the goals and the quality of experience one seeks. The child's character develops through the experience of inquiry; but it does not develop through problem-solving alone. For problem-solving is a technical enterprise, and it is amoral.

As I see it, then, what has happened is that, in line with the technical temper of the times, we have ground out students who can solve problems but who will forever have to be guided by someone else.[5] We have turned out people who can, for the most part, be replaced by machines in modern industry and, in fact, are rapidly being so replaced. The present hue and cry for leaders and creative geniuses is really a cry for people who can think as whole people, with commitment, emotional response, sensitivity, self-awareness, and self-knowledge. These capabilities are firmly "conditioned" out of many children by the time they are four years old; but in the life of inquiry these capabilities know no ceiling. In short, the emphasis on education as a process that begins only with someone else's statement of the problem denies the most fundamental human need: the quest for autonomy.

Our leading educators are clearly asking for development of the autonomous man.[6] They place highest priority on the "intelligence principle" (Clarence H. Faust); "freedom and discipline" (William H. Cornog); "understanding and ability to apply principles" (Ralph W. Tyler); "self-motivated inquiry" (Francis S. Chase); "proper relationships between values, attitudes, knowledge, skills, and overt actions" (Robert S. Gilchrist); "ability to deal with practical and persistent problems" (Lloyd S. Michael); "education to fit the goals of each student" (Kenneth W. Lund); and "self-direction" (Howard A. Latta).

Let's look back at Johnny. He has left the park; he is entering school. What will his experience be? Will anyone answer his question: "What's that?" Will he be free, even, to ask the question? Will he be able to walk slowly, rapidly, from side to side? Will he discover any rocks, precious in his eyes and capable of absorbing all his attention? Who will see to it that rocks are there to be found? How will Johnny decide what to keep and what to cast aside? What advice will he get? Will he ever experience the thrill of mastering anything? How often will he encounter a day of challenge or adventure? Will inquiry become part of his way of life, enriching and ennobling it? What kind of man will Johnny, the boy, be father to?

The problem of educating the child to be a more adequate and autonomous person himself is part and parcel of the problem of educating people who can get along together and communicate for the mutual survival of societies. The justifiable fears of rampant nationalism push the whole problem to the level of nations, but the process is similar. As long as the people in nations see only the economic and objective aspects of life—as long as they firmly clamp a spiked heel on their inner wisdom—and go hell-bent-for-election to maximize profits for their own countries, they will in the long run lose the capacity for recognition of their membership in the human family. And the animal instincts within us and our tendencies to mobilize reflexive action without thought will be reinforced by a kind of think-

ing which takes for granted self-interest untempered by humanity.
→Education is needed to correct these tendencies, and its instrument
of correction is knowledge. Education at present focuses too exclu-
sively on rational processes, on "objective" formulations of data, and
on knowledge over which there can be no argument because it is the
kind of knowledge than can be authoritatively demonstrated by culturally given scientific canons of proof of acceptability. But this is only
a small part of the knowledge we live with, and we now must examine
the kinds of knowledge and, in more detail, their relationships to education.

NOTES

1. Weston La Barre, *The Human Animal* (Chicago: University of Chicago Press, 1954), p. 371.
2. W. R. Bion, "Experiences in Groups, I-VII," *Human Relations,* I (1948), 314-320, 487-496; II (1949), 13-22, 295-304; III (1950), 3-14, 375-402; IV (1951), 221-228.
3. Dorothy Stock and Herbert A. Thelen, *Emotional Dynamics and Group Culture* (New York: New York University Press, 1958), p. 296. Five years of experimental research with Bion's concepts are reported in this book.
4. For a description of the basic dilemma of acting out as opposed to inquiry, see "Emotionality and Work in Groups," by Herbert A. Thelen in *The State of the Social Sciences* (ed. Leonard White) (Chicago: University of Chicago Press, 1956), pp. 184-200.
5. Herbert A. Thelen, "The Triumph of 'Achievement' over Inquiry in Educa-tion," *Elementary School Journal,* LX (January 1960), 190-197.
6. Francis S. Chase and Harold A. Anderson (eds.), *The High School in a New Era* (Chicago: University of Chicago Press, 1958). See chapters by the educators named.

3

Knowledge:
The Instinct for the Jugular

In which we distinguish between information and knowledge, note that the educative part of knowledge is a disciplined approach to life, and spell this out in detail for physical, biological, social, and humanistic (or subjective) domains of experience. We suggest that educators must themselves learn the knowledge disciplines of their subject fields, and that the way students and teachers can learn these disciplines is through engagement in genuine inquiry.

The school is one of the places in the community where students live a good part of their lives. In school they learn through firsthand experience to get along with others, to curb expression of their more destructive impulses, and to be sufficiently obedient to adult authority. These things they learn in other parts of the community, too.

The thing that makes the school "educational" is its concern with knowledge. The school is expected to go beyond conditioning to understanding. Its orientation is partly to the future, to the person each student could be and to the society we want. The school testifies to our faith that man and society can be improved, and that the way to improvement is through the trained use of intelligence.

What teachers think knowledge is and what they do with it in the school probably determine how far the child's education will go beyond simple conditioning of the sort that makes it possible to live in the same house with Rover. If one judges by prevailing practices in

29

many high schools today, the most plausible assumption about knowledge is that it is a packaged commodity to be given in exchange for the time of the student, and that neither it nor the student is much affected by the transaction. The package will contain instructions for the use of its contents—like an Erector set—and as long as one is content or unimaginative enough to build only the adult-anticipated objects, the contents of the package will be adequate. Fortunately these limitations don't matter much, because the chief educational product is a certificate saying that one has had the right courses and bought the same packages as the Jones boy down the street.

The purpose of this chapter is to take a good hard look at the nature of knowledge and the implications of this nature for education. We shall ask, Why do we have knowledge, where does it come from, what interesting and necessary purposes does it serve? We shall go at these questions inductively.

THE MEANING OF AN IDEA

If you go into the library and look over all those books—big and little, comfortable in their fatness, nervous in their thinness, inky or musty-smelling, with bindings opulent, or mean—what do you think about? Do you visualize a long unbroken line of nearsighted patient men, hunched lovingly over parchment, trying to pour their best thinking and life's blood into the imperishable? Or do you think of a lot of monkeys in a zoo, each endlessly and witlessly pecking away at typewriters, with the more grammatical results swept up and bound? The former identification predisposes you to think of the books' contents as insights hinted at in the pattern of words, the sequence of ideas, the description of vital, living experience; the latter view predisposes you to think of the books' contents as random jottings, the results of chance and idle curiosity but without meaning for you beyond the relief of boredom or the acquisition of some secondhand phrases to work into dinner-table conversation.

Do you agree with my feeling that books may be of either kind? But even if you do, I wonder if we would agree on which books were of which kind? I doubt it. For the meaning and importance of a book is not given alone by its contents nor by any other of its characteristics. Meaning is the result of an interaction, perhaps an argument, an image created in some living person's mind; an emergent feeling of excitement, or peace, or restlessness; a release of tension in a sudden, "By Jove, he's hit it!" But we react differently, and the same book to which you say "By Jove" may well be one to which I would say "Oh shucks"—and vice versa.

But why do we have these different reactions? It is partly due to our interest in words and language, in writing as an artistic product and an end in itself. But I think a greater reason is the fact that our experiences, both past and anticipated, are different, and that these experiences have left us with different nerve endings exposed, different wishes to have or to avoid certain images or thoughts, different questions, vague, general, precise, and specific, that startle us into attention when we chance upon something "significant" for us. If you had never been anywhere, never done anything, never been angry or loving, never tried and failed at anything—what would you get out of a book?

The thing that changes a grammatical phrase into knowledge is somebody's reaction to it. If you want to be tough-minded about it, you'll insist that this reaction result in insight—a shaking up and reorganization of thoughts into some new, more powerful pattern. But note that this can only happen when the written idea, as perceived by the reader, explodes among his previous beliefs, insights, understandings, hunches, and apprehensions. Let's consider a phrase, known and generally approved by all of us: "Honor thy father and mother." If I were to take that phrase by itself, I would find myself rather puzzled. But since I know my father and mother, seldom confuse them with other people, and have all sorts of expectations and feelings about them, the phrase attracts my attention, and the instant it does that it no longer stands alone. Of course, if it never occurred to me that the phrase was really meant to apply to me personally, then it would remain isolated, or perhaps part of some jargon along with nine other similarly empty phrases. But in my case, the perplexity begins with the word "honor" as connected to my parents. When do I honor them? All the time or just on occasion, and if so, on what occasion? Is honoring something I do in private, like picking my teeth? Or do I do it in their presence, like clearing the table? Or do I do it in larger gatherings? And where does this honoring business occur? In the dining room, church, outdoors? And how is honoring done? With slips of paper like report cards or checks or letters? Is honoring a do-it-yourself activity or does one need others to help?

Does it hurt or is it fun? Where does it lead? What, incidentally, do they do while I'm honoring them?

These questions may seem cynical and possibly irreverent. They are technical questions, asked simply to find out the specific behavior called for. Grammatically, at least, the phrase is a command— or Commandment—to do something, and if I am to follow it, don't I have to know how to behave differently than if I weren't following it?

But perhaps it isn't intended literally; perhaps it is intended as a statement of policy, whose ramifications have to be worked out fresh in each situation. For example, maybe one honors his parents on some occasions by doing what they want and on other occasions by doing what they don't want. In that case, it is a statement not about behavior but about relationships, and the appropriate behavior is that which maintains the desired kind of relationship in each situation. Maybe expressions of gratitude, obedience, or flattery might each be appropriate under some conditions.

Now I have to worry about a host of new things. What did the author or authors of the injunction have in mind. Who were they, anyway? When did they live? For whom was the book written? Why did they write down the idea? For that matter, how did they dream it up in the first place? And is the idea just a fragment, pulled out of an argument of some sort? Maybe it is only a cry in the night, an expression of hope or exasperation? Maybe it is the projection of a frustrated person, who thinks it's all somebody else's fault? Is the idea somehow an end in itself or is it the means to some other end? If so, what other end? If only I knew these things, maybe I'd know what to do—that is, maybe I'd understand the idea.

What has our investigation of this phrase revealed?

First, it makes clear that words are not experience, not reality, not actions. They connect with reality only as someone "reads meaning into them."

Second, they arose out of somebody's experience and he had something in mind when he set them down. They are not produced at random nor are they the result of idle curiosity. They are attempts to represent one's experience or the products—such as wisdom or enjoyment—of that experience.

Third, they are expressions of needs of the author and, possibly, of the needs he thinks his readers will have. Ideas and the knowledge they stimulate come from needs. If the Eskimos have, as Whorf pointed out, many different words for something we collapse into the one word, "snow," it is because in their way of life they need to distinguish between snow you ski on, snow you build an igloo with, snow you sink into, snow melted into water, and so on.

Fourth, the experiences one can have are limited by his culture—by its interpretations of what one may talk about or do. Kinsey's books attracted as much interest for their defiance of taboo as for their factual content; and this content was kept remote by dealing with the phenomena for the most part statisically. But the culture is limiting in other ways too. For example, in discussions of education or love one is immediately frustrated by a lack of precise vocabulary; we have as much trouble discussing love as an Eskimo would have if he attempted to discuss snow in English. We could use sixteen different concepts for "love" and we need at least eight for "learning." Drawing pictures doesn't help us much, either. And what about "justice," "need," "honor," "respect," "tolerance"?

Fifth, ideas, when reacted to and thus converted to knowledge, have consequences. Some of these are dangerous and our natural prudence keeps us from understanding them; after all, Man ultimately develops knowledge to help him survive, not to destroy himself. The knowledge, for example, that continued inflation will pauperize the large segment of our population living on fixed incomes is at present seen only as an intellectual point; but nobody in the public eye has dared to act on any of the obvious conclusions.

Sixth, the consequences of an idea may be rewarding or punishing, and this has much to do with whether it will be heard and what it means. We always try, like Alice, to make ideas mean what we want them to mean, and what we want them to mean is whatever is rewarding, gratifying, pleasant, justifying, or exciting to us. And if we want people to "learn" ideas—or better, to gain knowledge and understanding—we have to worry about their readiness, their needs, the rewards they may be seeking. If we start with a book full of ideas, we have to ask what kinds of meaning these ideas can have for different students, and what reward, in increased adequacy, power, autonomy, or satisfaction they will get from bothering to understand the ideas.

What can ideas give to students? If merely memorized as words, nothing whatever (except good grades on some tests). If converted into knowledge useful for guiding experience, everything that Man is capable of.

The difference between an educated man and an uneducated man is the ability to ask fruitful questions; when he has formulated such a question he can always ask another one: Where shall I go for the answer? It is quite possible that within the lifetimes of most of us there will be machines that can give us all the available information just by pushing buttons; but what buttons shall we push?

The ability to ask fruitful questions is not the result alone of having information nor yet of having experience. It is the result of being able to translate the one into the other; of having understandings within which symbolic verbal behavior and overt participative behaviors are joined. There is an ingredient over and above both information and action. A thumping technical name for this ingredient is "an intuitively valid metatheory"—but perhaps an illustration would make it clearer.

The story goes that a big diesel locomotive refused to run. The engineers and technical experts wreaked their respective wills on the brute but to no avail. Finally a wise old bird was called in. He circled the machinery a few times, twisted a knob or two in an exploratory manner, and then, seizing a tack hammer, delivered two light taps on the whatsis. The locomotive gave a snort and started to roll. Asked for his bill, the old man said that $10,000 would be satisfactory. Asked for an itemization of the bill, he replied: "Information about diesel engines—50 cents. Tapping whatsis with tack hammer—50 cents. Knowing where to tap—$9,999.00." "Knowing where to tap" is the ingredient most usually missing from our educations.

Having information is good, and practicing tapping a whatsis may be good, too. But information and practice alone do not carry us very far. "Knowing where to tap" is what John Dewey had in mind when he wrote that for knowledge to function it must be "internalized"; it is what Edward Tolman, the great psychologist, had in mind when he said that the most important ability for a researcher experimenting with rats is to be able to "think like a rat." It is what an artist or machinist might refer to as "having a 'feel' for the materials," and what a human relations expert would call "the ability to put yourself in the other fellow's place."

The "instinct for the jugular," this "knowing where to tap," is developed through reflection on experiences in situations that have importance for the student. To reflect on anything means to separate oneself from it enough so that it can become an object of thought. Reflection is a quest for the essential elements, for the "essence" of an object, which, according to Aristotle, makes it what it is. It is the search from within one's own experience for the line that captures the "pine-ness" of a pine tree in a drawing, or the "going-ness" of a diesel engine. Such a search requires one to have a well-developed "frame of reference" which includes knowledge of basic factors and how they operate along with sophisticated hunches about what the needed idea would look like if we could find it. We need not only thoughts about objects; we also need thoughts about "how to think" with these ideas.

"How to think" includes both methods and orientations. Each field of knowledge comprises ideas about phenomena and also thoughts about how these ideas are to be manipulated. What is geometry without the concept of proof? Physics without its basic systematization of length, mass, and time? Biology without a feeling for tendencies? Poetry without openness to emotional response? Foreign language without a receptiveness to other ways of life? Chemistry without experimental controls? Philosophy without humility?

Knowledge exists within its own context of expectancies, attitudes, and propositions. Both the facts and the context are different from one domain of knowledge to the next. In short, each domain has its own discipline, its own prescribed way of life with respect to the phenomena it encompasses.

THE DOMAINS OF KNOWLEDGE[1,2]

To get the meat of the discussion for education, I shall assert that there are four different domains of knowledge and that they enable us to comprehend four corresponding kinds of realities. My proposition is that within these several domains of knowledge are implied quite clearly the objectives of education and the kinds of learning activities that schools should be concerned with.

These domains are, by recent tradition, physical science, biological science, social science, and humanistic studies. These four domains can be arranged along a continuum. Physical science is concerned with events and phenomena far out from the self—the stars, for example. Biological science comes in a little closer, and social science

still more. In fact, we find social knowledge always partly from the
point of view of a participant in the phenomena we are studying.
Humanistic study is subjective and "inside"; it has to do with the
unique thoughts and expressions of indivduals. It is the record not
of the world "out there" but of the experience that an individual has
with the world.

These domains of knowledge are not catalogs of information; they
are not "areas" to be limned in outlines and survey courses, endlessly
detailed. An encyclopedia or textbook gives only answers, but from
where come the questions that give these answers meaning?

The Physical Domain

The physical world is composed of rocks, mountains, brooks,
houses, railroads; beneath these lie pooled oil, ores, layers of sand,
and the fires of molten rock, and above are the wheeling constellations
and the shifting winds.

Compared to the other worlds, the properties of the physical world
are stable and unchanging. Iron is iron, not $iron_{1750}$ and $iron_{1958}$.
Mountains stay where they are, and my house is always—thank
goodness—at the same address. Because it is stable, the physical
world is the "frame of reference" within which we note the life of the
other worlds. It is the world of space-time, the coordinate system of
the universe, however large or small, within which we live.

There is change within the physical world, but it has dignity about
it. I may be disturbed and embarrassed by the crumbling of the
bricks in my wall (do you know what tuck pointing costs nowadays?),
but the bricks themselves are crumbling in an entirely orderly way.
The grandest and most dignified changes—which have always inspired
awe in Man—are the regular progressions of the planets and stars
across the heavens. If Apollo carted the sun in his chariot, at least he
did it regularly: you could count on it, not just now, but in eternity.
These things, along with the ebb and flow of the tides and the falling
of apples are lawful; and these laws hold throughout the physical
world. The laws of physics and chemistry and meteorology hold just as
well in Patagonia as in Chicago, on the top of Mt. Everest and in
Death Valley. The same phenomena, wherever and whenever studied,
resolve themselves in the same way.

One may speculate that the recognition of lawfulness, order,
grandeur, and reproducibility may have been the beginning of faith,

although I won't insist on it. But faith that the physical world is lawful, must always be lawful, and is lawful in every part is well rooted in Man, and so far as I can make out, this is the only area in which our faith holds firm, even though it gets shaken up every so often. But our faith in these things is so strong that when we discover nuclei of atoms whose goings on don't fit with our ideas of the laws governing objects with other, apparently similar properties, we assume that the laws governing both situations are simply special cases of some larger grander law. So we go back to the laboratory, not down on our knees or to the Federal government.

Because of this lawfulness, events in the physical world are predictable. If we have the kind of discipline I have described, we can rehearse events in our minds (using equations and formulas and tables to help) and anticipate what will happen if we do thus and so. We ferret out the laws on the assumption that given described causes lead to certain effects. The notion of relationships between two things, like height above sea level and the temperature at which water boils, is not only lawful, it is explainable in cause-and-effect terms. This model of "concomitant variation" to ferret out relationships is a way of thinking about physical phenomena, but it is also a habit of mind that we use when we start thinking about many other regular behaviors in man and nature.

Our faith in explainability leaves no room for accidents. In physical science there are no accidents. The story goes that workmen in a paint factory some years ago were horsing around at lunchtime. One of them translated an irresistible urge into action: he chucked a piece of cheese at another fellow, who ducked; the cheese sailed over his head and fell into a vat of lacquer. The workmen decided to keep mum, but the vat told on them! All its liquid contents hardened to stone. The boss took one look, yelled with delight, and said, "We've invented something, namely, quick-drying lacquer. Our fortune is made. Now how the devil did we do it?" In physical science what happens once can happen again, and all things are explainable.

Moreover, we have another faith about physical science, that all discoveries are worthwhile because they will be useful—sometime. It took Marconi to realize that Hertz's spark, jumping across a gap in a coil of wire, pointed to the principle for wireless transmission. Bernoulli's principle of fluid flow had been well known in the laboratory for years before it was set to work to lift the first flying crate off the ground. The laboratory curiosities of today are the social utilities of tomorrow. Thus we support "pure" research, which differs from workmen throwing cheese at each other in that it is programed and in that, when some new reactions or properties appear, they are described, studied, explained, and added to scientific knowledge.

Physical science is proof against human tampering. It doesn't matter who you are or what your education is or what age you live in, you and any other student of the same phenomena are likely to find out pretty much the same sort of things. Of course his language may be quaint and his grammar awful and he may dream up a different theory to explain his findings, but the rules of argument are well laid out: his findings are true if they can be reproduced by someone else and his theory is useful if it can predict results in new situations. "Right" and "wrong" mean only fidelity to nature, not to man's wishes.

This fact of hard realities and independence from wishful thinking says something about what man does with his knowledge of the physical world. Given a particular end that he is trying to achieve, he has the job of learning to encourage those processes that are "going his way" and to slow down or inhibit tendencies headed in other directions. The whole field of chemical technology and the production of everything from Scotch whisky to structural steel is based on a sort of rapport in which the environment speaks directly to man and in which his ideas are tested directly against the environment. The rules for this conversation are well known and simple. Any ten-year-old can take a piece of string and a few rocks and discover the laws of the pendulum for himself.

The discipline of physical science is a way of thinking about events in the physical world. Education in this field should be concerned with this discipline, learned through direct transaction between the student and the environment and reflected on under the guidance of the teacher. The fundamental cornerstones of this discipline are acceptance of stability, regularity, reproducibility; the pursuit of consistency, generalizability, and explanation; the habit of cause-and-effect thinking; and the habit of demonstrating one's conclusions by testing them. All this implies the ability to distinguish opinion from fact; the recognition that wishful thinking gets nowhere; and, finally, the readiness to work with Nature rather than against her by utilizing her processes and properties to open doors to a better life. And, in the understanding of these things, there is always that striving for rapport with Nature—the rapport or "feel" that distinguishes the creative researcher from the technician, just as it distinguishes the good sculptor from the hack-and-chisel brigade.

The Biological Domain

The physical world encroaches upon the biological: your blood may be "tired," as the TV huckster would have you believe, but actually the troubles of the blood would be easier to unravel using concepts of hydraulics and chemical balance. Certainly in our lifetime there has been a persistent and spectacular yielding of the "vital principle" to the instruments of physical science. The old-time "vital processes" are molecular, and as the structure of the participating molecules becomes known, their properties and functioning become predictable. Thus the operation of the Salk vaccine, of insulin, of hormones, of rat poison, and, just recently, of chromosomes, are understood and predicted in physical-chemical terms. Physical and biological sciences both rest on theories of matter and energy as understood in the behavior of molecular, atomic, and subatomic phenomena. The theoretical biologist and the atomic scientist speak much the same language, and it tends to utilize the vocabulary of mathematical functions.

The biochemical-physiologist hopes ultimately, from theoretical knowledge of the "microscopic" world, to predict the visible behaviors of such complex organisms as cancer cells, livers, and mammals. These behaviors will include muscular and physical movements, metabolic processes, and the delicate systems of balances through which the cell, organ, or animal maintains life. There is the further exciting possibility that what we have learned to think of as mental and "psychological" behavior will someday be explained by means of extensions of the same underlying physicochemical theories. It was seriously suggested at the Darwin Centennial Celebration at the University of Chicago (1959) that within the next fifty years the last "secrets of life" will have been penetrated by the nose cone of the electron microscope, the spectroscope, and other extensions of the inquiring human nervous system.

In the basic microscopic world of natural science there is no distinction between living and nonliving, between animate and inanimate. But in contrast to this invisible realm, not directly available to the unaided senses, there is the macroscopic world of common experience in which objects are directly apprehended by sight, touch, and other senses. The objects in this realm are large and complex organizations of the processes and materials of the invisible realm. The nature of their organization itself both depends on these ingredients and regulates their interactions with each other. Thus one can study the complexly organized liver or brain by determining the chemical and electrical interactions of their ingredients, but he can also upset the liver or brain (e.g., through drugs, hormone, electrical stimulation, or removal of some portions) and then observe how it reorganizes its functioning under these new conditions. This approach concentrates, not so much on the action of each part by itself as on the relationships among the parts during the operation of the organ.

In addition to the part-whole relationships within the cell, organ, or animal, the whole animal may be studied in relation to its environment. This is the pursuit of the psychologist and zoologist. In their macroscopic visible realm of large "whole" organizations, the distinction between living and nonliving and between "biological," "physical," and "psychological" (or "subjective") can be made. In this gross world of everyday experience, concepts of time and space have intuitive and useful meaning. The physical world is seen as the backdrop against which animals live out their allotted cycles, species emerge and die out, civilizations flourish and decline. Life is here viewed as the struggle for existence in a particular environment, and he who would say anything intelligible about any animal must give some account of its environment. To understand Johnny, the boy, or Marilyn, the dinosaur, we have to know the "situation" being coped with. To understand how Johnny or Marilyn changes or grows, we have to have some dimension of time, some notion of a stable frame of reference—and this is found in the physical world. This ecological insight and habit is part of the discipline of the macroscopic biological sciences.

One may consider a single living creature during a period of a few minutes or days; he may also consider a large number of creatures over a period of years or eons. Studies of individuals impress us with their *differences,* which may be genetic or constitutional (inherited) or learned through conditioning or insight (situational). Studies of large numbers, such as the members of an entire species, impress us with *similarities;* and these similarities, described in words, are viewed as norms which describe the species. The existence of these norms enables us to spot the "deviates," and these are of special interest because they may represent mutations (i.e., biologically "new" characteristics) or because they may simply represent some "normal" tendency carried to an extreme (and therefore easy to study). In either case, these deviates will have somewhat better or worse chances of survival than the parent species, and over time (and assuming the mutant change is passed on through biological or social heredity) a slight individual advantage over the norm may foretell the nature of the species to come. As applied to human beings, a species which defies natural selection by protecting its defectives, certain deviates who seem to be spectacularly successful tend to become our ego-ideals and we try to learn to be like them (or teach our children to be like them). The deviate we shall be considering at length is the educated man.

Living plants and animals have two "dynamic" characteristics. First, they exhibit growth, conceived in terms of beginning, middle, and end; of spurts, consolidations, and phases; of change "from within," continually going on. We comprehend growth through building models which are "normative," such as the picture of what is expected of an "average" (dull and fictitious) individual. These models portray the progression from simple to complex and from the un-differentiated to the differentiated. And they are further concerned with the harmony existing among various aspects of growth and with the rate and extent of growth. To understand Johnny, we must know not only his environment but also his location along the model of growth, and it helps to know in what ways he is *not* "average" so that the model won't be taken too seriously.

Second, the living creature is self-regulating. It is not merely acted on by forces (like a high school student in a dull English class); it operates on its own behalf to maintain vital conditions within itself and to maintain its integrity as an organism. It senses and takes into account a variety of conditions in the environment; and it maintains itself by changing itself (except that man can change his environment as well).

This process of sensing and responding to the environment is also the process of getting knowledge. The difference is only one of complexity between the one-celled animal, getting information about the conditions of its fluid surroundings, and Man, gaining a thousand kinds of knowledge about his tremendously complex surroundings. Survival for man is not a simple thing of "hot" vs. "cold," or "nutritious" vs. "poisonous"; it is a proliferation of needs for food, shelter, relaxation, activity, and so on. La Barre[3] makes the interesting point that with the first solitary cell, as with all later organisms and man, purpose and knowledge came into the world. But it is only man who is conscious of using knowledge consciously to achieve his purposes.

Considering the life of the functioning animal, methods of thought tend more and more to take account of behavioral "tendencies" and "probabilities" (or modes of action) in relation to needs, drives, and purposes of the animal. Needs, drives and purposes are conceived as part of the inner state of the animal, and are inferred from his observed behavior. They are useful to account for consistencies in his behavior: thus stealing a pie, lighting the gas stove, dropping in on a friend at dinnertime, and daydreaming about roast beef are all consistent and understandable symptoms of a man driven by hunger. Unfortunately, there are other possible explanations: he steals the pie to anger the cook; he lights the gas stove preparatory to sticking his head in the oven; he drops in at dinnertime because that is when he gets off work; and he daydreams about roast beef because it is Mother's Day, and that is what his mother always cooked on Tuesdays. One's chances of ruling out such hypotheses are greater under experimental conditions, in which one may systematically vary environmental (or stimulus) conditions. The animal may be thought of as a system (the so-called "black box") which is acted on by a stimulus (input) and then reacts visibly (output). Knowing the input and output, what events within the system would be required to connect the two? Thus when you stimulate a child with a big box of candy (input) and the child looks pained and refuses the candy (output) you might infer that the child (black box) is already full to the muzzle with peanuts, cookies, and hot dogs. (Unless, of course, he is ill). Educators use this notion, too: we stimulate the child with a test (input), examine what the child writes (output), and infer what mentality would account for the relationship (such as it is) between input and output. (Unless, of course, the child is frightened, fatigued, or defiant.)

The behavior and functioning of a civilized person is influenced by an extraordinary array of causes (needs, drives, purposes) except at times when he is overwhelmed, as by hunger, guilt, or fatigue. Ordinarily he weighs several values or goals and makes choices; and it is terribly difficult to predict a specific course of action in a single particular situation. But if one speaks of a large enough collection of similar animals, he can assert with considerably accuracy the probabilities of given events. The National Safety Council is impressively accurate (usually within 10 per cent) in its predictions of the number of people killed over the Labor Day weekends, but it would throw up its hands in horror if you asked it to name the people. Generalizations about the functioning of animals refer to classes of things, not to particular individuals.

Studies of the economic, political, religious, and other functions of groups of people and of societies belong in the realm of social science, and will be considered in the next section.

It seems to me that the unique contributions of the biological domain to education are: the habit of seeking an understanding of living creatures from the way they behave in their own environments; the development of wholesome respect for the organism's genius for self-maintenance and adaptation in the face of environmental change; learning the limits to adaptation possible under adverse conditions; the acceptance of the inevitability of growth and its accompanying organismic changes; the acceptance of the fact that no individual is quite like the "norm," and that individual differences from the norm are normal; the development of the habit of inference from observed behavior to function and purpose; the development of tolerance for tentativeness in situations governed by probabilities rather than certainties; and, finally, the acceptance of one's own self as a living creature with a full range of biological attributes.

These insights arose from the needs of men and they can be useful in helping pupils meet their needs. As educators we should teach biological science to illustrate and demonstrate these things, to help children notice and accept the fact of variability and the ranges of individuality and to encourage children to test how far their efforts to predict behavior of various sorts can be counted on—and all this should be understood in its application to themselves as living organisms.

The Social Domain

The development of society is required for meeting the gamut of biological needs—sex, food, and protection. Society is also the storehouse of accumulated knowledge and the interactive environment for individuals.

The development of society is the development of interdependence among men, and society mediates between man and his environment. In the old frontier days, a man and his family were self-sufficient— or else. They raised their food, made their clothes, and looked to each other and nature for entertainment. Nowadays, there is hardly a thing you can do for yourself by yourself. Everyone is dependent on every- one else, for everything—except, possibly, playing solitaire or reading a book, if you have already got the cards and the book.

Generalizations in the social world describe the agreements men live by, and by which they will determine their conduct. Some of these agreements may be clearly stated, as in laws. For example, Okla- homa$_{1955}$ was a dry state. Some agreements may be given in custom. For example, a lot of Oklahomans drank whisky. Some agreements are simply informal expectations. For example, politicians are clowns, or students are in class to learn. Other agreements can only be inferred by an observer to account for consistencies in the behavior of many people; an example is Riesman's[4] hypothesis that Americans are becoming "other-directed" rather than autonomous. In social groups—which are miniature societies—we all begin to "know" what to expect from different individuals without a word being said about it. One realizes the force of such expectations when some- body behaves unexpectedly, as when a former nonparticipant comes to life during a meeting.

Agreements are part of the "culture" of a society or community or group. They are or were held by identifiable people at some time and in some place. They arose as needed to help their society cope with a problem—such as protecting the power of the in-group—or simply to resolve conflicts among individuals who can't all have their own way because their ways are mutually exclusive. Within a society, each sub- group develops further agreements of its own about such things as acceptable modes for greeting each other, receiving strangers, demon- strating "belongingness."

But once agreements have become incorporated in habit and ration- alized in thought and attitudes, they tend to live on with a life of their own. Thus Eggan writes, "Much of our school society and cul- ture is traditional and wrapped up in a long enough history to give it a semi-sacred quality which has kept it from being disturbed."[5]

The very cement that holds a society together in the face of challenge and internal disruptive tendencies also makes it resistant to change. As the pressure for change mounts, the stage gets set for revision— the Reformation, the "managerial revolution," the New Deal.

Cultural agreements and the social order they maintain were constructed by men and can be changed by men. The means of change range from orderly processes of re-interpretation of consciously understood rules, as by judicial review—to the imposition of new rules by force—as in the initial legislation requiring nondiscrimination in jobs and in housing made available through the Federal government. A major dynamic force in society is the continuous process of becoming aware of dislocations and inadequacies that show up when the agreements no longer fit the facts of life. New purposes then have to be clarified and new agreements have to be found to implement these purposes; and, as the changes are made, the way of life has to change, too, in order to accommodate and maintain the purposes. We are living through a striking instance of this process right now in connection with the Middle East, beginning with the Suez episode; another example is the American high school now and in the next few years.

Within this kind of broad orienting view of society, the various social sciences select certain aspects for study, and each of the social sciences contributes uniquely to our understanding of the societal domain. Partly to indicate some of the content of social science as a domain of knowledge, and partly to anticipate some of the considerations in the remainder of this book, I shall introduce into the record at this point a brief résumé of themes or problems central in eight social sciences. This summary, written with Jacob Getzels, pulls together eight articles contributed to a published symposium[5] by eight of our colleagues at the University of Chicago.

Our geographer points to the natural environment of man and suggests that the character of the lives of any particular group depends on the opportunities and the limitations set by the environment. In his terms, the social order may be conceived as the set of provisions by means of which men determine and enforce policies regarding the use of natural resources, in the broad interpretation of this term. Our anthropologist is impressed with the observation that groups of men develop a common way of life, which is reflected in unique instrumental and expressive patterns of behavior. This way of life is maintained through the transmission of cultural norms, which provide the principles for patterning human activity from among the range of available alternatives. Our political scientist is concerned with those activities that are the outcome of policy decisions held as authoritative by most members of society most of the time. The political system is mainained through action and counteraction with respect to these policy decisions, and the stability of the system, and of course of the society of which the system is a part, depends on the extent to which a common political orientation is shared by the members of the society.

Our economist, like the geographer and political scientists, is also concerned with the processes of choosing among alternatives in one segment of society and the effect of such choices upon the other segments. But his concern is in a slightly different direction. It is related not so much to environmental opportunities or to the location of the authority for decision-making as to the values that particular alternatives, as represented by scarce resources, have for particular groups or institutions in achieving their particular goals. Our sociologist sees society as constituted of interlocking institutions, and he is concerned with the relations among the institutions and with the extent to which each institution allows the persons in it to fulfill their expected roles. He is concerned, too, with the origin and the resolution of institutional conflict and role conflict. Our lawyer centers his inquiry on the exercise of power by the state for the protection, through coercion, of the rights of individuals and groups. Our psychologist changes the focus somewhat and tries to look *within* the individuals fulfilling the various roles. He seeks to identify their unique needs and motives stemming from what he conceives to be, at least in part, their organismic being. He is interested in the way each individual solves the problems posed by society and by his membership in institutions that make different, sometimes conflicting demands upon him.

As this summary demonstrates, the social sciences among them deal with at least some aspects of every human activity. Their methods of study range all the way from statistical inquiries such as are used in the biological domain to track down drugs useful for combating disease to empathetic and introspective inquiries such as those used in the subjective domain for the appreciation and understanding of literature. Probably the most significant thing that can be said about methods in all the social sciences is a consequence of the fact that social realities are made by men. This means that the social scientist is studying something he may have helped create, is probably party to, has attitudes about, and identifies with; and that his own way of life may be changed by his research experience. Moreover, to the extent that his findings have social importance and he feels a social responsibility, the scientist is likely to find himself in the role of consultant to various groups and agencies. Also, as a citizen, he may become an advocate for social changes whose need is suggested by his studies.

This participant involvement in the phenomena he is studying may —and often has—seduced the social scientist into sitting in judgment on the individuals and groups he is studying. His judgment may be that of God, using the behavior of others to point up or justify moral principles. It may be that of a national chauvinist, trying to prove that his own time and country has a civilization superior to others. It may be that of a chap like you or me, using the experiences of others to explore and perhaps support our own view of the world.

There are two kinds of antidotes to these blinding and distorting possibilities. One is given in the hoary phrase, "Know thyself." For bias stops being bias and becomes "sensitivity" when one can describe its workings accurately. The second antidote is the belief way down deep that human behavior is purposive and that by and large it is reasonable in the eyes of its perpetrators. To understand it, then, means to get inside the lives of the people one is studying. What the historian "essentially does is try to re-enact in his own mind the thoughts and feelings of a previous age."[5] The student of the Hopi must be able to know what it is like to think and feel like a Hopi, at the same time that he studies his own reactions to that experience.

To a high degree the generalizations and methods—the discipline —of the social studies overlap with the ordinary mortal's ideas and conduct in everyday living. One may choose not to become deeply involved in the domain of physical science, but he has no choice at all with regard to the domain of social science. He lives right in the middle of it. Intelligent understanding and control of one's own participation in society, requires that one solve for himself the conflict between individual and society (or between one's biological and social natures). Only then is the individual sufficiently free to reap the advantages of his other learnings, deep though they may be.

All of us are practicing, if amateur, social scientists. The contribution of the discipline of the social studies to education is to make us better practicing, even if still amateur, social scientists; and therefore better citizens, parents, leaders, and autonomous individuals. Note that once again I insist on the discipline, not just the organized information, of this domain of knowledge.

The relationship between participation in the classroom and learning social studies can very clearly be a two-way street. Social science illuminates and thus can contribute to development of a productive way of life in the classroom; we remember that the social scientist is always to some extent a participant in the phenomena he studies. The students in a class are generating and dealing (somehow) with a great many (not all) of the kinds of phenomena the social sciences deal with. Certainly it is intriguing to think of the classroom partly as a social science laboratory in which the problems and processes the student is engaged in supply at least some of the experiences to be studied in the social science curriculum. And the same notion could be extended to the school as an example of a small institutional community. Just to test this notion, I have listed a few of the kinds of questions that arise in every classroom and I have indicated particular social sciences which could increase the participants' understandings of these questions:

What is the nature and definition of authority (political science)? How "free" is the individual to influence others (political science, sociology, and anthropology)? What agreements as to conduct are needed, and with what degree of explicitness must they be detailed (anthropology, psychology)? How can outmoded or unsatisfactory or sterile ways of doing things be changed (social technology)? What sorts of information does the teacher need to get from the group in order to find common cause, motivation, and involvement (psychology)? What recourse is there for the individual who cannot, for whatever reason, go along with the group (law)? How are individual needs to be met within general group purposes (psychology, sociology)?

The Subjective Domain

There is a whole field called the humanities—philosophy, literature, the arts—which includes primarily the products of subjective reaction. These are the efforts of individuals to explain the world in their own terms, to express things that are universally felt but difficult to comprehend—things unique, idiosyncratic, rich, colorful, touching, wonderful—referring to parts of the world which are mysterious, curious, and exciting. More important, such explanations provide the grounds for adaptation, as these germinal ideas somehow throw light (probably through anxiety reduction and a sharpening of perceptual sensitivity) on problems to which the society must adapt.

The purposes of the humanities are to enrich comprehension of one's inner life, one's subjective world, not to produce a small-bore literary critic or professional musician or an argumentative escapist from commitments to causes. For their correct purposes, the humanities have to be met selectively, voluntarily, and sympathetically, and one can be helped by a good companion who can encourage one's strivings for awareness and meaning. The humanities belong to the greatest and most important quest of all: the quest for selfhood, without which all else is dust and mockery, empty and foolish.

Each individual student acts in accordance with the ideas in his subjective world. He does not act in accordance with the ideas in a textbook unless he has incorporated them without change or distortion into his own system of thought—a most unlikely event. As has been pointed out often enough by our psychiatric colleagues, individuals try to maintain this private world within, and it is the conflict in this world, generated from new experience, that drives learning and creativity. We have said that *many* aspects of human activity lie in the social domain. We may now add that *all* aspects have roots in the subjective domain. And education as the quest for meaning must be seriously and explicitly concerned with the relationships between the subjective domain and each of the other three.

We have already hinted at much of the importance of the subjective world in our discussion of inquiry and autonomy. Let us consider this matter of subjective meaning with respect to some items of knowledge. Suppose we are going to teach a unit on the Westward Movement. We all get maps, look up old journals and diaries, examine relics in the museum; we try to reconstruct the situation. We bring out facts: there was a lot of danger, a lot of hardship, perhaps a lot of camaraderie; there were moments of great tension and excitement, and greatness. And so we make our picture. But what does the child get from this? There are at least two conclusions he may choose. One child might get the notion that the world is a very hostile and dangerous place, and by all means the best thing to do is stay home where it is safe. Another child might get the idea that to become a real human being and realize all you have in you—to be alive—you have to go out and seek adventure, and hardship is part of it. He might even glimpse the faith that man can overcome hardship if he has courage. These are two altogether different meanings.

What we call school achievement is only a part of what is learned in the classroom. From the standpoint of future performance, some of the other learnings from classroom experience may be at least as important: learning mathematical skills along with a determination to avoid mathematics forevermore; a decision to be a scientist even though one has little aptitude for rigorous symbolic manipulation; a decision to stay in school only until one is big enough to drop out.

The humanities, however, are concerned not just with the enrichment of the physical, biological, and social worlds. They contribute uniquely to the development of the life of the spirit. They help people discover in themselves the universal experiences of the human race. The human quest is inquiry into what it means to be human, to have aspirations, to experience tragedy, sorrow, delight, and love. To be able to hear the bell that tolls and to have a sense of sharing in fundamental and universal experiences gives meaning to one's partnership with the human species just as surely as sharing in common attitudes and values gives meaning to one's belongingness in the social group. The kind of meaning one finds in being a human being is at the very center of one's cosmos; and an individual who, through lack of education or opportunity, has never come to terms with these larger questions feels deprived, hollow, and restless.

The contribution to education of the humanities and their disciplines of self-expression are, in summary: to perceive in one's own experience universals which enable him better to understand all experience; to "free" one of verbal straitjackets so that he can express his impulses and feelings through a variety of media; to help one become "open" to the evocative stimulation of artistic expressions; to sensitize one to the existence of a variety of human aspirations; to develop aesthetic sensitivities leading to the discovery, pursuit, and enjoyment of beauty; to free one's spirit to soar through all the expanse of imaginable time and space.

KNOWLEDGE AND INQUIRY

We conclude from our examination of the four domains of knowledge that they were constructed through different methods of investigation; that they refer to different kinds of realities. They arose from basic human needs; they have different degrees of coerciveness, usefulness, and subservience to man's wishes; each of them has its own modes of thought, and all these modes are needed to navigate in this complex world. And finally, these domains must be understood in their own terms and not violated.

Organized information is a by-product of knowledge. It is the verbal sign of knowledge compressed into cells, and the meaning is not there. Knowledge is unborn experience; it is the universals incorporated in the nervous system; it is a predisposition to approach the world with inquiry; it is meaningful past experience living on within oneself; it is the seed of potential internal reorganization through which one keeps in touch with the changing world. Knowledge lies in the basic alternative orientations—and the propositions through which new orientations can be built—by which we grasp the essence of events, comprehend them, and through comprehension, maintain and extend our own autonomy and captaincy of self. Knowledge enables us to not be caught flatfooted by the throw of the die; it enables us to understand in their own terms the phenomena with which we must and do deal.

In Chapter 2 we tried to describe the nature of inquiry. In this chapter so far we have approached inquiry, not from the nature of the human animal but rather from the other side: the nature of the way experience has been accumulated and gradually brought under control within the tribe. Through reflection, testing, talking, controversy, language and logic, a great deal of wisdom (in the form of conditioned orientations) has been built into the assumptions on which we live. A great deal more wisdom (in the form of alternative orientations) has been tucked away—by implication—in the records of men's thoughts and in the facts of their deeds. These implications, internalized within students, are felt as universals, guiding ideas, predisposing hunches, and so on. They represent, for that student, his knowledge. And his knowledge includes both concepts and the disciplined understanding of how to use these concepts.

For a student to gain knowledge, a number of things must happen.

First, he must give attention to something. This means that out of the flux of the perceptual inputs of living, certain things must arrest his attention—bring him up short, poise him in mid-air. Our jargon for this is to say that a need becomes felt, or that he has run into some discontinuity or gap, or that some external demand has hit him, or that some stress has arisen in his established mode of interacting with the environment. But even without the jargon, his attention must be focused on something.

Second, he must, as I have described for our little boy in the park, puzzle over something. This involves processes of the emergence of ideas into consciousness, where they can be dealt with. Dealing with ideas includes such things as associating other ideas to them, classifying them (as, for example identifying the domain to which they belong), trying to recall past experiences, rejecting notions that seem bizarre or inappropriate, engaging in speculation. Thoughts are cheap and mental processes are as lush as tropical vegetation. The wonderful thing is that you can spend all kinds of time mulling things over and thoroughly enjoy it. (It is said that John Dewey brought a particularly muddy two-hour seminar to a close one time by remarking: "Well, I think I can say that I now have a better understanding of the meaning of the word 'this.'")

Now there is one aspect of this process of puzzling that has been seriously slighted and denied, especially by scholars, which is that it goes on in a social context. Just as knowledge is the accumulated and conditioned wisdom of a society, so puzzling always goes on in reference to groups to which one belongs. The kind, penetration, enjoyment, and richness of speculation depends a good deal on the culture in which one has been raised. Moreover, one is stimulated by the challenge of newly perceived alternatives and by controversy with other people when they are similarly puzzled. They help one become aware of many meanings that would otherwise lie dormant in one's nervous system. Even if other people are not physically present, the processes of speculation are interactive. Lincoln is dead, but I mean no disrespect in saying that in many situations it is not merely whimsical to ask "What would Lincoln have done?" We will talk about group process in relation to inquiry a little later; let us merely note that a second process in knowledge getting is interaction with other people who are puzzled by (or imagined to be puzzled by or at least concerned with) the thing one is puzzling over.

Were we to stop here—which is where many classroom discussions stop—we would be settling not for knowledge but for gratifications. The discussion has been fun, even though nothing was learned. No, we must go on. What is needed now is *reflection*.

I suppose that for a great many people the need for reflection manifests itself in sleeplessness. Things hang over which have to be settled. One has to complete the internal reorganization of his own world, whose bits and pieces were shaken around by the interaction with the ideas of others. One has to resolve his puzzlement, find peace and closure, and tuck his new meanings tidily away within the framework of the old ones. And because one's world has been tidied up and strengthened through the comprehension of his own experience, he becomes free to give attention somewhere else tomorrow. But his nerve endings are more sensitive and his perceptual apparatus is sharpened: he has knowledge, and because he has knowledge life becomes a quest, not for answers—the only final answer is death—but for the significant questions to ask.

Can any or all of this occur in a classroom? Possibly, but little of it does at present. How are we going to bring it about?

NOTES

1. The basic organization of ideas in this chapter was presented in Herbert A. Thelen, "The Curriculum and the Domains of Knowledge," *The Elementary School Journal*, LV, No. 7 (March 1955), 369-376.
2. The notions were examined further in light of the Reality Principle in Herbert A. Thelen, *Dynamics of Groups at Work* (Chicago: University of Chicago Press, 1954), pp. 262-273.
3. Weston La Barre, *op. cit.*, Chapter 2.
4. David Riesman, *The Lonely Crowd* (New Haven: Yale University Press, 1950), p. 386.
5. Herbert A. Thelen and Jacob Getzels, "The Social Sciences: Conceptual Framework for Education," *School Review*, LXV, No. 3 (Autumn 1957), 339-355.

4

Society:
The House that Jack Lives In

In which we consider the social context of the school: its place in the community, the community-inspired needs of its students, and the dying out of the values on which education was once based. We suggest that improvement of schools will require us to take proper account of community pressures, and that this can be done only through continual, shared concern by both the community and the school for the welfare and education of youth.

It is no doubt as flattering to the egos of schoolmen at it is relieving to the anxieties of parents to believe that schools educate our children. Nothing, of course, could be further from the case. The school, like the meat market, pool hall, church, and streetcar company, contributes *something* to the education of children, no doubt, but one would be hard put to know just what, how important it is, how central in the student's life, and how much it contributes to the over-all development that we refer to as education. In our society it is the community's responsibility to educate its children; and in fact, the community does educate its children—one way or another. Our pious assumption that the educational job is done entirely by the schools is patently false as judged by our knowledge of what really goes on.

The false belief that the school is the community's sole educative agency leads to a rather seriocomic state of affairs: every group or individual with any kind of vested interest in education immediately

54

gets out its snickersnee and goes out after the schools! Service clubs, religious groups, merchants, police safety squads, charitable institutions needing pennies, colleges wanting students—not to mention the 100 per cent Americans, the regional chauvinists, and the foundations with pet notions about education.

ⅩThe learning of the child is actually influenced willy-nilly by all of his experiences in the community. Such an authority as the play *South Pacific,* in a rare burst of insight and courage, points out that race prejudice has to be "carefully taught"—presumably in the home and neighborhood, although if the schools would like some credit for this I won't stand in their way. The notion, held by one school of psychiatric thought, that the basic character structure of children is formed by the age of four is acknowledgment with a vengeance of the role of other parts of the community in education.

We need a complete reinterpretation of the place of the community and the school in the enterprise of education. In Chapter 3, I used the discussion of the knowledge discipline of the social sciences as an occasion to identify some of the kinds of questions we need to ask. I shall develop the remainder of this discussion around three major questions: (1) What are the relationships between the school and the community? (2) What is the place of youth in the community, and therefore, what are the needs of youth as a group? and (3) What is the relationship between the community's values and the education it provides?

SCHOOL-COMMUNITY RELATIONS: SYSTEMS

To get into this exciting topic, I'll need your help. Gather together the following materials: a large sheet of paper, a pencil (with eraser), and a bowl of popcorn.

With the pencil put a large dot in the center of the paper, and label it "school." Now on the corner of the paper—which we will throw away later—practice drawing ellipses or ovals (more or less egg-shaped). Now draw a dozen such ellipses around the dot, in such a way that the dot is down near one end of each, and they all point every which way out from the dot. Now sprinkle labels, one to an ellipse. It doesn't matter too much what the labels are—I'm sure your imagination is as good as mine, and you can't go wrong on this—but I have a preference for adjectives like "economic," "politi-

cal," "religious," "civic," "social," "business," "artistic," "charitable,"
"military," "aesthetic," "romantic," etc. If you buy these, you have
one left to make for yourself—try "educational." Now that you
have finished this visual aid, help yourself to a handful of popcorn.

The ellipses represent various "systems"—religious, political, and
all the rest of it; and what you have shown is that the school is a
part of each, and that they all to some extent overlap each other. This
is called "field"[1] theory. Each ellipse, or system, is composed of the
institutions, groups, and people who are concerned with that system.
Thus the community's religious system contains the people whose
attitudes, philosophies, hopes, conflicts, and behavior, taken together
determine whether the community will be tolerant in religion, battling
over religion, united with high morale, discouraged, and so on.
Through the communication of these ideas, attitudes, and feelings,
there has gradually developed in your community a network of
expectations within each ellipse. Each person or group or organization
"expects" some things of each other person, organization, etc. Moreover, each such agency expects something of itself. Finally, each
agency expects others to expect different things of it. It's the same
thing with a youngster whose hand stops halfway to the cookie jar.
The reason he hesitates is that he is in a conflict of expectations: he
expects that his mother halfway figures he'll swipe the cookies (he's
smarter than his mother on this point); he expects his father to remain out of the picture unless his mother tells on him—and it's
hard to figure the percentage on that; he expects the gang to compare
him favorably to Zorro—if he brings back the loot; he also has
expectations of personal enjoyment and remorse, of what the Sunday
school teacher would think if she knew, and all the rest. We might
call this the "cookie-system" for Johnny.

Well, it's like that for each agency, including the school, in each
system. The behavior of each is influenced by its understanding of
the expectations they all have for each other. In other words, the
school's attitudes toward religion, and its activities that have to do
with religion, are influenced by the whole "field" of expectations
within the community's religious "system." The school is by no means
a free agent with respect to most of its decisions; whether it knows
it or not, all these other groups and their attitudes and expectations are
going to enter into the decision. Also, the school, unlike most other
agencies, is part of *all* the systems of the community: economic, edu-

cational, civic, etc. This means that some part of everything it does is likely to be influenced by one or more such systems.

From this, we may deduce two notions: one is that the school is going to be a football for the other groups, in the other systems, to kick around. Consider an example: look at the idea of "released time" during the day for various religious denominations to give "religious instruction" to the students. Within the religious system there wll be controversy, probably because some denominations have the manpower to do this and others don't. Within the political system, there will be a lot of noise around the issue of separation of church and state. Within the economic system, there may well be raised the problem of what the teachers, who have less class time, will do with their now freed time; and, in the larger view of economics, there will be the notion that school time is a scarce commodity and the alternative ways of using it must be weighed and compared. And so on. There is hardly a single thing, from proposed methods of reading, course requirements, the use of field trips, freedom of speech of the teacher, the number of boys and girls dropping out of school, etc., that will not arouse conflict and static in several different systems.

Secondly, if a decision is carried out, the school has now redefined its role—which means that the agencies in each system have to revise their expectations of the school's behavior; and along with this, they will revise their own expectations of each other and of themselves. They will plan new strategies, either supportive or combative; will form new alignments; will make new friends and new enemies. Thus it is truly said that "a change in any part of a system results in changes in all other parts." In social enterprises we may add: "Change of any one part of a system is likely to be resisted by many other parts who know somehow that their turn will be next."

SCHOOL-COMMUNITY RELATIONS: FORCES

The concept of systems—political, economic, religious, educational—is highly theoretical. You cannot touch, taste, smell, or see an abstraction like a "system." The practical fact is that what one deals with is people. The concept of systems gives us a way to represent some of the social facts about these people: they have identifications, feelings of belongingness in groups, and attitudes and values consonant with their position and place in society. This position and place is given partly in the fact that they have jobs to do, and it is through the interlocking activity of these jobs that the economic, political, and other needs of the community are met. Each person thus has "functional" interdependence with a good many other persons, and each person has identifications and attitudes toward the other. A group of people having similar functional and social relationships comprise or are a "part" of a system.

The purposes and needs of each system generate pressures or demands, and these are brought to bear by individuals who in some sense, either officially or informally, speak for parts of the system (e.g., the pastor speaks for his church, which is one part of the religious system). The person who is thus spoken to feels the communication as a *force,* demand, or pressure put upon him.

We wish now to consider the typical situation in which the communication from one system to another is perceived as a pressure or demand. Would you mind getting an apple and twelve knitting needles? And, while you are at it, why not refill the bowl of popcorn? Now hold the apple in one hand and push each of the knitting needles through it, from twelve different directions. Aim for the center of the apple.

Think of the part of each needle that sticks out of the apple as an arrow pointed right at the school. Each arrow represents a "force" or pressure on the school, and each force is opposed, on the opposite side of the apple, by another force. One force in each opposed pair may be longer or shorter or equal in length (or intensity) to the other; that depends on how far you pushed the needle. This represents the balance-of-forces theory, or, if you want to be fancy about it, a modification of the "quasi-stationary equilibrium"[2] theory. The only place learning theory enters is with the bowl of popcorn, which represents reinforcement of effort through reward.

Now pretend that you are the apple's administrator, and look around you. What do you see? You see all those pressures, and you feel them impinging right on you. These pressures are generated by the expectations of the various groups in the various systems. You encounter these pressures as demands made by individuals, and they are expressed in different ways—in the form of pronouncements by professors that the school ought to "meet the needs of youngsters," or in the mildly expressed hope of the PTA president that something can be done to teach Johnny to think. These particular demands are gentle, as you can judge from the short length of knitting needle sticking out of the apple. You can probably deal with these demands through an innocuous program of public relations. But some of the other needles don't feel good at all; they are threatening. For example, here is a long-needle demand from teachers to let the first graders out at noon for the first two weeks—countered by that long-needle bureaucrat in the State Department of Education who insists that if you do you cannot claim state aid for these days. In this case you have two long needles jabbing from opposite directions, producing what is known as a "squeeze." Other examples: the United Friends of Human Misery want you to take up a collection for their Center and the Brotherly Comrades of the Downtrodden claim it will be over their dead body—which seems, temporarily at least, like a good idea. Your last consultant got your teachers all fired up about an "experience" curriculum, and the noisiest history professor in the local university is screaming bloody murder. The town's loyal alumni want you to hire a football coach (and they are willing to pay him more than you get) and a delegation (from six different systems) is waiting in your office right now to urge you not to (and they don't have a cent).

The apple—if you still have it—portrays the psychological side of the normal conflicts between and within systems. These social realities tend to be interpreted and responded to, not as acceptable, proper, and necessary conditions of life, but as personalized and willful pressures. Psychologically, our tendency is to react not to the legitimate issues involved so much as to the "ulterior motives" we think people have. A squawk is a squawk, not a communication, however inefficient, of needed or useful data.

Caught in what is perceived as a pressure squeeze, many an administrator feels trapped and anxious; he sees no escape. He reacts as you and I might: he gets counterdelegations together to "interpret the program," he writes fancy-sounding pronouncements to hurl, he knuckles under or lashes out, and then, if "they" won't leave him alone, he starts looking for a new job.

The superintendent, school board, and teachers association feel trapped in the same anxious squeeze. They know intellectually that things like changing employment practices, industrial developments, and political upsets have some sort of importance for the school, but when the community is perceived and reacted to primarily as a network of groups each anarchically pressuring the other, this intellectual knowledge remains empty abstraction. The practical problem becomes all-important: to maintain the school—not the educational mission—as if it were a fortress besieged. The maintenance of the school as an organization is the same problem as the maintenance of the local pickle factory, or of the economic balance in the Near East; and knitting needles and apples, translated into "public relations" and political and economic pressures, are the time-honored custom.

If the schools are trapped, so are other community agencies. And much of what we see and at which we cringe represents reactions to the feeling of being trapped. The schools are used by many in different ways as a stage for acting out problems that didn't arise there and which are aimed at the schools simply because they are an easy mark; you can always take out your aggressions on the school when you can't find some better target. Thus, for example, the school in some communities is the pawn in political battles, and such communities have incorporated the annual school fight among their traditional ways of maintaining the community. The fact that they can fight over such matters probably arises out of feelings of impotence in their legitimate spheres, reflects incompetence in the use of leisure time, and suggests that it is too dangerous to fight over anything important. So issues arise over the teacher who smokes (especially if she is pretty), the teacher who exercises his right as a citizen to express political views, the teacher who does not go to church, the unmarried teacher who lives alone and likes it, and so on. One is reminded of the account of New Zealand miners, who, deprived of the old-time fights over wages by paternalistic arrangements for socializing labor, would spend hours in the bar making bets on which of two flies would first take off. They would explain, "It gives us an interest."

We are all familiar with a striking recent example of the use of the schools to channel widespread unrest, or, to be technical about it, "free-floating anxiety." This is the only theory that can associate the launching of Sputnik to the requirement of an extra course in math or science for high school graduation. One can only assume that the children are being punished for the laxity of adults, or that this is a fright reaction—a political move which gives the appearance of doing something but without doing anything that would threaten the comfort of citizens; it has the appearance of change without upsetting the vested interests of adults.

Another illustration is given by the groups that try to push the school into teaching things like the "evils of alcohol." One can readily see how such a group of adults, feeling trapped and frustrated at their inability to deprive other adults of the right to drink, might, as next best, settle for scaring the devil out of children.

Thus we see that the knitting-needle concept of the community may result in the schools being imposed upon (for the wrong reasons). The reverse of this ploy is that the school can also be strongly supported (also for the wrong reasons). This is seen in the generally conceded usefulness of the school in providing entertainment to adults via football games. These may be important to provide a focus of interest and togetherness for adults, to increase morale, and to provide an activity which serves as a symbol of unity for the community.

PUBLIC RELATIONS AND SCHOOL IMPROVEMENT

The school administrator usually holds to the ellipse theory intellectually at the same time that he operates with knitting needles. Probably the best evidence of the way the school perceives the community is its public relations activities. Generally speaking, most schools engage in public relations in order to maintain themselves. The school recognizes that it must have good will, public regard, and money. Its opportunity to hire additional teachers, add a new gymnasium—even to get money for routine operation in some cities—depends upon "the public." The feeling of school as fortress is strong: dark and sinister dragons—some of them laughable in other contexts—are constantly ready to take a pot shot at the school and any one of these might be lucky enough to tumble the walls. In an uncomfortably literal sense, many schoolmen and teachers are simply holding the fort. To head off anticipated raids, we see schoolmen engaged in "public relations," and note their ulcerous anxiety about saying the right thing to the right people. Their goal to a large extent is to get people either to leave the school alone or to get them behind things the schoolmen want.

Public relations may be conducted in a wide variety of ways, as, for example, in calling for "advisory help" from groups like the PTA which exist primarily for other purposes. The chief problem here is the fear of the administrator that the advisory group will run hog wild, actually expecting to have its advice taken. The committee itself is equally fearful of making a suggestion, and especially a creative one. It projects its power fantasies (those knitting needles again) into the thought that its suggestions will be taken as a mandate from "the people" rather than reflected on, considered, and viewed simply as data for professional schoolmen to use in making wise decisions.

I am sorry to run on so long in this vein, but there remains one further depth to plumb. We must recognize what goes on inside the school. In a word, when there is distrust in the school's external relationships to the community, there is likely to be distrust also within the school. Thus in a certain large school system the rule is that any time a parent comes to talk with a teacher, the principal must be present. This suggests that he expects a fifth column at work within the school, and, of course, such expectations tend in the long run to be self-realizing.

The way educational problems are solved is very much affected by school-community relations, and many schools are doing about as well as can be done under the knitting-needle concept of group anarchy. In some schools there is a feeling of seriousness and responsibility for the educational mission. This involves trying out new devices for improving the efficiency, scope, or "depth" of experience provided for educational purposes. We have seen many movements over the years—movements toward teacher-pupil planning, the whole development of guidance services in schools, the growth of work experience (supervised by instructors), workshops of various sorts (sometimes shared by members of the community)—all for the purpose of invigorating the instructional program. Current innovations include the use of TV with classes of 200 or even of 400—which of course *does* take some explaining in view of the plea for money over the last fifteen years to reduce class size as much as possible. The creation of an élite group of gifted children is another experimental innovation; and here public relations are rather delicate, what with the concern of parents for "equal opportunity" and the trauma of having to decide at some point—but at what point?—who should be given additional "challenge." There is no doubt that the ferment involved in *any* experimental program does tend to wake teachers up, to get them interested in their work, to generate some enthusiasm, and to cause them to pay more attention to children than is their usual wont. This is all to the good, although just how much of the improvement is due to changed teacher attitude and how much is due to the actual innovations is extraordinarily hard to measure.

Generally speaking, the improvement of schools costs money, and it takes a great deal of effort and new learning by teachers—a fact perhaps insufficiently recognized in the rush for administrative gimmicks and do-it-yourself "group dynamics" magic. The money may come through governmental legislation, such as the Smith-Hughes Act; from foundations of all sorts which have interests in the improvement of education, as they see it; and from local support, through the usual tax channels. One of the stronger concerns of some school superintendents is whether all the taxable real estate in their district really is being taxed, and whether the taxes are being collected from everyone. The layman, who visualizes the head schoolman as poring over learned professional literature to discover hints to gives his teachers about why Johnny can't read, would hardly recognize this chap at work in the offices of its tax assessor and tax collector. This attitude implies a certain amount of inefficiency in the town government, and the administrator is serving as watchdog. I suppose this is hardly much different in kind from the various taxpayers' leagues who watch the other way to be sure the schools do not get the tax rate increased.

The illustrations I have been discussing all represent the knitting-needle assumption: that demands made by one agency or system on another shall be met as if they were attacking forces. This is a natural concomitant of a way of life in which decisions are based on power or the threat of power wielded by various groups. Under these conditions there is lack of trust, and one must be continually on the defensive; he must protect himself from the demands of his friends, offered in the form of "advice," just as from the attacks of his enemies. And because the school is a part of so many systems, impinging in so many ways on the life of the community, it has many friends and enemies. Under the present system of group anarchy, behavior reflects vested interests (however muted the expression) rather than the common weal.

It is clear that something terribly important has somehow been forgotten, and that is the educational mission of the school. Its energy has gone into the struggle for institutional survival, for making its relatively less and less adequate resources do an astronomically expanding job. There has been very little left over for studying and improving its educational functioning. Moreover, such contacts as it has had with the other systems for which it is supposed to prepare pupils have not been germane to education but only to the demands of vested interests.

What is needed, of course, is to use the existence of demands as data for understanding the social realities of the overlapping systems discussed in the first part of this chapter. We need to move from "acting out" to "inquiry," from animal reflexes to social enlightenment, from emotionality to thoughtfulness. What I have been discussing in this chapter has already been discussed in Chapter 2. The difference is that there we saw the fundamental conflict within human nature manifested within the individual; here we see it projected in group and institutional action. But the source of the difficulty in both cases is the same—and so is the solution.

There are some communities and schools that are taking exploratory steps toward this solution at the community level, through joint inquiry. Conflicts of interest between groups, as between individuals, do not have to start a fight; they can also lead to open debate which clarifies the issues; and these can be studied, facts obtained, and action taken. The participants in debate, study, and action generally include the parties between whom the conflict arose, plus experts and—this is essential—"neutral" citizens whose allegiance is to the whole community rather than to either of the erstwhile adversaries. In such communities, the rule of law is superseding the law of the jungle.

I shall return to this beachhead in the final chapter, after we have gained some image of the nature and means of the education we need.

THE PLACE OF YOUTH IN THE COMMUNITY

The second major question is, What is the place of youth in the community?—and therefore, what are the needs of youth as a group? This is no sentimental question; it is highly practical. Every teacher and leader knows that he must put forth special energy to get acquainted with his co-workers and students, for only then can he know how to work with them. Or, more accurately, only then can he lead them in ways they can and will follow. They have, in short, wills of their own. But it is not enough for teachers to content themselves, as they have always done, with trying to know the students in class, for all they can show us in class is their reactions and interests to the selected possibilities we present there. That is, the only choice they have is to try to make the best of what may be a bad lot of alternatives, none of which is of much interest or importance.

We must step back and take a broader sociological view, not concentrating on the individual differences among individuals so much as on the characteristics of the whole group of youth. And the first, most startling, and dramatic fact is that *youth has little or no functional place in the productive life of the community*.

This does not mean that youth has no place of any kind in the family and community. Children are loved, protected, valued; they are objects of our adult concern, and the surest way to get run out of town is to be mean to children. And children do not expect to be a part of the adult community. They find security in being responded to by adults, in being recognized as human beings and in being encouraged to grow up. Parents find delight (and release of their lurking anxieties) in such accomplishments of the child as learning to talk, eat food efficiently, and make bright remarks. The child's accomplishment is a source of gratification to parents, and he earns and has security and self-esteem because of their regard.

As adolescence comes along, however, there are changes in the situation. The achievement of the child is now taking place in school, and the parents learn of it only through secondhand reporting via more or less ambiguous marks. For some fortunate children of educated middle-class background, school achievement can keep up and enhance self-esteem, and thus make up for the loss of possibilities within the family. For a few other fortunate children, helping out with the family routines can be a route to self-esteem, although in most families I suspect that it is more often a cue to the feeling of being exploited, which is not the same thing at all. But for a great majority of adolescents, less fortunate than these, there is no satisfactory way to earn the esteem of adults. Moreover, the adolescent finds himself making more and more demands on the family budget, and he senses, regardless of reassurances to the contrary, that he is inconvenient if not downright resented. Parents by and large continue to love their children, but the adolescent has no way to earn or justify this love, and he is likely to believe that it has diminished. Thus Professor

Robert Hess[3] found that adolescents tend to believe that parents have much less regard for them than the parents actually have.

Under these conditions, adolescents become impatient either to break away from the family, with its continual reminder of their superfluousness, or to seek a job or other role in the productive life of the adult community. But these possibilities, for youth of pre-college age, are difficult to manage. Youths are too young to marry; there are many pressures against this and against entering the world of work. They do not participate in elections and there is no effective way in which they can participate in the political, commercial, financial, or cultural aspects of the life of the community.

Teen-agers, however, are granted a place in the community as consumers or as inciters to consumption by various commercial interests, which contribute such bits as the following to the community's educational effort:

Your boy: are *you* helping him to do his best? When is he most likely to do his best? Ask his teachers or principal. They've learned by experience that when a boy looks his best, he's more apt to do his best . . . if he's dressed for serious schoolwork, he's more apt to take school seriously. Make sure wherever he is—at school, at church, at play—your boy rates "A" in appearance. It can help him win "A's" in other things too![4]

I guess no group is too deprived to be exploited!

Adolescents may try to find a place by imitating the one segment of society they can identify with as most nearly at their own level of maturity. I refer, of course, to the night life, the café society, the entertainment world of TV and the screen, the pseudosophisticated high society, the conspicuous consumers, the multiple-married— all the adults who have not yet grown up and whose place in the world is given by their ability to express for other adults their remaining immature impulses. These are the people who can provide a model gratifying to frustrated adolescents, for they show that adolescence can be rewarding after all, if you are lucky. These people differ from the adolescent in that they can carry their tendencies to an extreme, which means that they can do the things "nice" people don't do, and this is precisely what a rebellious and insecure adolescent would like to do.

Such adolescents may form minority groups banded together in a feeling of impotence and deprivation, however well they may over-compensate for such feeling. These groups develop their own symbol system, their own language, gods, flamboyant customs, fetishes; they are restless; denied any legitimate way to channel their energies they have only such possibilities as conducting "drag" races up and down the main street of Sheridan, Wyoming, participating in gang "rumbles" in New York City, and otherwise filling in time, trying to build their egos through demanding and (at any cost) getting attention. Their object, fruitlessly sought, is to make a place for themselves—a fact perfectly well known and validated by the experience that many juvenile offenders can be reclaimed through work experience.

As parents, we have enough guilt feeling about the lack of a meaningful role for youth in the community and the home that we give them a large allowance, the family car, or their own convertibles. We lavish every privilege of irresponsibility on them, thus robbing them of even the most minute opportunity to earn any real self-esteem.

The few places we might give youth approval and self-esteem—through legitimate educational achievement—lie in areas of indifference to adults. Of course, the parents, recouping their own losses and living in dreams of the future (to be acted out by their kids at no risk to them) are interested in their own children's grades and, sometimes, in their education. Indifference does not extend to the contests sponsored by the local service club for patriotic essays and for the best neighborhood cleanup poster, but these circuses seem rather an affront to one's dignity and the kids can hardly be blamed if they take the cash but otherwise remain aloof from such games.

The notion that going to school and doing schoolwork is the student's *job,* comparable to an adult's running a service station, misses the meaning of work in the adult world: a productive venture paid in a commodity of immediate value, with return commensurate with effort. The notion that the school is a playing field for working out strong feelings in games (and vicariously in watching games) is a commendable try, but probably less and less important as violence and pornography, widespread in TV, the movies, advertising, pocket-books, and even in family magazines continually step up the size of dose needed for a satisfactory jolt.

The school as an adult-organized set of children's societies, a place not so much for social and emotional growth as for gaining social status within the peer group, has a good deal of potency. But for many youngsters, this socialization is second best and has a goody-goody quality, since it is captive to adult authority and therefore something of a mockery. The mockery stems from the pretense that there are no socioeconomic differences, nor differences in maturity, among the students. Dominated by wishful pseudodemocratic principles, the adults are likely to create the expectations that all students can "belong" equally, and that any red-blooded American boy or girl should be able, with a little effort, to be reasonably popular, outgoing, and socially adequate. Any child who would prefer to stay within the protection of his own gang, who is too fearful to buck the larger group, is looked upon as a snob; and the possibility that stratification may in fact exist is briskly swept under the ideological carpet. Actually, of course, the heterogeneity of the average student body would aggravate the social-psychological proclivities of a saint. And the high school student is no saint; nor are his teachers, who are notoriously self-selected into highly homogeneous social groups.

The heterogeneous school society can become a laboratory for a great deal of worthwhile learning; and it can help students to satisfy some of their needs for striving for position and role. But this will call for a much greater disposition of parents, teachers, and students to face the sociological facts and to accept existing social realities. The principle to be learned and applied has been unequivocally demonstrated in many communities: that socialization within heterogeneous or mixed groups cannot be forced or made an end in itself; it is rather a voluntary elaboration of relationships which are initiated within the activity of *working* together for common goals. This principle is implicit in Model 3, Reflective Action, Chapter 9—a kind of *educative* activity which is, nonetheless, motivated by the need of youth for a legitmate role in an adult-recognized society.

THE COMMUNITY'S VALUES AND THE EDUCATION IT PROVIDES

The basic premise here is that the values of modern American communities are changing. Many observers have pointed with alarm to the slippage of the old-fashioned virtues which don't change so much as they die out. Investigators who have taken cross-sections of the community find that the old people tend to stick with the old virtues and values, which tend less and less to be important to young people. The old-fashioned ways of thrift, planning for the future and expecting satisfaction in work are being displaced by the virtues of getting along with the group, measuring achievement by political and social skill rather than by contribution to society, orientation to the present and a lack of commitment to any virtue.[7,8] All of this bespeaks and fore-shadows an empty and vacant existence.

These forebodings, incidentally, are clearly represented in the widespread disappointment in the use people are making of their new-found leisure time. People don't seem to do anything worthwhile with their leisure; they either frantically pursue the mob pleasures of the moment or they sink into TV apathy. Both of these, in my view, indicate the use to which leisure is put under the new value system: as an escape from nagging emptiness through highly superficial activity or fantasy. For the psychic energy of a man who is deprived and hollow is preoccupied and tied up; it is not available for crea-tivity or for commitment to causes or for personally important, civilized activity. I think we may suggest that the use of leisure time already shows the shape of things to come in the creeping other-directed nonautonomous society.[5]

But what is causing these changes? It can be argued, and I will so argue because I believe we should give schools their due credit, that the schools have powerfully reinforced this change of values. The high school student, working for several years in the culture of a deprived minority, does develop a set of habitual expectations and ways of looking at himself and the world. Graduation from high school is not a character-shaking event; in fact, it's mostly a calendar matter, a matter of waiting it out. Graduation changes nothing. An increasing percentage of adolescents go to college, and there they consolidate their high school tendencies and learn to implement them with greater biological, physical and economic capability. And it is these college people who set the standards to be imitated by the others in their age group.

Nothing happens in college to change the adolescent value pat-tern. Even marriage, which used to have a sobering effect and used to be associated with true and ultimate acceptance into the adult world, now is assimilated with no real change of value within the protected and insulated peer-group world. Even preparing oneself for a job, which used to mean identifying with and striving toward adult work values, has pretty much lost its potency for change. The fact is that shortages of "trained" people are so great that industries and businesses have wooed the students; it is they who have adjusted to the student by offering to make his immature high school dreams come true. We have given our youth privileges of irresponsibility and these privileges have not had to be shaken off—far from it. The times have made them stick.

Thus one may quite seriously propose that the change in American values has come about through the injection into the body politic of the values of the adolescent. The astonishing similarity of the values of the organization man[6] and the high school adolescent simply cannot be laughed off, and this similarity helps us, I think, to a better understanding of the nature, place, and function, however it may have backfired, of the school.

The schools' methods of teaching have, of course, aggravated the problem of lack of commitment to any enthusiasms, causes, inquiries, or values. There is a tradition of teaching with words, and these are abstractions. Words are fine things for discussing and analyzing experiences one has had; but they can never take the place of experience; at best they can remind one of selected elements of past experience and that is all. If a person is never really immersed in any situation, with feelings, interaction with phenomena, embarrassments, the need to extricate himself, disappointments, wrong guesses, rewards and gratifications, why would he develop any needs or sense of urgency, any identification with horrible or delightful possibilities? In a sense nothing is real because reality hasn't engulfed him.

We are too good on dissection and we forget to put pieces back together. We have learned the usefulness of analysis from science, and this is a rational need. But the need for synthesis, beyond the simple enumeration of the numbers of situations about which one can say the same thing, is not rational: it comes from the desire to comprehend. It has to involve the reorganization of ideas, seeing wholes, sensing the broad sweep of movements, the large ideas, the basic proposition. It is a "reaching for the jugular" in situations, but to do this you have to want to do it with all your soul. Analysis is like working a puzzle; synthesis is like growing up. But one never has to seek for essences until he has been immersed in details; and this doesn't happen in the schools. Such details as one gets are presented one at a time because, using language, that's all you can do; but the whole overwhelming pattern of cues, relevant and irrelevant, strong and weak, consistent and inexplicable, never inundates one. There is nothing to internalize.

The child in school has very little opportunity for contending directly with the environment. Hence he doesn't know that he can challenge the world in direct transaction, and that it can challenge him right back. Instead, what happens is that the environment speaks to the child through the teacher or the book. These are faulty transmission media because the student's attention is directed by language to preselected aspects; the real start of inquiry in the voluntary arrest of attention is simply impossible. Ideas cannot be tested against the environment, they can only be tested against the teacher's or the book's ideas about the environment. Under these conditions, the teacher's authority as classroom manager is confused with the authority of substantive ideas. The result is that for years and years, the child is exposed to the false assumption *that truth is the opinion of someone on whom you are dependent for well-being.* And this is the assumption of the organization man. He is forever the consumer of the results of inquiries of others, and he does not learn to inquire on his own behalf. Thus our methods of teaching have aggravated the frustration of the adolescent's position in the world of men.

We have made a cursory field trip guided by three main landmarks: (1) Relationships between school and community, (2) the place and needs of youth, and (3) the change of community values. These are large chunks, like plums in a pudding. There are plenty of other large chunks that could be identified, too; but I have picked the ones that seem to me to talk most directly to administrators, teachers, parents, and community leaders.

Our task now is to try to pull the whole thing together. I shall make a sequence of statements, each of which emerges from the one before and leads to the next. The list could be pasted on a cylinder, because it is circular; the last statement leads right into the first. It does not matter which statement you read first so long as you keep going until you get back to it. This is like improving schools: it does not matter much where you dig in, so long as you keep going until comprehension is achieved.

Item 1: Each person or group in the community holds expectations for the behavior of other persons and groups.

Item 2: These expectations may be sorted out among networks or systems, e.g., political, religious, economic, educational.

Item 3: Each person or group belongs simultaneously in several systems, each of which has expectations for his behavior or role.

Item 4: The overlapping of these systems and roles is likely to generate conflict because the expectations of the various systems are not compatible.

Item 5: This conflict is felt as a conflict of interest among the groups belonging to the different systems.

Item 6: A person subject to this role conflict perceives others as putting pressure on him, and he assumes in action at least, that decisions are to be made through the alignments of groups for and against, with the larger pressure decisive.

Item 7: In this power struggle, schools use public relations tactics to appease everyone, because they think their survival depends on it. Thus educational issues are indistinguishable from political issues.

Item 8: School and community alike are caught in the common assumption of group anarchy as the way of life; and neither can change unless the other changes too.

Item 9: The only way out of this mutually reinforcing neuroticism is through joint inquiry, in which awareness and diagnosis of conflict is the basis for defining and studying issues and problems.

Item 10: The purpose of the joint inquiry, involving all persons or groups whose behavior affects the education of youth—the community's educational system—is how to do a better educational job.

Item 11: The better education of youth must be oriented to increasing capability for inquiry, and inquiry is educative only when it takes off from "real needs" of students.

Item 12: The "realest need" of youth is, in general, to find a place in the productive life of the community.

Item 13: The community effort to improve education should be through inquiry into the ways to help youth improve their lot through their own efforts, using school and community educational and welfare facilities.

Item 14: The whole community—aside from those most centrally in the educative "system"—must also be involved in the educational effort because as youth's roles change, other parts of the community structure have to change, too; and if they won't, then youth cannot move and education cannot encourage autonomy.

Item 15: The difficulty of giving youth the opportunity to better its lot (through education) is compounded by the fact that society in general is moving in the direction of lessening personal autonomy for all.

Item 16: The lack of autonomy is, in fundamental terms, a loss of commitment to important values; and with this, a lack of sense of common cause with others.

Item 17: The cement that holds organizational life (and community life) together is no longer faith in the other fellow's intention to contribute in his own way to joint effort toward shared goals, and common aspirations; instead it is specific expectations of how he shall behave. The seeds of change and innovation have been smothered.

Item 1: Each person or group in the community holds expectations for the behavior of each other person or group in the community.

Item 2: These . . . etc.

Items 9-14 are the part of the vicious circle that can be broken—and must be broken—in the name of education; and the rest will follow. But the educational effort will have to be an all-out one. This, however, is a practical requirement that can be met. For whatever our faults and ambivalences, the strongest communality left in the American community is that we love our children, and we are still capable of concern and effort for their better lot and education. And in working together for this goal, we shall be educating ourselves to the ways of inquiry and thus contributing to our chances of survival.

NOTES

1. See, for example, Talcott Parsons, "Some Ingredients of a General Theory of Formal Organizations" in *Administrative Theory in Education,* (ed. Andrew Halpin), (Chicago: Midwest Administration Center, 1958), pp. 40-72. For complete treatment of many ideas in this chapter see *Toward a General Theory of Action,* T. Parsons and Shils (eds.), (Cambridge: Harvard University Press, 1951), p. 506.

2. Kurt Lewin, "Frontiers in Group Dynamics: Concept, Method and Reality in Social Science; Social Equilibria and Social Change," *Human Relations,* I, Nos. 1 and 2, 1947.

3. R. D. Hess and Irene Goldblatt, "The Status of Adolescents in American Society: A Problem in Social Identity," *Child Development,* XXVIII, No. 4 (December 1957), 459-468.

4. From a full-page ad in LIFE, August 18, 1958, p. 58.

5. David Riesman, *op. cit.,* references Chapter 3.

6. William H. Whyte, Jr., *The Organization Man* (New York: Simon and Schuster, Inc., 1956), p. 429.

7. G. D. Spindler, "Education in a Transforming American Culture," *Harvard Educational Review,* XXV (Summer 1955), 145-153.

8. Jacob W. Getzels, "The Acquisition of Values in School and Society," Chapter in F. S. Chase and H. A. Anderson (eds.), *The High School in a New Era* (Chicago: University of Chicago Press, 1958), pp. 146-161.

5

Suppositions:
Four Models for Education

In which we summarize the preceding chapters and discern three fundamental dynamics in man and society. We then sketch, as an overview for the rest of this book, three educational "models" based on the three dynamics—and then add a fourth model to service the other three with pinpointed development of "basic skills."

Somewhere in one of his stories, O. Henry describes the experience of going by train at ninety miles an hour through a small town. The speed was so great, he says, that the watertank and the Episcopal church blended together into the image of a saloon. I am afraid this sort of thing happens not only to small towns but also to survey courses, such as Chapters 2, 3, and 4. We have been traveling pell-mell through an assortment of ideas, and perhaps we had better take the time for a brief review before moving on to the educational implications of the ideas.

Education is a process, a sequence of actions. The participants are teachers and students, individual human beings. Each has a human nature, which in turn is compounded from constituent interacting animal and social natures. The animal heritage tempts us to deal with problems and stresses by acting out reflexively and impulsively, i.e., "emotionally." The social nature, developed through consciousness, language, memory, and learning, inclines us to deal with problems through the effort to comprehend what is involved. These two

74

methods of dealing with situations, acting out and inquiry, have to be reconciled, and they have to be reconciled in every new situation.

The effort to resolve conflict between the two modes of reacting is the central drama of individual human lives. The ideal is neither to compromise nor suppress one or the other, but rather to integrate them within a way of life which is enriched by both—which has the color and richness and involvement that come from emotional response, and that has the control, purposiveness, and effectiveness that come from understanding. The active quest for integration which is most self-realizing in the seeking of autonomy or captaincy of self, goes on in all human beings, regardless, as the saying goes, of race, creed, color, or national origin.

Thus runs the lesson of Chapter 2.

The process of education deals with "subject matter." Subject matter is that part of recorded knowledge which is introduced as material for thought in classrooms. Since subject matter is already written down (for the most part), one way to deal with it is to memorize it. Another way to deal with it is to use it as reference material to answer questions which arise from one's efforts to cope with situations. Memorization produces walking encyclopedias, and it views education as basically a process of consumption. Using subject matter to answer meaningful questions views education as inquiry, and it produces persons who ask questions, connect causes to effects, and learn principles.

When inquiry is consciously guided by method, and when the methods are appropriate to the phenomena being studied, the fruit of knowledge is "discipline," an effective way of life with reference to the phenomena in the field of study. The person who has learned the disciplines of natural science, history, human relations, etc.—and knows when to employ each—may be said to be educated.

The motive power for inquiry is generated in a feeling of perplexity and challenge when one is confronted (under favorable conditions) by things he cannot cope with. The creative aspect of inquiry is in the diagnosis of the problem as it is felt and perceived by each individual. The solution of the problem is the application of rational methods of collecting data, making plans, taking limited action, studying its consequences, modifying plans, acting on these, and so on. The life of inquiry is one in which the experience of each step in problem solving changes one's perceptions and leads to reformulation of the problem.

In a literal sense, problems do not get solved, they only get reformulated in terms that are increasingly meaningful.

The various domains of knowledge all enter into life. The knowledge disciplines are learned as part of the quest for autonomy; and in this quest, the person learns to give conscious guidance to his own processes of inquiry.

Thus runs the lesson of Chapter 3.

No man stands alone because his behavior influences other people. It may influence them directly, as when he deals with them face to face; or it may influence them indirectly as when he changes some aspect of the environment with which they also are in contact. Thus people are interdependent, and form a society.

The society coordinates efforts of individuals for the purpose of providing food, shelter, protection, recreation, education, etc., for all. These different purposes are societal functions, and each person, through his job, his hobbies, his votes, his consumption, his participation in activities—has a role with respect to each function. One purpose of education is to enable the student to discover and understand a variety of functional roles within his own society as well as in the adult world. Since roles are defined partly by the expectations of others, one's sense of belonging is contingent upon the roles he occupies—and the extent to which these roles facilitate his own quest for integration and "wholeness."

The development of roles is a joint enterprise. The individual or organization cannot define his or its role in isolation from others. The topic of discussion through which roles are clarified is the job to be done or the function to be carried out and the contribution each can make to this function. When such conversations and consequent mutual accommodations do not occur, the person or organization may react in various ways to the lack of any mechanism for finding a place in the community's functional systems. Thus the school very often withdraws into defensiveness and tries to legitimize its own conception of its role through "public relations" (selling and persuasion) rather than through public discussion of the educational function and the various contributions to the educational function needed from home, church, businesses, schools, and other agencies within the community. Similarly youth, who also do not engage in public discussion through which role expectations can be clarified and defined, form their own society. This is a society in oscillation between two ways of finding self-esteem; through maintaining the privileged status of childhood versus seeking a place in the productive life of the adult community. The resulting behaviors, frequently excessive, reflect the indecision of the youth group and their frustration over the lack of means by which it can be resolved.

Finally we note that the workings of a society are based on some underlying principle, such as that social change will come about through the processes of group anarchy; and that having established its principle of operation, the society is trapped in it. The lesson of Chapter 4 ended with a picture of the vicious circle, and designated the part of the circle where a breakthrough might be possible.

MODELS FOR EDUCATION

On the strength of these ideas, I now propose that there are three fundamental quests going on in the world of man. I shall identify and discuss each one, and will sketch a model of education that can be built around it. Then I shall comment on the common element of inquiry central in all three models, and will end the chapter with a fourth necessary model which is dependent on the other three but which should be implemented separately. In succeeding chapters, I shall consider each model in turn.

Model 1—Personal Inquiry

The first quest is for selfhood or integration. In this quest, we see persons trying to reconcile their tendencies to "acting out" and "to seek reality" in a variety of everyday situations. Note that such seeking has both particular and general aspects: the need, for example, of acquiring not only the abilities of the scientist but also the scientist's way of life; the purpose of testing, not a few prejudices against the world, but an emerging philosophy of life; for seeing, not just a few fascinating ways to make a living or to evaluate the world, but, more fundamentally, discovering alternative ways of life and finding oneself as one creates his own or makes choices among them.

For us to help children in their quest for autonomy, we must first be able to diagnose and understand the nature of this quest. At the present time, with our existing crude diagnostic tools we can identify three sorts of children who should undoubtedly be dealt with on an individual basis.

First, there is the child who already knows and is committed to a particular profession, field of study, or way of life within the adult world. He may, at age twelve, be clearly cut out for physical science, music, languages, or mathematics; and he is, by adult standards, "talented." The talents we have so far been able to recognize seem to be with respect to fields of study which can be logically and rationally organized, skills developed through imitation, and artistic expressiveness. We also note such characteristics as an inquiring mind, an impressive fund of all sorts of information, and a startling ability to deal with abstractions. Many (if not most) students can give evidence of great talent, skill, or ability which should, both for their own and society's sake, be encouraged and maximized. According to investigators DeHaan and Havighurst,[11] about one child in five is "gifted" in some way. And we can try to foster such talents.

A second sort of child who is ready to learn is seldom thought of as talented. Such students may be coping, often unsuccessfully, with real and present problems of relationship, of orientation to authority. They may be lacking in overarching goals that can give their lives focus; they may be badly crippled psychologically, and be unable to perceive with any accuracy what goes on around them. Such a child may be continually "acting out" an inadequate theory about the world: he thinks everyone is against him, he regards the world as hostile or unfair, he transmutes every situation into a battle with authority. In short, this is an antisocial child, and he needs to be confronted with situations in which the falsity of his theory is patent, even to him.

(The passive antisocial child, withdrawn and fearful, probably cannot be reached through instructional groups. He is likely to need professional psychiatric help.)

A third sort of child who is ready to learn is the child whose range of experience has been so narrow that he has simply not had the opportunity to try to cope with very many aspects of life. It is fashionable to think of "lower class" children in this way, and to refer to them as "culturally deprived." I would include under this term, in addition, children whose families have been so preoccupied with making a living, achieving social status, being intellectual sophisticates, maintaining piety, etc., that the child has never had the chance to recognize, let alone explore, the possibilities of any other way or kind of life. Such children often appear to have no goal or direction in their own lives, for they have not had to make choices, and therefore they have not had to think through "who they are" and where their commitments lie.

We believe that most normal children have some recognizable degree of talent, of antisocial orientation, and of cultural deprivation. The resulting quest of each child is different, and this calls for individualized instruction. For each quest, a different kind or quality of social opportunity or confrontation by reality is indicated. The talented child, anticipating adulthood, seeks experience in that part of the adult community which uses, challenges, and stretches his talent: the laboratory, studio, library, shop, or counting house. The antisocial child requires confrontation by expectations from the "real" (i.e., adult) community which give the lie to his unsophisticated and partial theory of life. Generally speaking, this confrontation may stimulate the child to seek (or accept) responsibility and reward for functioning as a social rather than as an antisocial person. The culturally deprived child simply needs participant-observer experience in families, groups, and organizations whose existence he could not have dreamed of.

Personal Inquiry with respect to all three needs is inaugurated by selecting an existing spot in the classroom, school, or community which can provide the environment most appropriate to the quest of a particular child. In this spot—shop, studio, store, field, business, work gang—the student participates in the work to be done. He will be encouraged to comprehend his experience to the extent that he is able; and this means thinking about it quite consciously. Thus, in so far as possible we will encourage him to note and mull over his thoughts, feelings, and performance; to try to set his own personal goals for inquiry; to plan strategies for dealing with parts of the job; to consciously collect evidence for his policies. He will be helped to find accounts of the experiences of other people in similar predicaments and circumstances, and to contrast their findings with his own. And, finally, he will be asked to help decide when to bring his inquiry to a close.

Personal Inquiry is the subject of Chapter 6.

Model 2—Group Investigation

The way each person acts to realize his own biological and psychological needs for self-maintenance and autonomy may very well conflict with like efforts of other persons. House rules are needed, and the most basic one is that "your freedom to swing your fist ends where my nose begins." Thus a social image of man is also needed, a man who builds with other men the rules and agreements that constitute social reality.

Interdependent men must and do, in one way or another, develop the agreements they need. In this respect, every collection of people in continual association with each other becomes a "group." Moreover, each individual contributes to the establishment and modification of the rules and thus helps to determine both its prohibitions and freedoms for action.

The rules of conduct, both explicit and implicit, in all fields—religious, political, economic, scientific—are elaborated, rationalized, explained, communicated, and interpreted within a larger body of ideas, purposes, ideals, aesthetic sensibilities, organizational assumptions, material resources, and plans. This larger corpus constitutes the "culture" of the society. It is through continual effort, through reflection, to understand our culture that we become aware of the implicit rules by which we live, the nature of our assumptions about our environment, and the possibilities for freedom.

Thus in groups and societies a cyclical process exists: individuals, interdependently seeking to meet their needs, must establish a social order (and in the process they develop groups and societies). The social order determines in varying degrees what ideas, values, and actions are possible, valid, and "appropriate." Working within these "rules" and stimulated by the need for rules, the culture develops. The individual studies his reactions to the rules and re-interprets them to discover their meaning for the way of life he seeks. Through this quest, he changes his own way of life, and this in turn influences the way of life of others. But as the way of life changes, the rules must be revised, and new controls and agreements have to be hammered out and incorporated in the social order.

The relationship of this dynamic to education has been only half understood. There has been a failure to realize that the development of knowledge, valuable in its own right, is a by-product of the continuously operating dynamic of changing and/or maintaining the social order. The great bulk of knowledge transmitted in schools is legitimized by the assumption that people must and do participate (whether or not they know or like it) in the social order; and they have no choice about this. Motivation for classroom learning should be high when the learner perceives that the restrictions and freedoms in the group are determined by his own state of knowledge and skill. One would expect motivation to be greatest when "rules" and "learnings" reinforce one another; and when increased autonomy can be earned through the gaining of skill, sophistication, intellectual penetration, or other facet of competence. Such relationships would associate the gaining of knowledge to greater opportunities in the way of life in the classroom, and the consequences could be exciting: granted that many students are not initially motivated to acquire some kinds of knowledge, nevertheless all students care about the way of life that develops in the classroom.

The educational model based on these working suppositions is Group Investigation. Given a group of students and a teacher in a classroom, some sort of social order, classroom culture, and "climate" is bound to develop. It may develop around the basic value of comfort, of politeness and middle-class morals and manners, or of keeping the teacher happy and secure. In these all too frequent cases, the gaining of knowledge collapses to the learning of information, and the meaning of the information is respectively to stimulate bull sessions, develop conformity, or provide the teacher with materials to show off with.

We propose instead that the teacher's task is to participate in the activities of developing the social order in the classroom for the purpose of orienting it to inquiry, and that the "house rules" to be developed are the methods and attitudes of the knowledge discipline to be taught. The teacher influences the emerging social order toward inquiring when he "brings out" and capitalizes on differences in the ways students act and interpret the role of investigator—which is also the role of member in the classroom group. Under these conditions, the gaining of knowledge could serve initially only to validate the student's portrayal of the investigator role; but as the way of life of inquiry comes to dominate the social order, the purpose of gaining knowledge—which by then will be inseparable (but not identical) with meeting personal needs in the group—will have a powerful appeal in itself. And, of course, knowledge learned in its essential, even if microcosmic, social context, will be utilizable in the larger arena as well.

The first requirement for group investigation is a teachable group: one which can develop a sense of common cause, one whose members can stimulate each other, and one whose members are psychologically compatible and complementary. The students are assigned to a consultant (teacher) who confronts them with a stimulus situation to which they can react and discover basic conflicts among their attitudes, ideas, and modes of perception. On the basis of this information, they identify the problem to be investigated, analyze the roles required to "solve" it, train themselves to take these roles; act, report, and evaluate the results. These steps are illuminated by reading, possibly by some short-range personal investigations, and by consultation with experts. The group is concerned with its own effectiveness, but its discussions of its own process are related to the goals of the investigation.

The dynamic of the investigation, as Bion has shown, is the need of the group to maintain itself, and the beginning of investigation is demonstrated incompatibility among assumptions underlying the reactions of the members to the planned stimulus situation. The need to deal with such differences is the primary psychological motivation for investigations by the group, but as the group "develops," many further kinds of gratification become available to individuals, and these add drive to the inquiry. We will expand on these matters later, in Chapters 7 and 8.

Model 3—Reflective Action

We have been considering the social order as a milieu within which each individual strives to develop and maintain his way of life. Because there is a social order, predictability is possible; one can guess with some accuracy the likely consequences of possible ways of acting, and he can govern himself accordingly. He can see his own behavior as a means to alleviate some immediate condition and, at the same time, as a long-range influence (through changes due to learning) on major social ends.

But in addition to being the social-psychological-humanistic *milieu* of individuals, the social order and culture is the *instrument* through which men provide food, shelter, entertainment, protection, and other conditions necessary for life or demanded by men's aspirations. In its operation as a functional agent, the social order must yield to a higher authority, namely, the demands and facts of the "real" world. In a word, the social order and culture mediates between the individual and his environment; it is the meeting place of desires that come from individuals and the stubborn realities and opportunities that nature makes men face up to.

In Group Investigation, the group transacts business with the environment primarily as a way of finding out how the environment will respond. Thus chemicals are part of the environment and chemical experiments are designed to reveal their properties. Artifacts from another age, such as journals and furniture, are also part of the environment, and the history class collects and studies these objects as part of its effort to reconstruct the life of an earlier period. In both cases the aim is to learn about phenomena whose occurrence depends in no way upon desires of the students.

Our third model, Reflective Action, visualizes the group transacting business with the environment both in order to change the environment and in order to learn the skills and insights necessary for changing the environment. Thus group investigation is directed to the learning of scientific and theoretical propositions, whereas Reflective Action is directed to the learning of working suppositions. Just as a teacher needs both in order to function intelligently, so also does the citizen, chemist, consumer, and everyone else engaged in the practical affairs of the world.

The model of Reflective Action stipulates that the classroom, school, and community are to be thought of as laboratories for the learning of the policy sciences and the engineering arts. Various aspects of the laboratories or of the way of life therein may be reacted to by students: the formal and informal organization of the student society; the methods for legislating and enforcing rules; the physical appearance or convenience of the plant; the program of studies; the lunchroom, gymnasium, library, conference room, and other facilities; and so on. The "climate" of tolerance and freedom will be such that at any given time certain students will feel that certain changes might well be advantageous. Such students will have the opportunity to recruit others to their cause; and a communications system will exist, so that their representations can be channeled in an orderly way to the appropriate deliberative bodies. These will (or will not) arrange for the necessary enabling legislation for the initiating group to act. All steps will be handled with rigorous concern for adequacy of data (e.g., in the sampling of perceptions of the student body); for formulation and weighing of alternatives; for prudence and foresight in planning; for tentativeness in acting; and for periodic assessment of consequences through which further plans and policies can be modified toward greater realism and efficiency. And finally, all action will be seen as illustrative of similar larger actions and underlying significant issues in the larger society. From an educational viewpoint, the student does not "learn by doing." He learns by planning, doing, and reflecting on the doing. This program is to have a first-class intellectual content; and it will demand the learning and exercise of wisdom in affairs impinging directly on the students.

The motivation for Reflective Action by students is the same as for adults: to improve their material and functional way of life and to protect individual rights and liberty in a world whose increasingly complex interdependencies threaten to extinguish individuality. The motivation of the adolescent is considerably stronger than that of the educated intellectual adult who has been taught that social action is "beneath" him and seems, for the most part, quite content merely to complain while his community goes to pieces all around him. For the adolescent has strong need to find, through some sort of participation in the productive community, an avenue to self-esteem. But the fact that this is the driving force in Reflective Action does *not* mean that this is also its educational justification. If students want to get together on their own time and in their own clubs to change the world, let them—and more power to them. But this has nothing to do with the school, which is concerned with social action *only* as a kind of experience indispensable to the learning of certain practical disciplines essential in our times. By and large the school is not out to change society, but only to produce enlightened citizens who will act intelligently. Considering the quality of much of the present operation of society, having people act intelligently would be a sure-fire way to bring about drastic changes; but the changes would come from the force of sound ideas, not from the particular biases or social attitudes of a group of schoolmen.

In the part of the school program concerned with reflective action, consultants from the school and community can serve as trainers in the methodology of action; experts can offer information to be considered and interpreted; working committees can study social, economical, political, and other policies involved in making wise decisions. And there must be continual encouragement and help to ascertain the consequences of actions as perceived by all those touched by the actions, to rediagnose the problem, and to take further and better action.

The educational model of reflective action is spelled out further in Chapter 9.

Inquiry, the Common Element

All three models involve inquiry. Each model is concerned to initiate and supervise the processes of giving attention to something; of interacting with and being stimulated by other people, whether in person or through their writings; and of reflection and reorganization of concepts and attitudes, as shown in arriving at conclusions, identifying new investigations to be undertaken, taking action, and turning out a better product. These characteristics were foreshadowed in Chapter 3.

In these models we have delineated three major situations or contexts of inquiry. Personal Inquiry is close in spirit to the basic human problems of Chapter 2. It is the quest for meaning, the reconciliation of man as animal with man (the same man) as member of society. Group Investigation is oriented to the domains of knowledge, Chapter 3. It is the development of common cause and culture around the pursuit within an interactive group of knowledge. Reflective action is built on the background and processes of Chapter 4. It is the mature effort of the student body (or volunteer fractions thereof) to bring about desired changes in the larger society.

When the three underlying processes—personal integration, development of the social order, and modification of the environment—are kept in balance, with each serving as a check of the other, they become the prime dynamics for achieving the major values of personal autonomy, predictability, lawfulness among groups and nations, and survival of the species.

All of these kinds of inquiry ferret out information and turn it into knowledge (the four domains) useful for inquiries.

Part of the knowledge of greatest educational value is knowledge of how to participate more effectively in these kinds of inquiry. And through participation in each inquiry, new personal needs, common causes, and action needs will emerge, and lead to further inquiries.

Model 4: Skill Development

I put this last because it is subsidiary to and facilitative of the other kinds of inquiries; if the other inquiries are not in existence, then this fourth type cannot exist. In a way, practice in skills relieves some of the burden from the other inquiries, but the reason for separating it is purely practical: it is organized differently and probably should involve different and special personnel of its own.

The fact of the matter is that students do have to learn to read, write, listen, memorize the multiplication table and the symbols of the chemical elements, learn the vocabulary of a foreign language, study, and speak effectively. But these learnings are skills which are not ends in themselves. One does not read just to read, he reads for information, to kill time, for enjoyment, etc.; and likewise for the other skills. The motivation for learning skills, then, is to enable one to carry out the other three kinds of inquiry adequately. The most effective pressure for learning skills will be the standard of performance the students themselves require in their own inquiries (with a bit of judicious inspiration and encouragement by adults). To learn skills they must want to learn, for a major requirement is paying attention to practice. Just going through the motions is—simply going through the motions.

The pressures may derive from group standards, but skill learning is an individual matter. Thus some students "pick up" the necessary skills in connection with the larger activity which originated the need. And dragging an already competent reader through the peregrinations of Dick and Jane, or an accurate computer through endless arithmetic problems is probably an excellent way to kill interest and desire to learn.

Students learn skills by different routes. Reading, for example, has been studied quite intensively, and the present conclusion is that the good teacher tailors the approach to each child. For one child, the key seems to be phonics; for another, word study. I suspect the same thing would be found with other skills, such as writing proper sentences. It is possible that grammar is actually useful to some students, but it most certainly is a hindrance to others who learn to write prose the way a "natural" composer writes music—through having something to say and a sensitive ear that tells him when he has said it correctly.

It is proposed to set up a skills laboratory to be attended by individuals when they need more skill—and know that they do. If a student needs more skill and doesn't know it or denies it, he will not go to the practice laboratory because that would do him little good. He will need to be helped, through assessment during inquiry to understand and accept his need.

The laboratory will be manned partly by student consultants; but it will be guided by ingenious teachers who know how to break skills down into manageable parts, and who can help the students make their own flash cards, practice tapes, record charts, test diagnoses, and similar devices.

In the next five chapters I shall attempt to answer: What would a school look like if it took these models seriously and adapted them to education? In anticipation, I assure you that it would look quite different from today's schools. For we propose to separate the three kinds of inquiries which now all go on together in a jumbled and inchoate fashion—deal with each in its own terms, and use the learnings from each to facilitate each other. And in this analysis we shall, whether we like it or not, be forced to see that the school cannot do the educational job alone—a conclusion foreshadowed in Chapter 4. So Chapter 11 will examine in the light of our understanding, the problem of the means by which action can be taken to improve education in the schools and community.

NOTES

The framework of ideas here presented has been emerging for some time. Previous papers by the same author that may help round out the propositions are:

1. Educational Dynamics: Theory and Research. Complete issue of *The Journal of Social Issues,* VI, No. 2 (1950), 96.
2. "Basic Concepts in Human Dynamics," *Journal of the National Association of Deans of Women,* XV, No. 3 (March 1952), 99-111.
3. "The Experimental Method in Classroom Leadership," *Elementary School Journal,* LIII, No. 2 (October 1952).
4. "Emotionality and Work in Groups," Chapter in *The State of the Social Sciences* (ed. L. D. White), (Chicago: University of Chicago Press, 1956), pp. 184-200.
5. With J. W. Getzels, "The Social Sciences: Conceptual Framework for Education," *School Review,* LXV, No. 3 (Autumn 1957), 330-355.
6. "Four Propositions in Search of an Educational Dynamic," *Adult Education,* VIII, No. 3 (Spring 1958), 146-152.

7. La dynamique des groupes sociaux: organization et group de travail, Chapter in *Psychosociologie Industrielle,* Paris: Revue Hommes et Techniques, CLXIX (1959), 72-95.

8. "Work-Emotionality Theory of the Group as Organism," Chapter in S. Koch (ed.), *Psychology: A Study of Science* III (New York: McGraw-Hill Book Co., 1959), 544-611.

9. With J. W. Getzels, "The Class as a Unique Social System," Chapter in *Yearbook of the National Society for the Study of Education,* 1960.

10. "Engineering Research in Curriculum Building," *Journal of Educational Research,* XLI, No. 8 (April 1948), 577-596.

11. Robert DeHaan and Robert Havighurst, *Educating Gifted Children,* (Chicago: University of Chicago Press, 1957), p. 275.

6

Model 1:
Personal Inquiry

In which we report some experiences with students when they are set free to inquire into things meaningful to them, and go on to suppose how education could capitalize on diagnosed needs and talents of boys and girls. We rather speculatively draw up specifications for the Program of Personal Inquiry, and visualize how it might be operated by the school.

It would be nice if we could hop on a bus, jog along to the nearest high school, and there slip around unobtrusively to observe personal inquiry going on. From reflection on several such experiences, we could then develop a sort of blueprint or set of propositions which could be adapted, with due respect to local facts, to another school. Actually and unfortunately, however, the bus we shall have to board to find our picture of personal inquiry will not be a product of Detroit. Our trip will be imaginary.

Yet I think there is no doubt of what we are looking for, nor will there be any difficulty in recognizing it when and if we find it. What we are seeking is a process of interaction between the student and his natural and societal environment. In this situation the student will be aware of the process of which he is a part; during this process he will be aware of many choices among ways he might behave; he will make decisions among these ways; he will then act and see what happens; he will review the process and study it with the help of books and other people; he will speculate about it, and draw tentative conclusions from it. These provisional conclusions will be of all sorts—about his own abilities, about the way others behave, about the nature of men and materials and society. Probably the most distinctive feature of the whole thing will be the deep involvement of the student—his absorption, his concern, his releasing of a great deal of effort and energy into the activity; and there will be a commensurate emergence of insight from the well-spring of this meaningful experience.

What I have been projecting here is the picture of the autonomous person. It is also the picture of a "significant" life. It is the human animal realizing the nature toward which he is pushed by his biological equipment and pulled by his spiritual aspiration.

But—this life must be learned. And it must be learned during the period when the child is growing up. It should be the major concern of the educative community and of the school.

The fact that our picture of personal inquiry is imaginary doesn't mean that it is a fantasy. We can hop onto actual busses and drive out to see many of its components. Thus we could observe some of the work experience of high school students, for here there is the quality of interaction between the student and a real world in which he is "playing for keeps" rather than trying to outwit the educational authorities. We could go another direction and observe a good psychoanalytic session in which the patient is exploring the meaning for himself of some challenging experience. We could go into a research laboratory and note how skillfully past experience, through reflection, is consciously translated into a new course of experimental action. Or we might just relax in a big armchair and watch a baby's delight as it takes its first steps.

Can all this be put together? One way to find out is to try it and see.

During 1957-1958 we tried it—in a limited way, to be sure. What we found out is that it can be done, but it will difficult and it will take time. Let me tell you about it.

During the last month of the school year in our Sophomore Project at the Laboratory School of the University of Chicago, six students were set free for personal inquiry during almost half of every school day. These students were part of a class of fifty sophomores who were together for three hours each day. Three teachers undertook to teach them Algebra, English, and Social Studies. To free the students for inquiry, the teachers agreed to give them A's in their course work, so they wouldn't have to worry about requirements. In place of the course work, the six students and the three teachers agreed to meet three hours a week in a "seminar" whose purpose would be to stimulate and provide some of the guidance needed by each individual. The time, incidentally, was taken from two "library" periods augmented by one afternoon after school. The students were encouraged to formulate any problems that intrigued them and then go after them in their own ways. They could ask for and get private consultation with the teachers, and what with one thing and another, this tended to occur in almost daily five- to ten-minute conversations about specific questions.

How did these six students take being excused from these three subjects? Jane, Paul, and Penny all decided to go ahead with Math anyway—they wanted to be sure to cover the ground. Accordingly they talked with the Math teacher and decided, in each case, what further work they would do. Jane did all this further work—the equivalent of a month in the regular course—over one weekend. The other two took five days and ten days respectively. All six feared to miss grammar instruction in English, and insisted on taking the regular examination. None of them minded missing the last month of social studies, and they let the social studies teacher off with his promise to give them a review session next year just before they took the college board examinations. Most of them sneaked into the classroom to see his movies, however.

What did the students do with their time for inquiry?

Penny, who lives in a changing neighborhood, set for herself the question: What causes slums to develop? She went after this problem with great enthusiasm, formulating quite specific questions to be answered. She looked up books and articles suggested by the teachers and she interviewed several of the University faculty. But somehow she could not find answers; the information she got just didn't fit together. Moreover, during the interviews her preconceived questions seemed to her irrelevant and she didn't ask them. After two weeks she came to a completely new and unexpected conclusion: she needed to work with other students. She needed them partly for emotional support and reassurance, but mostly to compete with. The meaning of study and learning for Penny resided in the drive to do better than others; without the other students as pace setters, she was confused. And without the reward of knowing that her achievement was superior, she lost her self-confidence.

Paul took the first two weeks of regular course work in the three subjects. He was a very "independent" boy, who had expressed his independence by falling behind. Now that he had been excused from the requirements, he again expressed his independence by insisting on meeting them after all. His question for inquiry was: To what extent is the press free? Who exerts control over the press, and by what means? His interest in this question arose out of an argument with his father. He read three books and reported on them to the seminar. His reporting was detailed, superficial, and without organization; it was undisciplined: ideas came tumbling out, but he made little effort to organize them until the other students and the teachers started questioning him. Thus challenged, he pulled ideas together to bolster what for him was clearly an argument. As with Penny, the meaning of study and learning for Paul was socially oriented: it was in the service of antagonism and rebelliousness. Unlike Penny, who gained a great deal of insight into her difficulty, Paul achieved neither self-insight nor intellectual satisfaction with his topic.

Mimi expressed strong interest in the history of mental hospitals and the condition of the mentally ill in society. She was unable to give any reason for being interested in this topic. She strongly resisted all efforts, however tactful, by the teachers and by the other students to find a reason either for this choice or for any other personal preference, opinion, or behavior. Her defense was tears, and the others soon learned not to probe. For the most part, Mimi seemed unnaturally happy. The other students, for example, were quite apprehensive about the selection of their topics for inquiry, but not she. She put off reporting her plans to the seminar as long as possible, and then—as the others were beginning to suspect—she really had very little to report. In short, she was unprepared.

All this was deeply shocking to the teachers, for throughout her classroom life, Mimi always had done assigned work beautifully, ahead of time, and to perfection. Following the rather painful revelation of unpreparedness—and the flow of tears—Mimi buckled down, read five or six articles and parts of three books, and wrote a well-organized paper. As with Penny and Paul, Mimi's study and learning was also socially oriented, but not competitively or antagonistically.

She was a warm, friendly, attractive, and popular girl, and she truly delighted in meeting and exceeding the expectations of others—not to show them up, not to reassure herself, but simply to please them and have their warm regard. And throughout her troubles, she never lost the liking and regard of her colleagues.

Penny, Paul, and Mimi probably achieved somewhat less in our experiment than they would have done within the ordinary classroom situation. They did less work, got less out of it, and had less satisfaction. They are "A" students and will continue to be "A" students. They are highly intelligent. So far, their learning has been captive to their social adaptation to other people. It has not, apparently, been a key to unlock the mysteries and realities of the world in which they live. These are people whose potentials—presumably for creative work and leadership—have remained unrealized.

Jane, Roger, and John, the other three in the seminar, are probably the kinds of students that teachers retrospectively would call "gifted" —if we forget that by all the screens so far used to identify "gifted" children, Penny, Paul, and Mimi are equally "gifted." Jane, Roger and John simply blossomed in the seminar. They were eager, enthusiastic, happy. They worked hard and loved every minute of it. Penny, Paul, and Mimi show us some of the kinds of problems we will encounter with this notion of personal inquiry; Jane, Roger and John show us that the game is very much worth the candle.

Jane started, as already noted, by cleaning up a month of math over one weekend. The topic she chose to work on was not posed as a specific question; she wanted to find out all about symbolic logic. This had been mentioned by her math teacher last year and she had been curious about it ever since. Her present math teacher, somewhat startled, suggested some references, and she was off. She reported twice to the seminar, and the social studies teacher felt no shame in admitting that she lost him halfway through the first talk. The paper she wrote is cherished by the math teacher.

Having had her fill of constructing "truth tables," Jane next turned to the rewriting and expansion of her 120-page manuscript on the history of the English language. She read a variety of books and rounded out and polished her discussion. What was she going to do with this manuscript? Nothing—she just wanted to write it.

Roger said he was interested in the relationship between intelligence and achievement. The teachers told him this had all been studied, and suggested some references. Roger said he didn't care, he wanted to figure it out for himself. So he was given the data on one hundred students: two scores for intelligence, achievement scores in five subjects, and several subscores from an aptitude test battery. He then went calling on the Educational Psychology professors—four of them—and left them rather dazed. He was soon haunting the statistics laboratory, calculating scores, running correlations, and moving rapidly into factor analysis. He didn't have time to complete the latter and decided to finish it over the summer. Part of the reason he didn't have time is that he also decided to write a long short story. It was about four men caught in the depression of the thirties. Roger developed the character and circumstances of each— a doctor, a farm hand, a clerk, and a merchant—all in bad shape. He had them meet at a bar, and the story ends with their pact "to see each other through."

John told the seminar he was interested in perspective drawing. He was fascinated by the way angles are determined by the vanishing points, and he wanted to look into it. The teachers, beginning to feel a little harried, sent him to the art teacher; the art teacher told John what he knew, and then turned him over to a student teacher who had just completed several courses on the theory of perspective. Out of all this, John prepared three sequences of drawings, showing the development of the final completed perspective for a TV table, a chair, and a bookcase. His demonstration to the seminar was impressive, to put it mildly. John then announced that he was troubled by a point in his Jewish religious doctrine and wanted to investigate it. The social studies teacher acted as adviser, and John lost himself in reading for three days. Then he announced he had found his answer, and wanted to read Machiavelli's *The Prince,* which he did, and on which he led the seminar in discussion for an hour.

You will be glad to know that the three teachers who were responsible for all this have recovered. The whole Sophomore Project, culminating in the seminar for our six students, left the teachers with two overwhelming impressions. The first is that we have terribly underestimated what students can do and that, given a chance, their capabilities and interests can be startling. For example: one boy took on the job of recording practice spelling tapes for the use of other students; a girl set up and ran the room library (including a system of fines for overdue books); one project group worked up a dramatic radio program on the use of nuclear energy, presented it via a public address system to a sixth grade class, and then led that class in an evaluative discussion of their program; a committee of students met with the teachers during three noon hours to design "task cards" for students to use in planning their own work; a group of students interested in math got the math teacher to form a slide-rule club for them; another group organized a reading circle and then demanded the English teacher's help in analyzing books (which they all read).

The second over-all impression of the teachers was that none of the students—without exception—knew how to define a problem. Topics, questions, areas, interests—yes; but not a problem in the sense of a formulated statement of an obstacle to be overcome in order to achieve a goal. Even with Jane, Roger, and John we have little idea what their inquiries were "really" concerned with. Thus there is some reason to suppose that Jane's total immersion in academic activity is used to avoid social interaction; but the fact that she is really gaining knowledge makes her inquiry legitimate also as an end in itself. I have discussed the same thing in somewhat different terms in Chapter 2, where I make the point that the crucial failure of education is in failure to relate achievement demands to the subjective world of the student, or to put it another way, it is the tendency to keep the student working on puzzles rather than on problems meaningful to him.

This was also the failure of the seminar with the first three students, who used learning as an indirect way of solving their social problems. It was in respect to these problems, not the intellectual ones, that their fundamental need for inquiry existed. What was missing in the seminar for these three was adequate diagnosis of their more basic needs and the supervisory and counseling skills which would have brought them to consciousness and, through reflection on planned activity, would have developed insights about them. It is with this in mind that I have labeled this chapter "personal" inquiry, rather than "individual" inquiry.

Let us, then, build on this experience to imagine how the sort of personal inquiry we seek might develop and lead to insights producing autonomy. Let me offer several illustrations, then try to formulate the educational principles involved and, finally, see what can be said about how personal inquiry could be built into a school's program. I give you Joe, Betty, Tommy, Grace, Robert, and Jack.

Also Miss Case, Reverend Thompson, the lovely Miss Steinzor, a firm
of industrial designers, some shadowy characters in Student Personnel, the doughty Mr. McCorkle, the motherly Mrs. Price, and assorted
other members of the cast.

Episode 1

Joe at fifteen has a rigid, intolerant outlook toward other persons,
and sooner or later he always finds some way to damn them on
"moral" grounds—which he rationalizes in "religious" terms. He has
great difficulty in relating himself to other people and his aggressive
self-confidence masks a real lack of self-esteem and a real confusion
of goals and purposes. Joe is spending a month—and more if needed
—between noon and 5 P.M. with Reverend Thompson. Together they
go calling on parishioners, answer the mail, talk with visitors of all
sorts, discuss Thompson's Sunday sermon, consider the problems of
staffing the Sunday school with volunteers, explore the church's possible participation and position with respect to a variety of civic and
interchurch movements. In addition, Thompson is having Joe do a
survey of his congregation, using questionnaires backed up by interviews of some of the members; and the survey, planned by Thompson,
Joe, and a local sociologist, is to assess the needs of the congregation
that might be translated into better programs run by the church.

Joe went into this experience somewhat less than wholeheartedly.
He liked Reverend Thompson and identified with him from the start;
here was a man who was "moral," "religious," and friendly. Joe's first
shock came when Reverend Thompson admitted that he liked and
enjoyed the comapany of Alderman X——, whom Joe considered to
be a dyed-in-the-wool sinner. There was a period of disillusionment
for Joe, in which he saw Thompson as a hypocrite, and it was during
this period that Joe entered into his first meaningful relationship with
a teacher, his inquiry supervisor, for he needed help to deal with his
disappointment in Thompson. But, as time has gone on, Thompson
has allowed Joe to try to make decisions about many problems, and,
confronted with immediate and practical matters, Joe has found that
religion is more an orientation to life than a prescription of specific
behavior regardless of the situation.

Joe's relationship with Miss Case, the inquiry supervisor, has grown,
and it was a real breakthrough for him when she gathered six other
students for three discussion sessions on "what religion means to

me." For the first time in his life (so far as Miss Case could tell) Joe actually listened to fellow students and came away feeling good about them. Joe is now talking with Miss Case about joining the school's Youth Welfare committee, and Miss Case feels that his inquiry is about ready to come to an end. She is setting up a two-hour discussion among Joe, Mr. Thompson, herself, and the social studies teacher, the purpose of which will be to help Joe reach "closure" in his experience through putting into words what he has learned (from these people and from the five books, including the Bible, that he has read) and seeing what sort of universality these ideas have.

Miss Case feels pretty good about the whole affair. The reports from other teachers had looked rather bad for Joe: overaggressive, intolerant, narrow-minded, somewhat disruptive. Punitive and disciplinary measures only seemed to make matters worse. And his parents, who had raised Joe to be a good boy, were terribly let down and angry with him. There are plenty of further matters to be dealt with by Joe, especially in relation to his parents, but it looks as if he may now be able to get help in the time-honored way of adolescents: from each other.

Episode 2

Betty is a "well-adjusted" happy girl. Her test achievements are satisfactory, she gets along well with teachers, she is secure at home and has many friends, both boys and girls. She likes to socialize in class, but a gentle reminder from the teacher sets her back to work. She gets A's, B's, and C's, and no particular "subject" excites her much. She is active in student affairs, is playing the field in her attachments to boys, and there is no reason to suppose that she won't make a good marriage, raise handsome children, and live usefully and pleasantly.

Miss Case, her inquiry supervisor, had troubles within herself when it came to Betty. Miss Case is unmarried, and she has not had an easy life. She has always "had to work for what she gets." In some ways, her ability to identify with disturbed and unhappy children grew for her own soul's salvation. Miss Case, like anyone else who has responsibility for others, understands some things about the bases for her mildly hostile feelings. She found herself tempted, for example, to try to find something "wrong" with Betty, and she found herself engaging in fantasies in which she confronted Betty with her defects.

Clinical interpretation of some of Betty's essays, for example, suggests
a certain smugness coupled with an expectation of what to Miss Case
appeared to be privileges. Miss Case found it hard to identify with
or find common causes with a child who seemed herself to have no
deep involvements or concerns, no problems—a child, in effect,
who already has a kind of middle-aged maturity and acceptance of
life without ever having had to go through the pain of being socially,
at least, an adolescent. Miss Case, as a former history teacher, realized
that Betty would be just as well off in a job, a camp, or even taking a
vacation as in school. Which left Miss Case feeling rather outraged.

Betty had no particular suggestions for a personal inquiry of her
own—or, more accurately, she had a great many suggestions but no
commitment to any of them. Miss Case offered the notion of working
in a second-grade class, helping the teacher. Betty, with her usual
aplomb and appearance of bright interest, accepted this suggestion,
which sounded like fun. For two hours each morning Betty helped
Miss Steinzor with her class. Betty accepted Miss Steinzor readily,
and the fact that Miss Steinzor has a good figure and is engaged to be
married to an architect raised her considerably in Betty's esteem.

The boys and girls for the most part immediately liked Betty, which
was no new experience for her; but they also began to trust her, and
to bring her their troubles, anxieties, and fears—and this was a new
experience. Her desire to please Miss Steinzor, coupled with the high
expectations of the children, led, in this unfamiliar situation, to a
new sort of feeling: a blend of real eagerness and involvement along
with a lurking anxiety that she might fail to live up to what others
expected from her. This came to a head when little Harry got into a
scrap with Bud. Betty tried to separate them; they both turned on her
and Harry threw a block at her. Of course he missed, and was sorry
immediately afterward, but Betty was rather shaken by the experience and asked for a long talk with Miss Steinzor. Unfortunately the
latter had to duck out early that afternoon because her architect was
coming to town and the meeting had to be postponed; and Betty felt
for the first time the loneliness that goes along with an unaccustomed
feeling of inadequacy. And Betty couldn't help wondering about Miss
Steinzor, too.

This is a long story, and I'd like to take you through the whole of
it, but we have so many other boys and girls to get to, that maybe
I'd better hit only the high spots. It was agreed all around that

Betty would be less anxious in a more "structured" situation—one in which there were more rules, in which the students were a little more conforming and had a better hold on their impulses. She therefore was moved as helper to a fourth-grade class and was quite successful. When the teacher offered to let her teach an arithmetic lesson, Betty was flattered and challenged: she worked for hours getting ready for it, and tried to anticipate all the questions the children would ask. Her first lesson went fairly well. Two weeks later, the teacher offered to let Betty plan and carry out a project with half the class. Betty, now thoroughly involved, rose to the occasion. She consulted with three of her high school teachers and the librarian and for the first time in her life had the satisfaction of engaging in a real inquiry.

So that's where Betty is now. Miss Case doesn't know where it will end. Betty's own high school work in classes seems to be rather better, and socially Betty seems to be playing the field with the boys rather less. She may be settling down on a rather serious boy interested in chemistry. The Student Council's Committee on New Courses was rather surprised when Betty, accompanied by three other students, appeared before them to ask for a short course in Sociology next year.

Episode 3

Tommy was something of a "square," but his basement, much to everyone's surprise, was full of model boats, trains, and autos that he had constructed himself. On the theory that you are more likely to help people by building on their strengths rather than on their weaknesses, Miss Case got Tommy working part time making models for a small firm of industrial designers. The firm's partners liked Tommy's work very much but he began to rub them the wrong way, and things got pretty tense. In fact, one of the partners told Miss Case that they "couldn't stand that boy much longer"; but she prevailed upon them to let her send a counselor to observe the situation for a few days before they took action.

The counselor watched and talked with Tommy and the people he was in contact with on the job. They then had a two-hour meeting together, during which a good deal of feeling was expressed and through which it appeared that Tommy's own difficulties were playing into those of the partners; that nobody seemed able to break the vicious cycle of insincere praise, hurt feelings, aggression, and blow-ups. Ostensibly to help Tommy but actually to help the firm, the counselor was invited to attend weekly staff meetings at which various problems and grievances were aired. By the end of two months, the firm had hired a new man who coupled design imagination with some of the human relations skills they needed, and the outlook was prom-ising. Tommy had become something of a mascot around the place, and, when the rest of the men prevailed upon the local adult education center to put in a course on design mathematics, they took Tommy along. He did very well in this course, and it was probably just as well that Miss Case let him drop the school's algebra course, at which he was failing.

In this adult-protected, work-focused situation, Tommy appears to be effective. He respects the partners because their ideas are better than his and because they are opening new doors for him, and this respect gives him the basis for self-discipline—for "staying in line." The experience has persuaded Tommy that somewhere within his design hobby, which he had not even mentioned to any adult at school, may well lie his vocation, and he is rather torn at the moment between improving his draughtmanship, learning a great deal more about strength of materials, and designing some model kits to try to sell to a leading toy company. He is also facing the uncomfortable idea that back of design there is a considerable amount of science—which has not in the past been interesting to him. But he can see that he will have to learn mechanics and electronics if he is to stay permanently with these partners, and that for furniture design—which is a new interest, not entirely disassociated from a little brunette who has taken to smiling at him—he will have to know anatomy and a great deal about functional analysis. All of this excites rather than discourages him. Acting on a hunch, Miss Case had him take another IQ test last week, and he was up 18 points—a fact that everyone concerned is still trying to assimilate.

Episode 4

Grace is a rather unattractive girl with a mediocre record of achieve-ment and intelligence. She pals around with a few other girls similar to herself and they talk endlessly about a singer whose recordings they collect. They are also the mainstay of the choir of a small church, and their crush on the choir director seems obvious to all but the persons involved. Grace has no clear ambitions, although she talks about "going to college next year"—an eventuality which, in view of her grades, economic situation, and aptitudes, seems rather remote. To all appearances, Grace's world is a tight little island, impervious to the machinations of well-meaning adults.

At present, Miss Case is arranging to chat with Grace an hour a week in the hope that she can get her to begin to think realistically about herself. Miss Case can see several possible ways to move but she doesn't know which makes most sense, and she has not yet assessed Grace's "readiness" with respect to any of these. The alternatives which may open up are: (a) getting Grace interested in personal grooming, or, if that is too threatening, in making her own clothes—knitting sweaters might be a good beginning here; (b) talking with the choir director to explore two possibilities: one, that Grace's interest in singing is genuine and may provide a focus, and the other, that the choir master develop some insight into his symbolic (or real?) relationship to Grace and be alerted to help her break through to a more mature understanding of her own needs; (c) talking with the Sunday school supervisor to ask whether Grace may have any flair for working with younger children; (d) visiting the home and talking with Grace's parents to see if she has revealed any special talents and interests unknown to the school and to assess the kinds of forces that may be encouraging Grace's resistance to developing commitments to some goal, and that may be nibbling away at her self-esteem; (e) putting Grace's case on the agenda for a "case conference" with all her teachers, to see if they have discovered any strengths that Grace might be encouraged to explore; and (f) asking the counselors of the student government program to get—by indirection—an assessment of Grace's interests and capabilities from some of the student leaders.

To Miss Case, these activities are all simply to get information about Grace—to help Miss Case and, later on, the girl herself, to accept and understand the phenomenon that is Grace. As Grace and Miss Case get hunches, they may decide to make use of various diagnostic and clinical tests and to call on psychiatric, vocational, and academic counseling skills. But these resources will not be used until the team of Grace and Case has developed some hunches worth inquiring into by these more elaborate means.

Episode 5

Robert, an exceedingly shy and withdrawn child, has already been studied by Miss Case. He was unable to help in any way, incidentally. The testimony is all quite clear: Robert has no relationships with anyone, and he is too tied up in his own misery even to be able to look at television with enjoyment. Miss Case has had to acknowledge that this is a case beyond the reach of the sort of "situational therapy" involved in the personal inquiries program of the school. She has discussed Robert with all his teachers, and they are going to make a special effort to bolster his ego with little failure-proof tasks like running the movie projector, giving a hand (very casually) in transporting books and materials from room to room, coming in after school to arrange a bulletin board, and so on. They will also make no effort to induce Robert to participate in give-and-take discussion, and will be prepared, if necessary, to defend the right of the individual not to participate.

But this is a case for psychiatric treatment, and the personnel services staff is consulting with a local clinic to find him this kind of help. Miss Case and the Personnel Director have added Robert to their list of twenty-six others (out of 800 pupils) whose existence demonstrates the need for some kind of special institution along "treatment camp" lines that will operate all year round; and they are getting ready a proposal to send through channels to the appropriate subcommittee of the Community Education Council.

Episode 6

Jack is an extremely bright boy who has been cordially disliked by most of his teachers. He is sarcastic and belittles the efforts of teachers and students alike. He actually studies assignments enough to maintain his A average, but he delights in pretending that he never cracks a book.

Mr. McCorkle, the physics teacher, burst his seams one day in class, but the bell rang in the middle of his tirade, so he told Jack to come in during conference period as he still had a lot more to say. When Jack came in, Mr. McCorkle had himself under control, and in a cold and analytical manner spent half an hour giving Jack a completely dispassionate picture of how his behavior was perceived and reacted to by teachers and students. Jack attempted to defend himself with blustery argument, but McCorkle just ignored the interruptions and went on with his bill of particulars. Jack used his real brightness to offer fancy, self-justifying interpretations of the incidents described by McCorkle; but McCorkle, who knew better than to turn the discussion into an intellectual argument (which he would probably lose anyway) doggedly stuck to the "facts" as he saw them. And Jack, finally confronted for the first time in his life by a completely steadfast adult, quieted down and began to listen. He seemed to alternate between the verge of tears and the verge of nasty comments of his own; but he said nothing for the remaining twenty minutes. McCorkle closed the "interview" by saying that Jack should give himself a couple of days to think things over, and then he should feel free to consult Miss Case, McCorkle himself, or anyone else in the Personnel Services Department.

For the next two days, Jack was absent from physics, and McCorkle discovered that he was going to the library instead; he had somehow talked the library teacher into accepting him because he had to get out a "special report." McCorkle went to Mr. Round, Director of Personnel Services, and rather shamefacedly described what he had done. Round reduced McCorkle's anxiety by pointing out that many teachers and counselors had tried to "get to" Jack over the last couple of years, but that McCorkle was the only one who had had success—probably because he had really given Jack information about Jack rather than just deriving relief for himself. Moreover, Jack was handling the situation very well. He was clearly not ready to make peace with McCorkle, but he had found an intelligent compromise: he had not left school or become destructive, nor had he accepted McCorkle's observations. Instead he had cut physics, but was apparently using the time rather constructively. Of course he had broken the school rule and lied to the librarian, which was not right; he should not have taken the law into his own hands, and if he had asked Round for permission he would have gotten it. He was probably acting out his own defiance in this rather innocuous way of flouting authority, which, after all, had been part of his pattern for a long time. Clearly, said Round, the next move is up to Jack. If, in the meanwhile, McCorkle bumped into Jack in the hall, he might comment that he had noted Jack was not in class and then move on unless Jack wanted to talk with him. And Round would check with Jack's teachers and the librarian so that he would know what was going on.

The next week turned out to be rather an unstable one. Jack himself showed more extremes of behavior than ever before, from long periods of holding himself in during the other classes to flashes of almost vicious attacks. In the library he worked as if the devil were chasing him. McCorkle found himself confused and wondered what he would do when Jack came back. Round got busy with other matters and forgot about Jack.

The situation broke on Friday. In English literature, Jack failed to respond when Mrs. Price called on him. She called his name again and he came to with a start. She commented that he seemed rather preoccupied and then repeated her question. He answered it perfectly, and she complimented him. After school Jack came into Mrs. Price's office and told his story. He mentioned that his library project was one on rocket fuels and that he was so far simply finding out what had been tried and how well each fuel performed; he also said he felt sure the librarian was aware of his deception, but she had given no sign, and the suspense was awful. When asked about McCorkle, Jack said he couldn't understand him; that he had seemed neither angry nor pleased when Jack passed him in the hall, which surprised Jack because he figured the old boy would be after him for cutting physics. Mrs. Price suggested that maybe McCorkle was waiting for Jack to figure things out for himself, and the fact that he didn't seem angry might mean that he would talk with Jack about it. Jack felt that anything would be better than leaving things unresolved—and there was his A in physics to consider, too.

Jack went to see McCorkle. McCorkle asked about his work on jet fuels, and after reading his notes, suggested some further sources Jack had not known about, including an instructor in the local college. McCorkle further suggested that the report looked promising, and asked if Jack had thought of science as his vocational area; if so, why not prepare for and try one of the Science Foundation examinations? After all, a four-year college scholarship was worth a little effort. Jack took all this with a slightly superior smile that began to irritate McCorkle, and when they finally got around to the physics class, McCorkle said flatly he didn't want Jack in his class. It had gone very well for the last week and that was the way he wanted it. The teacher said he was sorry, because Jack could be very helpful to him and to the class if he wanted to, but there seemed no point in just returning to the old pattern. Rather to Jack's surprise, he found himself suddenly very eager to be back in class, and the next forty minutes was spent negotiating the conditions for this return.

Jack was back in class for a week before he began to get bored again. He and McCorkle were on friendly terms now, and the teacher suggested Jack take the final examination immediately just to see whether he really needed the class for academic purposes. Jack's grade was an A, and they decided that he would drop the class and that he, McCorkle, and Miss Case would consider other ways to pursue his inquiry in physics. It all ended with Jack attending a seminar on rocketry given by McCorkle's friend at the college; and with Jack establishing a quasi-counseling relationship with Mrs. Price. In the seminar Jack had to work very hard to keep up, and Mrs. Price was quite successful in helping him reflect on his feelings in this situation and develop some feelings of identification with classmates on whom he had earlier vented his scorn. Mrs. Price opened Jack's eyes to an entirely new sort of role he could take—that of helping others—and he signed up with the Student Council to give coaching aid to students in science.

I wish we had time to thumb through the other record cards. Here's Sandy, for instance, a quiet bright girl who has just finished her book on folk dancing. Carl has been spending his afternoons practicing pipe organ and has composed a prelude which he will play at the Music Festival. Three girls made a survey of the food choices of the students and ended with a series of recommendations for the cafeteria. Two boys have a responsibility for working up unique window displays for four merchants, and their last display was a real traffic-stopper. Five girls are working part time as nurse's aides, one boy is doing accounting (under the supervision of a CPA) for two small businesses, other youths are working with florists, groceries, museums, nursery schools, and so on, in an endless list. But perhaps we have said enough to make clear what we mean by personal inquiry.

Personal inquiry, in the sense of acting out and satisfying needs, however commendable, is not enough. For over and above this it must be educative. We are concerned not only that needs be met but also with how they are met. It is insufficient to help students cope with immediate situations; they must, in this process, learn to cope with other situations as well. Our aim is not adjustment as such but learning.

Our little vignettes do not tell the whole story. Let's see what part they do tell, and then we can consider the portion of the inquiry process which must be added in order to make the experience educative. In the vignettes, then, I have intended to make clear a number of things.

First, inquiry must be based on careful diagnosis. It is not a matter of grasping at any old interest or enthusiasm of the moment; we cannot select from a list of precooked and rehashed possibilities; it is not what some authoritative adult thinks the "student ought to have"; it is not a way to get housekeeping done around the school; it is not a transmission of some particular teacher's pet enthusiasm; it isn't even what some clinical test (when placed alongside somebody's model of health) suggests is needed. It is none of these. Inquiry begins with a problematic situation which represents a whole class of problematic situations. The "problem" may be one of channeling strong creative drives into situations that will produce ability, as with the girl in the sophomore project last year who wrote the linguistics book. The "problem" may be one of working out relationships between oneself and other people, as with Joe, Grace, and Tommy. The "problem" may be one of finding a goal in life, as with Betty and Grace. But whatever the problem, it must be a central one, whose solution can illuminate many other situations.

The finding of the problem and its acceptance or formulation by the child himself is what I mean by diagnosis. You will note in the examples above, the stress I place on confrontation of the student by data about his behavior in carefully planned situations. Joe was confronted by Mr. Thompson's different interpretation of "religious" principles, and Joe's inquiry really revolved around dealing with the feelings and confusions this produced in him. Betty was confronted with a situation in which the expectations of others got her emotionally involved and the challenge of responsibility forced her to clarify her own goals and values. Tommy was confronted—in a situation where he was "safe" to accept it—with the disturbing results of his interpersonal behavior, but the work on his models was kept sufficiently central so that he could edge into the inquiry at his own pace and as he developed readiness for it. Grace's problem was not identified in our vignette, but the first step in diagnosis was illustrated: that of getting hunches about what sort of confrontation under what conditions could lead to inquiry. Robert's problem, that of emotional crippling, had to be referred for professional medical aid. Jack's problem was not too dissimilar to those of Joe and Tommy; the difference in Jack's case was his greater ego-strength that made direct confrontation, really without any supportive relationships, effective.

The second point I have built into these little stories is that inquiry involves firsthand activity in real situations. In most cases, the inquiring student is aided by working close to some adult with whom he can identify—some adult he would like to be like, perhaps, but at the least an adult he can easily trust. This adult must be without ulterior motives in dealing with the student. He has a job to do; he helps define the role of the student on the job, and the demands the student has to meet come either from the nature of the task or from the nature of the social conditions obviously required to get the work done. In other words, I want the student to transact his business directly with the work and the work environment; I want him to discover that there are realities outside of his own personal desires or those of "authorities," for it is only within such a stable framework of action that his own behavior can be assessed unequivocally by himself. It is only thus that he can discover and learn to depend on his abilities and that he can face up to weaknesses, because they cannot be blamed on other persons.

The third point I have tried to illustrate is that inquiry is an ongoing business, one in which experience itself continually generates new data for consideration. It is a process in which the student is always changing, developing new perceptions and insights, new feelings, new evaluations of new kinds of experiences, new attitudes toward old experiences. In short, it is a process which calls for continual guidance through reflection on the results of one's own experience. It is because of this aspect of inquiry that the student needs a great deal more than mere job supervision. He needs a Miss Case— someone always available to talk with him not about the job but about the meaning for him of the job-related experience. This counselor must also be someone with whom the student can identify, and he must be able to establish rapport with the student. The student may have to select the person himself, as with Jack, who decided on Mrs. Price. It may well be that another student will also have this sort of role; certainly many parents will, too.

The fourth point I have worked into my accounts though with less emphasis than I would like, is that it will be valuable for the student in most cases to have images other than his own against which to compare his experiences and project his thoughts. I refer here to books and other sources of information of all sorts. For many students, the counselor's main role may turn out to be that of getting into his hands some book, journal, or other written material which, because it is organized and objective can give him a useful view of the technical processes and social meanings of his work, or which because it is personal and subjective, can stimulate an awareness of personal meanings and issues for the student. The combination of books, counselors, supervisor, and others falls flat unless it can stimulate an awareness of new attitudes and unless it can give the student enough information so that he sees there is something to reorganize in new insights.

The fifth point is that the student must be quite consciously inquiring. The diagnostic process should give him a clear commitment to goals to be sought. The work experience should give him data to consider. The interactive process, with books and persons, should raise questions. And finally, the student, with whatever guidance he needs in order to reflect, must reach his own conclusions and formulate them quite consciously. It is not enough to say, as most adults do in summer workshops, that they "got a lot out of the experience." Granted that much of what the student will "get" will never enter into his awareness—or at least not for a long time—nonetheless some part of the experience must be available to consciousness and be guided by a recognition of the nature and steps of inquiry.

It is at this point—of reflection and explicit formulation—that practically all work experience now set up through schools and colleges actually fails. Education is always a slightly schizophrenic business: one is walking through experiences at the same time that he is conscious of himself as a person walking through experiences. It is this little bit of extra consciousness that distinguishes inquiry from simple satisfaction of needs. And it is the absence of this part which, in Chapter 2, I labeled the crucial failure of existing means of education.

It follows from this that the student must be helped to learn to inquire. This is what the knowledge disciplines ought to contribute far more extensively than they now do, even at the Ph.D. level. The method of inquiry can be worked out partly with the aid of a counselor, but you will see that it is also a major objective of the group investigations to be discussed in the next chapter. For the method of inquiry is basically a social process, not a private and individual process, even though we expect the individual to incorporate the method into his own way of life.

The student, whether he is a second grader or a professor, needs procedures to help him inquire. There must also be checkpoints at regular intervals—sessions in which the student reviews his progress and attempts to assess how far he has come and what steps are needed next. Reporting to a group of peers has real advantages, too, provided each student is adequately interviewed by the group at the close of his report. The chief advantage here that is difficult to attain by other methods lies in the fact that the reporter is likely to gain a strengthened commitment to his inquiry as a result of his semipublic declarations; he is reinforced by the expectations others now have for his performance.

Finally, one of the products of inquiry is further inquiry. The diagnostic processes I have illustrated all assume that this is the first inquiry by the student, and I have given attention to this because the first will also be the hardest and because I hope some reader will be encouraged to give it a try. But at the end of the first inquiry, there should, I think, be a council meeting, composed of the student, his counselor, the supervisor, possibly his parents, and anyone else who has a legitimate interest in the inquiry. Not only the personal inquiry but also the student's other experiences should be considered, for it is the student as a whole person that we are trying to describe and locate along the pathway to maturity of thought, emotion, and behavior. The perceptions of all these people are the data from which the next inquiry will be adduced—either because a need emerges clearly in their agreements or because their confusion suggests a critical confrontation to be used next in order to see where the student really stands. And all such testimony should be written into the record —including the agreed-upon evaluations which fairly sum up the student's accomplishment in the inquiry proper.

ORGANIZATIONAL MATTERS

At this point I rest my case for personal inquiry. I hope that as you have read you have been thinking about the boys and girls you know and have been testing the relevance of these notions to their lives.

What differences would such experiences have made for your son or daughter? Or, for that matter, in your own school experience? If you feel that the model is worthwhile in these terms, then you are ready to join me in tussling with the formidable problems of organization; but I beg you not to decide for or against an educational idea simply on the basis of "practical" considerations.

The first problem of organization is deciding what needs to be organized. The only way to discover this is to begin in a small way to get the wheels rolling and then gradually to define special responsibilities as their need becomes apparent. Successful organization has to be developed over time. So where do we start?

I think a fine place to start is in a high school summer session. Here we won't have to worry about "courses" and we can also begin to train ourselves in the necessary skills. We can begin to find the people in the community who can help and the kinds of students we can work with to make a beginning—although ultimately we must try to reach them all. So let's turn the summer session over to a committee of teachers and let's give them a school year to talk with other teachers, get into the community, select students, and so on.

The next year in school, let's go on with some of these same students plus a few others, and free the teachers who learned most during the summer to work with them. They will probably have to select some from among the many students who for one reason or another can give two school periods plus time after school to the experience.

Maybe the next year, by saving time through the reorganization of the rest of the school program along the lines indicated in the next chapters, we will be ready to deal with the whole freshman class. This, of course, assumes an all-out school effort, with faculty workshops, consultants, and the beginnings of a functioning Community Education Council—as delineated in Chapter 11. Assuming, then, that we are ready for a large scale operation, involving at least a quarter of the students, then I think the following sorts of things will have to be provided:

The Director's office should contain two sets of files, one with folders for all the students, the other with folders for all the community resource people—who have already been identified as willing to help. Both sets of files should be coded and summarized on cards for the rapid "fitting" of student to opportunity. The Director will be in charge of this fitting process. His job is to see to it that the files are fed regularly and systematically and that they are kept up to date.

On the community side, the Director will have to keep contacts alive, and everybody from the Superintendent of Schools down may have to help make contacts, interpret the program, and report results through television, newspapers, mass meetings, and programs for sponsors. The Director will probably need assistants to do the leg work; they should be hired as needed. Some of them may be teachers who have been relieved of some of their class work. Others may be housewives who have been trained during a three-week summer program.

On the students' side, the Director needs machinery for collecting revealing "incidents" from teachers. He will need the help of a full-scale testing clinic—which may not be located in the school. He will need a corps of supervisory counselors—probably one for every twenty-five students. These counselors are the key supervisors, and I suspect they will develop their own specialties, determined by their relationships to particular kinds of resources in the community, their own competence in supervising different sorts of inquiry, and their own ability to work with certain kinds of students. The director will have to help this group decide how students will be divided among them.

Each supervisor will need to train several assistants who are to be on-the-job counselors. The ideal assistant would, in my opinion, be one of their own former high school students who had been through the program and was now in a nearby college. And ideally, these assistants would themselves be planning to be teachers and could get college credit toward their own preparation through this experience. Failing this, there is always that hardy perennial, the trained housewife, to fall back on.

The supervisor, counselor, and student should meet together for all critical purposes, such as launching inquiries, defining or redefining the responsibilities of each participant, and making decisions about necessary changes.

Whether the program will roll depends on something else, which I shall call the Spirit of the Organization. The necessary spirit is that of inquiry. Mistakes will be made and confusions will develop; lines of communication will get snarled, people will get disaffected from time to time; the mimeograph machine will break down, and there will be occasional invasions by irate parents. But if the staff will think of themselves as learners too, will see in each failure a new lesson, a new insight, will deal with their internal problems directly, face to face—then the problems will be challenges. But the minute the staff thinks of itself as a factory, in which time is money and efficiency the god of the machine—all will be lost.

7

Social Order:
The Subterranean World of the Group

In which we let Flight 716 show us some of the richness and complexity of group behaviors, and we note the fundamental conflict between the emotional and work tendencies of the group. We propose that group development proceeds as a continuous undercover investigation of how to resolve this conflict in each situation. We suggest that the social order emerges to provide the "ground rules" for dealing with this conflict; that the most educative classroom is one whose social order incorporates the chief features of the knowledge-discipline to be learned; and that its members are selected to facilitate this quest.

There are many things the ideal (or educated) citizen needs that the child does not: ability to judge political issues, control economic practices, safeguard the health of the community and the world, communicate with other peoples raised in different cultures, and so on. We believe that these abilities are the resultant of two things: a generally enlightened and civilized mind and heart on the one hand, and specific knowledge and practice on the other. Presumably this provides the rationale for general and technical education.

The learning of algebra, Shakespeare's plays, and French grammar, if taught properly, would contribute to the enlightenment and competence of the citizen. But the last thing most children have any

113

real and present need for learning is algebra, Shakespeare's plays, and French grammar.

The question before us, then, is, How can the task of learning things that children don't (as children) need, be incorporated within their basic striving for an effective way of life? This is where the group comes in, and in this chapter and the next I shall try to show how. The question, rephrased in anticipation of the plan of group investigation, was introduced in Chapter 5: What sort of group arrangements will help a child learn all sorts of things "society" requires of him to learn even though the child has as yet no particular "felt" need for these things?

Since the idea of group participation has been frequently associated with the ideas of conformity, manipulation, and thought control, I wish to point out that our thinking precludes these devices. They are not what we are seeking. What we are looking for is understanding of the kinds of social-psychological dynamics which develop readiness for learning, extend experience, and enable a person to gain new insights and socially useful skills that are meaningful to him.

The sort of basic idea we need is a theoretical one. For personal inquiry, we have isolated a universal drive toward autonomy as the process available to drive education. For groups we need a similar fundamental concept of drive: What is the dynamic in groups that can be geared to education? We shall start with this question, and pose a series of propositions to cover the matter. Then, in true pedagogical spirit, we shall show the application of these propositions to a couple of dramatic events in the lives of groups; and following this we shall pause to comment about the effects of "culture" or "background" of members. Then we shall pull ourselves back on the main road with some experiments on group composition and some speculations about what is involved in obtaining "teachable" groups, which are groups whose fundamental dynamic can be most readily channeled toward educational outcomes. We shall close with the question of just how the teacher can accomplish this channeling, and that will be the central concern of the next chapter.

THE GROUP'S DYNAMIC

In all groups there is a common and universal dynamic. It is a natural process that is just as fundamental and universal in groups as the quest for integration is to individuals. And it is this dynamic which we intend to harness to education.

The nature of the dynamic is, as always, the generation and resolution of conflict between two natures. In personal investigation, the two natures were the animal and social natures of the individual, expressed in conflict between his tendencies to act out emotionally and to inquire intelligently into the situation. In the group, the two natures in conflict are its tendency to seek comfort through development of interpersonal friendships and alliances and its tendency to seek out and deal with situational realities. Let me explain.

When a number of persons, strangers to each other, happen to find themselves together for a period of time, they start to interact with each other. They may not say anything—at least not at first—but watch their eyes! You will note that after a quick look around, they begin to give attention to each other in a highly selective manner. Harry may be watching Susan across the way—a fact she is going to be conscious of pretty soon; then the two may engage in the game of watching each other surreptitiously, with each quickly turning away when the other is about to catch him or her at it. Another person in the group, with his loud clothes and exaggerated movements, is being watched quite openly (but with different expressions) by many people. He is playing to the gallery, even though he may not know it. Yet another person may be mostly invisible to the others; but he has eyes, too, and in his gestures, posture, and facial expression you can read his acceptance of the role, invited by him and already accorded him, of isolate.

Now let us suppose this is an airline waiting room. It is ten minutes until departure time. An event occurs: The well-tailored voice from the loudspeaker suddenly announces a thirty-minute delay due to "mechanical difficulties." To carry my fantasy any further I'll have to make a few stipulations about the social conditions. If this is La Guardia, and the delay occurs to a red-carpet flight, nothing much will happen. But if the flight is tourist class and the airport is in the Southwest, somebody is going to say something. What he says, and to whom he says it, will depend on the relationships that have already become tentatively established. We can bet the gallery player will make a wisecrack or a hostile remark to the whole group; and that if his remark is responded to spontaneously by someone else ("You said it, boy") the two may move closer and into conversation. Harry and

Susan—again depending on the assessments they have been making—may or may not get into conversation; and, again depending on the further assessments this would provide, may or may not fly together when the plane finally leaves. The isolate, supported by the feeling of disappointment and resentment which he knows is shared by all, may venture a remark to whoever sits closest.

I have been showing you the development of what Jennings[3] calls the "psyche-structure" of a group. There is no goal for the group as a whole, and people enter into interaction voluntarily—there is no requirement to "participate." Each person is dealing with highly personal matters, and each seeks something from certain others. What he seeks may be an active overt response or it may be only an impassive expression into which he can read whatever attitude he would like to see there. The persons have meaning for each other. They form alignments and identifications with each other. A group is born, with subgroups and communication channels. This waiting-room group is a trivial impermanent group; it will dissolve readily into smaller groups and isolates just as soon as everyone gets seated in the plane. But this group has the makings. Suppose, for example, the plane doesn't take off. It turns out the passengers will have to wait overnight. Lifelong friendships can form on lesser occasions than this; and when the plane does take off the next day, I doubt that the fixed seats, arranged in twos and threes, will seriously stand in the way of sporadic conversations involving many different combinations of passengers. And the stewardess, who hasn't had the opportunity to read this, is likely to encounter a general group spirit manifested in good-natured kidding, sullenness, or whatever shared attitude has developed among the passengers. She will note the "cohesiveness" of the load.

All groups have a psyche structure. It is oriented to personal "psyche" needs of individuals. Through this structure individuals deal with their anxieties, doubts, and private desires. It is a structure for seeking comfort and reassurance. It is also interactive, and what one person needs for comfort may be upsetting to someone else. In this case, assuming that the people are together every day for a period of time—as in a classroom or business office—a shared opinion will emerge in the group about what sorts of behaviors will be sanctioned and what sorts punished. Boundaries to the expression of feeling and to the development of intimacy (and distance, too) will emerge.

My little teaser about La Guardia vs. Albuquerque and first-class vs. tourist flights was put in to make an additional point: that the boundaries and behaviors are strongly conditioned by the mores of the "larger" community. No group has unlimited choice in the nature of its controlling climate and unspoken agreements; it has to operate within the range of possibilities already available in the larger society to which its members have, through the years, become conditioned.

Restrictions and demands come also from the task, and these generate a different sort of group. Let us suppose, for example, that old Flight 716 in our above fantasy is really in trouble: after two hours of doing whatever mechanics do, the certo system is still "kaput." The man in charge hastily calls together a high-level group to diagnose the difficulty. Let's consider this process of calling the group together. When he gets on the phone, whom does he call? Obviously, those individuals who are believed to be experts with certo systems; the criterion for selection is past achievement and therefore presumed ability to contribute. Moreover, these men are not asked if they would like to come; they are instead given the front-and-center routine. Further, this is all right with them because to be available for such emergencies is part of their jobs, and they are being paid for it.

So now we have the diagnostic conference, with its individual members absorbedly poking, peering, testing and inspecting the parts of the plane which are most unlike Caesar's wife. One of the obvious things to do is to test the tension in the golly-worbus, an operation calling for skillful use of the transmerz. When Norton, from the Iron Filings and Grit division, wanted to use the transmerz he found that it was already in the possession of Stark, of the High Temperature and Holocaust Lab. So Norton said to Stark: When you are through, if you please. And Stark said to Norton: A minute more, and it's yours. From this bit of civilized interaction you'd never have guessed that on the long walk to the hangar Stark had confided to Turnquist (Audio Thumping and Vibration section) that Norton struck him (Stark) as being only a little bit less intelligent than a blind goat on whom a lobotomy had been performed by a thumb-handed moron who, at the age of four, had been rejected by his mother.

After each expert had poked to his heart's content, Gridley, being ready, suggested they proceed to compare notes. Nobody was sure what the trouble was, although four experts had each noted at least one suspicious condition or symptom. Their job, said Gridley, would

be, first, to hear what each individual had observed; second, to weigh
the observations as possible evidence for speculations as to where
the trouble lay; and third, to plan a program for attacking the ailing
certo mechanism in such a way that each operation would throw
maximum light on the possible causes of trouble. As the group moved
from speculation to hypothesis and recommendations, Stark and
Norton argued together that the trouble lay in the grubblepusher,
whereas Turnquist seemed to feel that the honk valve was a more
likely culprit. Gridley, who felt that his expertness was not on a par
with that of the others, privately thought maybe the problem lay in
the generators—but that's what he always thought, and he considered
that it would be inappropriate to mention this because his task was
really to coordinate the thinking of the experts. Of the two other experts in the group, one had almost nothing to say, looked at his watch
often, and finally begged to be excused, commenting as he left that
all he could see to do was take down the grubblepusher and the honk
valve. The other expert, when finally pushed for an opinion, went
to the board and presented three alternatives which he had arrived at
by symbolic logic, and he nailed down the problem as the "faulty
extenuation of the threshold level in the over-all working system."
When asked for further explanation, he admitted that this was basically an heuristic notion, and that he probably should not have mentioned it.

As we look back at this slice of life, we see that the fact that there
is a task to do makes a difference. The difference comes from the demands of the task. Data must be gathered, pooled, and speculated
about. Thoughts must be spoken out loud, and they have to be put
together, which may require concentrated attention by one member,
the "coordinator." The right to talk depends on the relevance of an
idea to the problem. Various members may find themselves in agreement with some members and in disagreement with others; if there
are two incompatible opinions each strongly held by a few adherents,
then the group in effect is seen as consisting of three parts: those who
hold opinion A, those who hold opinion B, and the other members.
Further, different persons are likely to be differentially "involved." For
one member, getting the plane in the air is terribly important; for another, making some mathematical deductions is the big thing; for the
man with the wrist watch, getting out of the meeting is the goal.
Finally, the members are chosen with reference to the nature of the

problem—they in no sense choose each other to work with.

Our diagnostic conference is a "socio" group. It is oriented to solving problems, or, in more general terms, taking action against the environment. The socio group has a structure of subgroups, and of functional roles and positions (status and authority) which define the expected relationships between the members and the group's task. Different kinds of contributions may be expected from the various members, but the differences of expectation (in so far as they are legitimate) are based on assessment of competence and contribution. There is a common purpose, namely, to solve the problem; and, the group has to organize its discussion with this in mind. The purpose is explicit, and it is easy to judge the relevance of contributions.

As we compare our passengers and experts, we see that the psyche and socio groups each contain elements of the other—in spite of my effort to present extreme and pure examples.

In the case of the passengers, the beginning of overt interaction (talking to each other) was the announcement to the entire collection of people that the plane would be delayed. In psyche terms, each individual experienced heightened anxiety, anger, or shock at the unexpected, and each had to deal with it in some way, using other individuals for this purpose. But in socio terms, the announcement threw a stress not only on each individual but upon the group as a whole. In effect, the voice imposed a demand—to wait longer than expected—from the "outside"; and the demand was made on the collection of persons as a collection, not as a series of differentiated individuals. From the airline's point of view, fifty-two persons, constituting the ambulatory load of the plane, had to be instructed to wait longer; and the reason for telling them this was that if nothing were said the group would begin to take action "against" the airline: asking questions, demanding explanations, striking attitudes, demanding sympathy, etc. A few passengers would initiate these contacts, and the others would listen in. Informally, then, these few would be acting on behalf of the group.

In the example as given, the stress tended to accelerate the psyche-group behavior and consolidated the psyche-group relations already partially established. My fantasy was probably not entirely realistic. Harry, for example, instead of turning to the girl, might be more likely to turn to some man who looked as if he were an old hand with airlines, and this would signify the suppression of a mild romantic interest by a stronger work need to get to wherever the plane was supposed to take him. For a moment, Harry must choose between personal interests and task demands. If something similar happens with the other passengers, too, then very little more in the way of a further announcement over the speaker would be required (in Albuquerque) to bring a socio group into full-fledged existence. But note that the psyche group is still in existence, even though partially suppressed.

In the case of the diagnostic conference of experts, I have planted a few psyche elements in my account. The most obvious one is the indication of relationships between Stark and Norton and Stark and Turnquist. Stark is seen to have antipathy to Norton, and to feel close enough to Turnquist that he can confide this to him. This, then, is part of the interpersonal or psyche picture. Now, however, look what happens in the course of working on the problem; Stark finds himself in agreement with Norton and in disagreement with his friend Turnquist. In my illustration I have portrayed an easy shift in alliances, as if persons can make common cause with erstwhile enemies, or can turn against their friends. Presumably they can deal with problems as problems, and check their "emotions at the door." Actually, of course, we all learn to do this to some extent—usually to a lot smaller extent than we admit. And it takes energy: we pay a price. This energy goes into solving the problem of what to do when one's personal private inclinations are in conflict with meeting the presumed expectancies of one's task role. One must give in to one or the other, or he must find a new basis of conduct that enables him to maintain both task and personal integrity at the same time. This inquiry into a new basis of conduct is the source of new learning and insight, and over time it develops the standards and values of the group.

I have been posing the psyche-group relationships entirely in terms of interpersonal attractiveness and repulsion, which is the phenomenon first used by Helen Jennings to differentiate psyche and socio structures within the group. But this like-dislike dimension is only one of many that belong under the general heading of interpersonal relations. Other aspects include obtaining stimulation, reassurance, dominance, punishment, reduction of anxieties, challenge, ego support, responses to all sorts of ideas and feelings, and so on.

To sum up:

1. All groups have both psyche and socio-group natures, oriented respectively to creation of the group as a milieu for personal need-

meeting and to creation of the group as an instrument for solving problems and tasks which come from "outside" the group.

2. The nature of the psyche needs and of the problem of harmonizing these with socio needs is largely determined by the particular combination of personalities in the group (e.g., who are the members).

3. The demands of the psyche and socio natures of the group are partly reinforcing, partly supplementary, and partly in conflict.

4. For the group to survive, it must somehow reconcile the demands of its two natures. This survival or maintenance need is a strong one, and is universal; in one way or another every group must deal with it.

5. A system of implicit and explicit agreements is developed by the group in order to combine its psyche and socio needs; these become incorporated into the standards, values, and operating assumptions of the group.

6. The rapidity, validity, and ease of maintaining the group in the face of its conflicting natures is largely determined by the leadership, whether it be from one person or from all the members.

THE PSYCHE NEEDS

The teacher can shut his eyes to the psyche system of the classroom, but he cannot make it disappear. For most high school students, activities have higher psychological reality and priority of involvement than do the planned learning activities of the socio system. The high school student, standing between childhood and adulthood, driven by sensed biological capabilities and felt emotional urges, harried by the need to belong but not knowing where or how to go about it—such a person has a lot more on his nervous system than a tension to find the root of $x^2 + 3ax - 6a^2 = 0$.

We have recently obtained some data at the University of Chicago that will, I think, serve to illustrate what I mean by the high-priority psyche needs. The data come from a current study, supported by the U. S. Office of Education,[7] on how to group students into effective, learning-oriented classes. By way of introduction, I might say that uncovering these psyche needs turns out to be quite a chore. They are not directly measurable. Each must be inferred from a pattern of attitudes, hopes, perceptions, and beliefs; and each represents, in effect, a basic theme or way of life which might be established in the group.

These psyche needs were identified from patterns of scores obtained from a three-hour test battery administered to 750 high school students in 11 schools. From these, we selected 216 students in grades VIII through XI. In the sample there were as many boys as girls; there was equal representation of three ranges of economic "class" (laborer to professionally trained executive); IQ was evenly and comparably distributed through the class, grade, and sex groups. We developed 172 scores for each child—IQ was one of them—and then set the campus UNIVAC to grinding away. The themes it came up with are eye-openers!

The largest factor, accounting for about 12 per cent of the data, is one we call the "goody-goody" factor. It is contributed to by all the scores through which a child says how well he likes things— teachers, ways of working, goals, other kids, and so on. It is also contributed to by scores which, taken together, give a picture of conformity: the student who is high on this factor likes everything expected of him, no matter what it is. It is accompanied by rather low-level work, and by lack of emotional involvement. There is rejection of fight and flight, and of all but rather muted expressions of feeling. We could not help but wonder if this factor doesn't portray a highly successful adjustment to the demands of the typical classroom; and, if so, it should probably be called the "survival" factor. It is more characteristic of upper- than of lower-class (economically) children.

The second factor, accounting for about 6.5 per cent of the data on these high school students, is a social-sexual factor. The sexual part has to do with discriminating between boys and girls, having different expectations for the two sexes—as compared with thinking of them as interchangeable. Along with this goes acceptance of emotion, preference for active rather than passive interpersonal relationships, and a distinct liking for decisions to be made by the "group" rather than by oneself, teacher, or large class. This factor tends to be more typical of the younger and brighter students in the seventh to ninth grade range, and probably spots a particular developmental task characteristic of this age.

The third factor, accounting for about 7 per cent of the data, is characterized by tentativeness and confusion with respect to participating with other people, in uncertainty about what values are important, and in variability with respect to items getting at deeper indications of personal security. There is confusion about one's own sex role, retreat into passivity, concern over personal-social relationships, and avoidance of emotional expression.

The fourth factor, accounting for about 4.3 per cent of the data, appears to be a combination of rational consistency with needs to exploit one's peers. There is great preference for "telling" and rejection of "listening"; moreover, what one tells about is himself, his feelings, his opinions. Working together for a common goal is rejected, as is acceptance of responsibility for one's own progress. There is preference for activities involving the class as a whole (i.e., in which one is anonymous, can't be checked up on easily, and can avoid responsibility). The most attractive value is sensual enjoyment. This factor is negatively related to IQ, and tends to be found with lower-class boys.

The fifth factor, also accounting for about 4 per cent of the data, is strongly female and is associated with low IQ; there is a tendency for lower-class and older students to enter in, also. The dominant note is identification with boys' activities and behaviors. There is strong preference for listening rather than telling, for submission rather than dominance, for comfort rather than work. There is a good deal of interpersonal "sensitivity."

The sixth factor, accounting for about 3 per cent of the data, is for boys. The strongest component is the value of social restraint, but it has nothing to do with altruism, which is the lowest rated value. It has instead to do with submissiveness, which shows up in just about every score that could be thus interpreted. The preferred teacher is the authoritarian, the most worthwhile activities are teacher-dominated; listening is strongly preferred to telling. Identification is with female behavior; judgments are made critically and evaluatively of other people; nothing is voluntarily revealed about oneself.

The seventh factor, about the same "size," is a classical textbook picture of counterdependency; that is, of denial of one's own dependency. There is strong rebelliousness against adult authority, against the discipline of working on tasks. Peer groups are used to assert oneself, not to listen to others. At the same time, there is a seeking of warmth from others, and a strong rejection of opportunities to "be on one's own." There is evidence of confusion about the male role, and of deeper insecurity and feelings of inadequacy. This factor is shown most by boys of high IQ.

The eighth factor, also about 3 per cent, is most represented in the younger children, and somewhat stronger for boys than girls. It seems to represent an effort to submerge oneself in group activities, preferably with a few other students. Probably likes to "do things" with a group of kids, but brings very little to the group. Tends toward passivity and avoidance of responsibility. It is the picture of a "fringer."

The ninth factor, also about 3 per cent, is for young, high IQ students. It shows a strongly teacher-centered person who wants the teacher to set out a respectable thought-out course of study, to stimulate the student and make demands on him, and to work closely with him. The student likes information and listening to reports. The value picture suggests thoughtfulness rather than mere "academic" achievement. The student rejects practically everything that has to do with the class, and probably has trouble coping with peers.

The tenth factor, also about 3 per cent, is rather similar to factor 9 in its teacher-centeredness. A different kind of teacher is preferred, however, namely the rule-giver or authoritarian. There is strong preference for working alone, within boundaries set by the teacher. There is rejection of the teacher who tries to plan with the student, and rejection of class activities.

And so on. The UNIVAC continues to grind away, and will, no doubt, identify many more factors. But perhaps this is enough to make the point that there are many ways of life and many kinds of psyche needs of the students. Most of these are ignored in teaching, yet their combination should certainly have a good deal to do with determining what sort of class group will confront the teacher. Most interesting of all, however, is the clear revelation of the very wide array of non-learning concerns of children. Conformity, confusion, sex identifications, reactions to authority, relating to (or avoiding) peers—these sorts of problems and needs probably "drive" the interaction in the classroom much more than interest, let us say, in *The Merchant of Venice*. One suspects that the prescribed "materials of instruction" and academic tasks set by the teacher may be useful primarily to provide a content vehicle for exploring and working on these higher priority social-emotional-sexual developments. After all, these *are* high school students.

To confound and confuse the picture further, no actual student can be represented by a single factor. Any of the ten factors presented above may be strong, middling, or weak within a particular student, and all combinations are possible. It is clear that the dynamic world of the group, out of which a social order is created, is a world of phenomena that lie below speech and usually mostly below consciousness. It is the world of motivations, tensions, and energy systems; and it makes insistent high priority demands on the realms of thought, memory and behavior. Events in this submerged world, manifested in the over-all problem of reconciling psyche and socio systems, have much to do with the quality, amount and meaning of learning.

Differences in culturally shared predispositions and attitudes are, of course, quite clearly seen as one goes from one country and language to another. Not merely individuals, but whole groups appear to operate on different assumptions. Not knowing how characteristic of each country were the groups I dealt with in Europe in 1956, I shall not identify the nationality of these groups, but I would like to put into our notes some apparent cultural differences with respect to the shift from psyche-comfort orientation to the commitment to work.[5]

In one country a group had to settle two matters before committing themselves: first, that what they were being asked to do was rational with respect to defined problems; and second, that the foreign trainers could beat them in a fair fight. The first requirement has to do with the cultural tradition of forgetting class and other differences when there is "something that needs to be done." The second requirement seems to be related to an acceptance of another person as "one of ourselves" and therefore trustworthy; the fight (verbal, thank goodness) was the initiation ceremony.

In another country, the two most prominent elements in commitment seemed to be, first, that the trainer accept an authoritarian role, for the image of the leader has throughout history been that of The Tyrant; to act in any other way would produce so much confusion that communication would end. But the second element was that outside of the meeting, the trainer must be friendly on a personal level; avoiding status symbols, mixing and mingling with all the members at meals, always being available for talk—these were important. The group would accept responsibility for problem-solving under these conditions if the leader would tell them what conclusions they were expected to reach. This last condition we ultimately were able to loosen up a little; they did not have to be told explicitly, they could be told indirectly through a leader-dominated give-and-take discussion.

In a third country, commitment could be given only after an analysis of the positions of each person with respect to the problem at hand. Each social level and each office has, it is assumed, clearly defined privileges and responsibilities. So once each person's social position and functional relationship to the problem is decided—and this takes time—then each knows how far, in what way, and with respect to what things he will commit himself to any purpose or course of action.

In a fourth country, the group could expose problems, swap opinions, listen to each other—but never reach a decision as a group, and even when the members seemed to want the same thing, they were very resistant to agreeing that they all wanted it. For commitment here is a matter of individual conscience, and no man may question or interfere or evaluate the beliefs or motivations of another. The way out of this is for some authority to lay down the law—not so much by telling people what they have to do but rather by manipulating events in such a way that each person has to act in some way. Thus we could not get the group ever to agree to analyze or study a problem, but when we confronted them with a problem, we could expect, usually, a high degree of involvement and cooperation. This would last until we wanted to pull out some conclusions, and then again no agreements could be reached because each man had to decide for himself.

THE DIFFERENCE GROUP COMPOSITION MAKES

It has occurred to a number of experimenters that groups of specified characteristics might be generated if the members were chosen rather carefully for that purpose. There is no doubt at all that, within the possibilities limited by the culture, groups may differ quite considerably, and that much of this difference may be due to the particular composition of the groups.

I should like now to show you some of the differences that can be produced between groups through careful selection of their members.

Here are two groups of six adults. They meet separately, and are given the same task: They are to consider a whole batch of objects that are on the table in front of them, and to choose any one of the objects to keep. Then they are to decide what to do with the object they chose. The objects include: a handsome diary, a phonograph record, a book of six impressionist paintings, an assortment of cheeses, three one-dollar bills, etc. This task was devised by scientists at the Rand Corporation and has been played with in laboratories all over the country.

The first group of six begins by asking each person which object he prefers. There is little agreement. Then they inquire into why each person likes the object, giving the members a chance to persuade each other. There is a short stalemate after that, and two members switch their preference to agree with a third. A fourth member, her heart set on the diary, gets into a strenuous but controlled argument with the fifth person, whose mouth is watering for the cheese. The other members intervene from time to time, and a new stalemate occurs when each says that he has a preference but doesn't want to obstruct the group and will yield to the group's will. Unfortunately, the group's will remains elusive. Finally one person comes up with a brilliant solution: Take the portfolio of six paintings and then give one to each member. The group is delighted with the suggestion and recognizes that it solves both the problem of choice and of disposal of the loot in the same stroke. The session over, the members hang around to talk to the experimenters and two of them say they would like to come back and listen to the recording of their session. Then they go out of the laboratory together, and they are headed for coffee and a post-mortem of their session.

The second group of six asks to have the instructions repeated twice. A member starts to tell his preference, but the members do not listen, and nobody volunteers a personal preference after that. Instead, they each cite pros and cons for different objects, and seldom are two members talking about the same object. On the average, six people talk during each minute (as compared to four in the previous group). There is a great deal of irrelevant conversation, as the record reminds one member of a night-club experience and the book cues off a two-person side conversation on modern literature. Moreover, one person never enters the conversation at all. They finally send one person to the board to write down the number of some object, and then they immediately decide on the three dollars. They get up to leave, but the experimenter tells them they still haven't decided what to do with the money. They express surprise that the money is theirs—they hadn't understood that the choice was for keeps. They half-jocularly and rapidly decide to give the money to another person not present. She is expecting a baby, and she can use the money to buy it something. The baby is expected to arrive in seven months. The job done, the members get up and leave the room rapidly, without a backward glance.

The first group accepted the task and got thoroughly involved in it, its members established and maintained good relationships to each other, and it arrived at a thoroughly realistic and satisfying solution. The second group never really accepted the task as something to work on, and practically all of their behavior indicates nonacceptance and flight from the necessity of facing up to personal differences and feelings.

Both groups were selected by the Gradolphs[2] from thirty adults attending a workshop at the University of Chicago. The instrument used for selecting them was a "projective" test which presented a series of incomplete sentences. The adults were required to complete each sentence as rapidly as possible, and in these completions they revealed the same sorts of behavior that they showed in the experimental task. In each group the members were chosen to be quite similar, so that their common characteristics of work or work avoidance got established as the basis on which the group then operated.

As a next step, the Gradolphs put three members of one group together with three members of the other group. This new group was unable to finish the job at all, had a terribly difficult and tense discussion into which a great deal of hostile feeling was released, and two of the participants never spoke to each other during the remaining two weeks of the workshop. The group contained two equally strong and opposite approaches to the problem; these approaches met head-on, and there was no way to resolve the conflict. Hostility and frustration were reactions to inability to deal with the conflict.

The theory behind this experiment is that in a stress situation people tend to react with different emotions. They may run away, fight, become dependent, or seek intimacy with another. Most people have all four of these elementary capabilities, but the people selected for the experiment were extreme, and hence the differences showed up with great clarity. But in addition to these emotional kinds of capabilities, people also can "work," that is, seek facts and try to analyze and deal with the realities involved in the problem. I have called the emotional way "acting out" and the reality-seeking way "inquiry." The first group was an inquiry group, with a fairly strong component of seeking intimacy with each other as a way of reducing anxieties created by the task. The second group was a classic acting-out group, and their dominant emotional theme was flight.

What about friends? Would groups be more effective and productive if all the members were friends? All right, let's try it and see. In 1953, my research seminar at the University[8] had all the members of the seventh grade in the Laboratory School fill out a sociometric questionnaire by means of which they rated all their classmates on a 7-point scale of friendship. Two groups of eight girls were selected for the experiment, and the members of both groups were equally chosen by the rest of their classmates—that is, members of both groups were equally "popular" in the class. The groups were made different, however, in this respect: the eight girls in one group had all rated each other as first or second on the friendship scale, whereas the other eight girls in no case chose each other. This second group was not composed of enemies; they simply didn't choose each other as friends. Both groups were given the same two tasks: (a) Look at a picture and make up a story about what is happening, and (b) look at another picture and tell how the people in the picture feel about each other. The stories were to be worked out by the group in any way they wished.

All the girls had been given the sentence-completion test so that we were able to assess their tendencies toward fight, flight, dependency, pairing, and work. Each comment made during the discussion was also keyed to these same five categories. It was thus possible to compare the pattern of emotion and work in the private individual test situation with the pattern as actually expressed in the social interactive situation. The correlation between test and group situation for the friends was .78; for the nonfriends, .32. Thus the popular notion is supported that one expresses his "real" feelings more spontaneously among friends than among mere acquaintances.

In the first story (tell what is happening), the friends and nonfriends expressed the same amount of emotion (36 and 32 "units" respectively). In the second story (how the characters feel about each other), the friends expressed six times as much emotion as the nonfriends (95 to 16 units). In the first story the friends directed 50 per cent more work to the assigned task and to solving their problems of working together (123 to 84 units). In the second story, the friends did 250 per cent more work (171 to 70 units). In other words, the friends expressed more work and more emotion in their second story-telling, whereas the nonfriends expressed less work and less emotion.

The figures give only the bare bones of the story. The friends were more emotionally involved as they went along; the nonfriends became progressively more apathetic. Neither group gave much energy to the story. The demand to tell a story only provided the occasion for some high-tension interpersonal and group dynamics. The friends, being friends, felt free to fight, and the fighting was of two sorts. First, there was a competition between two members for leadership of the group. Each contestant had followers, too. One of them seemed to engage in interpersonal fighting for prestige and status; the other expressed the desire simply to run away from the assigned task. Second, the group projected into their stories a great deal of hostility toward adults. In a word, the group fought each other and together they fought the world. And more so as they went along. But this fighting also generated a lot of creativity. They tried to top each other in thinking up details of fantasy; the competitiveness increased the number of ideas about the pictures. It is true that the fantasy tended to be rather hostile, and at a couple of points the observers were downright embarrassed. The girls also defied the experimenters, refusing to follow the instructions with regard to the second story.

In the nonfriends group, the dynamic was simpler: one difficult person had to be dealt with. She was badly out of step with the others, who were inclined to follow the instructions in a dull and obedient manner. The group was not sufficiently cohesive to deal with this girl, and they simply gave up on the second task. They were bored and uninterested, and we took this to be withdrawal from their unsuccessful efforts to deal with their problem child.

We were astonished at all the hostility among the friends, and we sought information that might account for it. We offer the following as a plausible explanation: The friends were all several months older than their classmates, and 8 to 10 points lower in IQ than the average of the class. They were also members of minority groups within the class, seven belonging to one minority group and one to another. We felt that all three of these conditions could very well add up to a feeling of "not belonging" in the total class—possibly even to the feeling of being rejected—even though in fact they were as popular with their classmates as the youngsters in the other group. Their "friendship" might be expected to be something of a defensive coalition, oriented not so much to their appeal for each other as to their perceived need to defend themselves and stand together in the total group. Their hostility to adults, as the visible and powerful symbols of the majority group, would be entirely reasonable.

We conclude that just selecting "friends" is not good enough. We also want to know the basis of their friendship. The research seminar was about evenly divided when I asked them which group they would prefer to try to teach. Certainly the nonfriends would be far easier to "manage" in class, but the friends would have a greater potential for learning—provided the learning activities also met their needs to deal with whatever motivations drove them together as friends. This would call for a rather shrewd diagnosis of needs and considerable ingenuity in devising learning activities that could capitalize on rather than be wrecked by these motivations.

It is becoming increasingly evident that children are "whole" people, and no one fragment of information about them will enable us to say much about the kind of group they will produce. You may know, for example, that they are friends, or have high IQ's, that they generally have highly positive attitudes toward school work, or even that they are intensely interested in some school subject. But you still don't know what to predict when you put them together.

TEACHABLE GROUPS

We do not know at present how to compose groups for instructional purposes, but we do know a good deal about what is going to be involved, and there is a growing belief that the composition of the group may be at least as important as the method of the teacher in determining the quality of the educational product. This is a difficult proposition to prove, because what is generally reported as educational achievement tends to be limited to memory of information, conditioned skills in problem solving of specified types, and more or less subjective opinion as to how "good" a student or citizen the child is in class. Unfortunately, "outcomes" defined in terms of specific behavior instead of in terms of meaning and understanding have something to do with education but probably not much. At any rate, these outcomes are relatively insensitive and unresponsive to group composition. A thoroughgoing drillmaster who suppresses all conversation among the children may teach them to spell quite as well as somebody who is more oriented toward inquiry. The differences

won't show up on a standardized spelling test, even though they probably will show up in whether the student goes on spelling correctly
when the teacher isn't standing over him—although even this has not
been demonstrated adequately.

When I talk with teachers about their classes, I find two common
agreements that: (1) Classes in the same subject differ markedly—
one may be easy to work with, productive, and stimulating, whereas
the next may be dull, resistant, and satisfied with little accomplishment and (2) many a class would be just fine to work with if only the
teacher could get rid of one (but more usually two or three) "difficult" students. The most common wish is to have a class with which
the teacher can work, be sympathetic, find common cause and mutual
respect. In different schools classes are selected by different criteria.
In some schools, students are asked to select the math (or other)
teacher they would like to have in the next year, and it appears
that this has some advantages. It communicates the willingness of the
faculty to concede that the judgment of the students about teachers
is worth considering, even though it may not be taken completely at
face value. It gets the student to commit himself a bit more consciously
to try to make a go of the class. It creates an expectation of better relationships and of the possibilities of reward in the class. On the other
hand, it may arouse anxieties in certain teachers who feel that they
have been plunged into a popularity contest. The reports I have
heard about this practice are favorable but not conclusive.

We hear a good deal about ability grouping, which involves selecting from the total population of the school certain classes of youngsters who are bright or dull in particular school subjects. It is by no
means established empirically that this is a good practice, and Bruno
Bettelheim[1] has presented strong theoretical objections. The teachers
I know who best like a high ability class appear to be teaching about
the same old material in the same way, but they find it easier to communicate to the class and they get the ground covered more easily.
Teachers who try to capitalize on what they suppose a high ability
class should be capable of—that is, who try to give the students something extra—seem less persuaded that segregation makes the job
easier than just teaching the youngsters as individuals within a "regular" class. And teachers who think bright classes should be more self-
directing and able to work more on their own have quite regularly
been disappointed.

Another kind of practice which is often found in schools is to have teachers or counselors select classes on the basis of their combined knowledge of the students as persons. Attention is given to separating friends (or putting them together), to trying to put each student with the "kind" of teacher with whom he will work best, and to distributing the "strong" students among the various classes. This sort of selection process, admittedly fumbling and uncertain in its judgments, seems to be generally considered worthwhile, if only because one feels better when he tries to use his intelligence instead of leaving choices to chance scheduling factors and IBM machines. An example of this procedure, which seems to be highly successful, is the selection of small "reading" groups of primary children. Here the groups are selected from all the primary classes and carefully matched to the various members of the teaching staff.

Turning from school practices to the sort of experimental studies reported in this chapter, it is amply shown that the productivity and characteristics of group operation are strongly affected by composition. It is less well demonstrated that the educational results, assessed with respect to each child, are closely related to composition. Those experiments which really give the child an opportunity to reveal the meaning to him of ideas to which he has been exposed do consistently show relationships between learned meanings and interpersonal relationships, but it would be a hardy enthusiast who would insist that one *causes* the other.

Having now, I hope, disarmed the reader by this display of fairness and caution, I shall proceed to comment on the problem of composition in relation to the grouping of students for instruction. The dynamic of the learning group is the continual interweaving of the tendencies of the members of the group to develop common cause and common culture (socio-operation) versus their tendencies, as individuals, to respond differently and to find different meanings in their common experience (psyche-operation). Three general specifications seem most important:

The groups for learning should be small enough so that each individual can be heard, can have a contributing role, and can become well acquainted with the others.[6] This suggests a maximum size of fifteen.

The groups for learning should be able to find common cause fairly readily; socially they should be able to speak the same language and in the some idiom, among themselves and with the teacher. This means that they should subscribe to similar values with respect to the importance of work, the kinds of contributions that are to be rewarded and punished, the expectations of the teacher's role as authority.

The groups for learning should be able to get into temperamental conflict. The members should react differently to the same reality stimulus; there should be the possibility of clashes.

The groups for learning should be composed of persons whose psyche affiliations will be compatible with the demands of the task and of the method of learning. The method of teaching should not make demands that deny needs for friendship, support, and some interpersonal communication by the particular students in the class; or, to put it another way, compatibility between students and method of learning should be good enough that energy going into psyche needs also promotes rather than hinders possibilities of learning.

The Sophomore Project at the University of Chicago suggested some specific aspects which may ultimately turn out to be useful.[4]

First, students do approach subjects differently. One child can make sense out of algebra presented symbolically and theoretically; a second child probably needs to have the symbols tied down to objects like blocks, moving wheels, and data-producing experiments; a third youngster needs to see algebra in relation to how people like himself can use it in everyday affairs; a fourth is mostly intrigued by its puzzle-solving aspects, which are attractive partly because they are so remote from "life"; a fifth child is struck by the beauty of the systematic organization and logical coherence of the subject. A clear implication is that very probably there is need for different methods of teaching, with different emphases upon symbolic and operational experience, different mixtures and sequences of induction and deduction, and different contexts (social, experimental, physical) for algebraic problems and principles.

Second, students do seem to work best in particular kinds of social organizations. Thus one student seems to work problems best by himself; a second works best with a buddy; a third does better with a small clique; and a fourth is least distracted and most stimulated in a larger group.

Third, students differ very markedly in the kinds and amounts of instructions they need in order to work effectively. One student works effectively only when he knows in specific detail exactly what he is "supposed" to do next; a second student makes the most out of activities whose purpose is defined in general terms but whose materials and resources are spelled out; a third student is more challenged when he can plan the activity as well as execute it; a fourth is stimulated by hearing the ideas of others and then creates something different for himself, and so on.

Students' ideas differ about who should make the decisions that guide learning. Thus when we ask students "who should decide" each of twenty-four matters about the class, one student answers that he, the student, should make twenty-two of the decisions for himself; another thinks the teacher should make all but one; and yet another student wants to leave most of the decisions to the class!

Fourth, students differ in the kinds of support and clash that stimulate them to learn. A student who challenges another to creative self-expression may drive a third to tears or sullen apathy; two friends may form a clique which is impenetrable to group purposes, or they may be a strong combination which gives the group excellent natural leadership; a student may be tied up in anxiety which can be released by the spontaneous expression of hostility by a classmate, yet the same kind of expression may tie another student in knots. And, to some extent, these considerations may apply to the teachers, too.

Fifth, students differ in the amount of knowledge and experience they can bring to bear in an investigation. This is the problem of resources for the group, and it probably reflects interest in the subject as well as more spectacular personal variations in experience. At any rate, it is likely that group investigation is helped by having students who can relate questions and concepts to a variety of observations.

Sixth, and to infinity, inclusive: physical energy, creativity, frustration tolerance, ego ideals, sex attitudes, spontaneity, self-concepts—all enter into the picture. In every classroom there develops a way of life. This way of life contains expectations, habits, values, and methods of working. It emerges from competing possibilities brought into the group by the members. The way of life becomes stabilized and institutionalized as it accumulates a body of folklore, tradition, memories, and relationships to other ways of life encountered over time. In short, the group develops its own culture, its own provisions for maintaining social order, and its own relationships with other groups to which the participants also belong.

Thus we see that every group is a growing, changing organism.

The individual changes through his experiences in groups. Some of the changes might be called the product of "conditioning." They are brought about through social reward and punishment consistently applied over time, and they tend to reinforce some kinds of responses to certain situations and inhibit others. After a time, these conditioned ways of responding become habitual, and the individual, who was not aware of the changes going on in the first place, now takes the "rightness" of these conditioned behaviors for granted—until he lands in the middle of a different culture.

Another kind of individual change might be labeled "learning." Thus to be a member of a group requires learning its doctrines; learning to like and hate certain objects, conditions, and people; learning to contribute in the ways expected of one; learning the skills of being sufficiently oneself at the same time that he is part of the group. Many of these learnings are quite consciously incorporated in his subjective world view, and they change his basis of action in many situations.

A third kind of individual change is a special kind of learning which we might as well call "educative" learning. This is learning for purposes to which one has conscious commitment. It is guided through a continuity of relevant experiences over time. It is reflected upon. It is dissected, explored, and put back together again in the form of principles and ethics useful for coping with a whole range of situations. It includes a sense of self and the meanings for oneself (being the kind of person one is) of the learned ideas and principles. It consciously seeks and takes into account the experiences and thoughts of others. And from this, it makes one able to be the observer and executive at the same time he is the actor in the situations of everyday life. Through group experience a person is bound to become housebroken, and he may become clever, but there is no guarantee at all that he will become educated.

We can see that the task of the teacher is extraordinarily difficult and complex. The educational requirements are: (a) to facilitate the natural processes of group development that are going to go on anyway so that they won't use up all the energy of the group, (b) to intervene in the group in such a way that the drives back of these natural processes are harnessed into potentially educative activities, and (c) to supervise potentially educative activity in such a way that educative learning actually occurs.

Can this be done at all? Why do we think so? And how is it to be done? These are the next questions for the next chapter, on the design for group investigation.

NOTES

1. Bruno Bettelheim, "Segregation: New Style," *School Review,* LXVI, No. 3 (Autumn 1958), 251-272.
2. Ida and Phil Gradolph, Unpublished research in the Human Dynamics Laboratory, University of Chicago, 1954.
3. Helen Hall Jennings, *Sociometry of Leadership,* Sociometry Monograph No. 14 (New York: Beacon House, 1947), p. 28.
4. Herbert A. Thelen, "Classroom Grouping of Students," *School Review,* LXVII, No. 1 (Spring 1959), 60-78.
5. Herbert A. Thelen, "European Groups: A Challenge to American Education," *Elementary School Journal,* LII, No. 7 (April 1957), 351-362.
6. Herbert A. Thelen, "Group Dynamics in Instruction: Principle of Least Group Size," *School Review,* LVII (March 1949), 139-148.
7. Research contract SAE7786. Development of Different Methods of Instruction for Different Types of Students. 1958-1960.
8. Dittoed report by seminar—Education 319, Spring, 1953.

8

Model 2:
Group Investigation

In which we compare group investigations to "projects" and "activities," present a lengthy case study of a genuine investigation, and develop the principles used by the teachers in the conduct of this class inquiry. During this discussion we try to communicate general policies for the method of guiding Group Investigations, and we close with some administrative suggestions for organizing this kind of educative experience.

Let us suppose you go with friends to see *South Pacific*. When the play is over you count your money and decide you can afford to keep the baby-sitter for another hour. So you go into a nearby joint, sit down, and have a little something. And you talk. There are two kinds of talk.

In one kind, your friends say, Wasn't the play wonderful? Did you know that Bloody Mary is only twenty-six years old? Boy, would I love to get to that island, the audience was responsive. Who was that dowdy blonde in the first box. I just love plays, don't you?

In the other kind of talk, someone says, You know the character of Bloody Mary as a mother puzzles me—do you suppose offering her daughter to the lieutenant was based on a kind of primitive expectation of noblesse oblige? And it occurs to another that if Nellie hadn't been from someplace like Little Rock the whole play would have been impossible. And that first introduction of Bali Hai really sent shivers up and down my spine; I'll see that mountain in my dreams!

The first kind of talk is acting out. It contains two elements—emotional release and stereotypes. In emotional release, we are simply blowing off without awareness our sense of wonder, excitement, competition, shock or satisfaction produced by the play. The words and ideas used for this purpose are unimportant; children use nonsense syllables. The words and ideas have about the same kind of meaning as the phrase "How are you?" when used in greeting. The language is ready-made, prefabricated, randomized, chewed-up, and chunky. Nobody listens. And when the conversation is over, about all you can say for it is that it was useful to maintain the interaction of friends. Since that was probably its purpose, there is no cause for complaint —or is there?

The second kind of talk is inquiry. It involves reality-seeking and knowledge. In reality-seeking, we are trying to get hold of aspects of our lives that intrigue or trouble or interest us; as knowledge, we are using universals and principles, which, because they apply in other situations as well, help to illuminate the experience of the play by connecting it to past experiences. People listen to each other. And when the conversation is over you can see that it was more than something for the group to participate in; in addition, you have new feelings about the other persons, you have new thoughts to enjoy and pursue, and you have found a brief respite from mundane life in the assertion of a side of yourself that usually lies dormant.

This second kind of talk is inquiry, but it falls far short of being educative inquiry. The emotional quality of the conversation, with its elements of self-discovery, groping for ways to comprehend experience, and responding to others is, however, a *sine qua non* for educative inquiry. Our friends discussing *South Pacific* are having the kind of experience as a group that Johnny, way back in Chapter 2, was having as an individual. In Chapter 2 we saw what sorts of things would be required to make Johnny's walk educative, and now we shall consider how to make a conversation—and its associated experiences—educative.

Since schools are organized in classes which discuss things, it seems only polite to pay our respects to existing classroom practices, selecting those that help illustrate or define what we mean by group investigation as overviewed in Chapter 5. Having done this, we shall try to explain how group investigation is different from personal inquiry, what makes it tick, and what it can do that personal inquiry cannot. Then we'll present and analyze a group investigation which was undertaken partly to test the usefulness of the very principles this chapter is about. We shall wind up by commenting on the problem of organizing group investigations as a major method of education within the school.

BITS AND FRAGMENTS

Inquiry in the school currently goes on in bits and fragments. Some of these bits and fragments are excellent, and it will be worth our while to spend a little time with them.

Here is Valerie, a snappy, black-eyed, six-year-old. The other day she came home from kindergarten, marched straight to her room, and shut the door. There was the sound of much tearing of paper. Then silence. Her parents, struck by the business-like air and the yen for privacy—so unlike their daughter—investigated. She was sitting on the floor methodically thumbing through all her books. Occasionally she would put one of the torn bits of paper in as a marker, and lay the book to one side. She was, it turned out, engaged in " 'search." The kindergarten class was going to make a city; cities contain houses; she was getting ideas about houses from pictures in her books. Thus here is a nice airy house—for chickens, with slats; here's a tall house with chimneys and windows; and this nice one in the garden says Rover over the door. The next day she trudged to school with an armload of books.

This fragment has the feel of inquiry about it. The four symptoms that seem most evident to me are: first, tremendous absorption in the task, shown in marching straight to the room and immediately setting to work; the job was so much on her mind that Valerie hardly said hello to her mother (which is unusual). Second, she knew what she was doing and could put it into clear language, suggesting both a focus and a consciousness of purpose; there was nothing vague or mixed up about her understanding of the immediate goal and of next steps. Third, her behavior was strikingly different from her usual after-school pattern of action; she was taking a new role, guided by acceptance of the "discipline" or way of life of inquiry. Fourth, she was acting partly on behalf of a group which expected individual work from her and which would reward her for it.

Here are two girls and a boy in high school. We have some new experimentally designed student desks, and this committee volunteered for the job of assessing the advantages and disadvantages of the new furniture. Four features of the operation of the committee pretty well cover their behavior. First, the social situation is almost a classic triangle, with the boy and one girl "going steady" and the "other woman" being a source of considerable anxiety to her sister Eve; the boy appears mostly unconscious of the interplay between the girls. Second, the projection of fantasy is continuous, fabulous, and brimming with emotional investment. The boy and his girl friend project fantasies of power, but these are related to the job: they wish to visit the company's designers, who need to be taught principles of design. (Later, the designers visited the school, and these students *did* set them straight.) Third, in addition to these goings on, the team turned out a first-rate study, making use of observations of students using the desk, of questionnaires, and of analysis of the strengths and weaknesses of the design when compared to ideal criteria they had formulated for student desks. Fourth, the committee made use of the Director of the Laboratory as a consultant, and much conflict within themselves swirled about their relationships to him. On the one hand, they showed the outward subservience of their exaggerated concept of an employee. The idea of the boss turning over important work for them to do was exciting, and they did everything they could to maintain the picture of the Director as their boss. On the other hand, a push for power manifested itself in a barely controlled rebelliousness, and what it meant practically is that they would accept the Director's suggestions only after reworking them in such a way that they no longer recognized the source of the ideas.

This fragment has an intriguing seriocomic flavor. It is worth noting that the three students formed their "committee" first and then volunteered for the job together. One suspects that the "research" initially, at least, was seen as an adult-provided *raison d'être* for their threesome. They had much to work out among themselves, but even social relationships cannot be worked on in a vacuum, and the activities of research provided just the sort of scope they needed. Certainly the interpersonal dynamics provided a great deal of the energy that was channeled into their competitive creativity, their assertion of bold ideas, their acceptance of the rules of evidence to settle some of their arguments. In a word, the demands of the research provided the rules for the interpersonal game. But the research group also did an outstanding job of research; the research in its own right had a strong pull. As an adult, I can only marvel at the group's having such a tremendous amount of energy and vitality that they could sustain *both* the interpersonal and the research interactions going on at such a continuously high level of intensity.

My next fragment comes from the second grade. The unit to be taught is social studies. I doubt that the teacher mentioned social studies to the class, but she probably posed a question such as "How do different people live?" At any rate, she proposed that they select some group of people, find out how they live, and then put the information together in a play which they would write themselves. After some discussion, the youngsters, under the Disney influence current at that time, selected prairie dogs for study. The teacher, Miss P, with years of second grade behind her, was almost but not quite startled at this choice. Not being ready to give up the Algonquin Indians without a fight—or at least a skirmishing action—she expressed a number of demurrals, each of which was countered successfully, Miss P was forced to admit, by a pupil. After ten minutes of her skillful opposition, the youngsters had committed themselves so strongly to prairie dogs that Miss P felt it was too late to put her foot down.

They started their study by naming the characters for the play they would write, and, of course, the characters turned out to be baby, children, mother, father, chicken, farmer's boy, snake, etc. They made lists of questions to be answered: What do prairie dogs eat? Where do they live? What do they do with their time? How big are their families? Who are their enemies?, etc. Individuals sought answers to the questions from science pamphlets, books, the science teacher, officials of the local zoo, and I have no doubt at least a few of the youngsters talked their parents into taking them again to see the Disney opus. They reported their findings in compositions during the writing lessons. The plot of the play gradually took shape and was endlessly modified with each new bit of information. The play centered around family life, and there was much discussion and spontaneous demonstrations of how the various members of the family would act. Most of these characterizations actually represented a cross section of the home lives of seven-year-old children, as perceived by the children. But each action was gravely discussed, soberly considered, and justified in terms of what they knew about the ecology of prairie-dog existence.

They built a stage, with sliding curtains and four painted backdrops —more reference work here to get the field and farm right. The play itself was given six times, with six different casts, and each child played at least two different parts. There never was any written script; only an agreement on the line of action and the part of it to occur in each scene. And after each presentation, the youngsters sat around and discussed what they had been trying to communicate, how it might be improved.

It is my impression that this unit of work was pretty good inquiry. The children worked by themselves to find answers to questions which they felt they needed to answer, and they translated the answers into action and agreement. They made and perceived many connections between their ideas of prairie dogs and their ideas about human beings, and I am not purist enough to be shocked by the flavor of anthropomorphism in the proceedings. They found out a lot about family life, ecology, plant growth (in connection with prairie-dog food), farms (in connection with the painted scenery); and they learned (and became consciously aware) of how information can be used to settle some arguments.

I was impressed all along with Miss P, who regarded social studies as a set of principles and understandings rather than as a pile of stacked up information. For her, a family is a family and a mother is a mother, and some universals about child-parent relations probably hold throughout the mammalian kingdom. She was more concerned that the children be "involved" and eager to learn than that they "cover" particular situations selected arbitrarily in advance. At no time did Miss P introduce any limit to the "subjects" of the children's investigations. Plants, rain, and energy, along with animal habits, were all looked into as needed. These were just extra dividends in social studies—and without them, what meaning would the social studies have? Her final word, after it was all over, was: "I never knew prairie dogs could be so interesting."

Just by way of contrast (and to underscore a point), let's consider another class in social studies. This is in high school, and the object is to put on a series of television sessions on the history of the community. The students looked up information, and they went out in teams to visit historical sites on which they reported later. Harry and Joe took pictures of an Indian mound, left there by "original" settlers. They took it from the south because the light was better that way; and they never discovered the northern slope where erosion had laid bare a burrow full of Indian relics. Mary and Sue spent two afternoons on a graph of corn production in the region; the graph was in a geography book the teacher gave them; and the time was mostly spent in making a neat, elaborately lettered document for the camera. The narrators were chosen for their handsome appearance, and much of the staging of the show (which used reports, mostly) centered around deciding the most decorative way to seat the students. A lot of old firearms and household implements were borrowed from a local museum and displayed with a sentence or two of comment for each.

There is no doubt that many of the kids learned something about their region. But where was the bulk of the energy going? What purposes dominated the learning? In what terms could success be measured? I guess the answer is clear enough: Success lay in the effectiveness of the television show, as a blend of entertainment and information-giving. The lesson Harry and Joe will remember best grew out of their inquiry on how to get a good photograph; drawing pretty graphs will never terrorize Mary or Sue again. Some of the students may also have learned that for some purposes (I hope not in general) beauty counts more than ability, and some more of them may have learned that the reason for getting information is to pass it on to someone else. The roles in which they inquired were those of the *reporter* with a keen eye for "human interest" angles, rather than the *sociologist or historian* with a disciplined concern for the course of human events.

Inquiry is not the same as activity. Our second graders and our high school students both engaged in much the same sorts of activities, and they produced the same sort of product: a staged communication. But one experience feels like genuine inquiry, the other does not.

All these bits and fragments, of course, have a lot more sense of inquiry to them than most laboratory experiments introduced with the comment, "Let's do an experiment today," and more meaning than most of the puzzle-solving of the usual canned math course, and more involvement than the surface discussions of assigned readings in history. Yet even these activities are potentially tools of inquiry in their respective domains, and would be meaningful if they were used to find out something that seemed important to the students. And, similarly, the class is full of dynamic possibilities, has energy to burn, and for the most part has curiosity. These drives, instead of being suppressed, could stir up the motivations and the climate which make the difference between a "project" and an "inquiry."

Let us linger with these bits and fragments a little longer to note their relevance to the problem of "grouping." In Chapter 7 we presented a few experiments which make the point that the particular combination of personalities in a group has a lot to do with the productivity of the group working on assigned tasks and with the meaning of the experience to the individual. In this chapter, we started by going to *South Pacific* and I presented two kinds of follow-up conversations. I suppose you have participated in both kinds at one time or another, and I might as well go on to make the point: that probably the particular combinations of personalities among the friends you were with determined which type of conversation emerged.

In the same way it seems reasonable to suppose that the amount of effort little Valerie put into looking up houses—and the meaning for her of this solitary experience—was partly dependent on her feelings about the teacher and the other kindergartners. Our furniture-research team was a group first, and the nature of the research activity was very much determined by why they were a group and what sorts of things a group like theirs can do. The second graders studying prairie dogs developed into an investigating group, but I have not introduced any evidence there to indicate the effects of the particular composition of the group. All I can add is what Miss P told me: that she composed the group by taking all fifteen of her second graders and adding selected first graders to them for the prairie-dog experience. In the social studies class with its television shows, we were impressed by the absence of the attitudes of group investigation—for which I am inclined to give the teacher a lot of credit. But it is reasonable to look to the composition of the group as providing its resources of picture-taking skill, graphing skill, and decorativeness on the screen; and to guess further that this particular class found the bases for prestige and status in the market-place value of individual contributions to the "show."

The ideal group would be composed in such a way that its emergent natural tendencies could easily be interfered with for educational purposes, using principles of group investigation for guidance.

RATIONALE FOR GROUP INVESTIGATION

Someone once said that a good obstetrician is a man who knows when to stand aside and let nature take its course. When a student's life already has a well-developed direction and thrust, it seems sensible to give him his head, take our cues from him, and help him find meaning in activities, which, for his own good reasons, are important to him. Sometimes, too, a student lives in a state of immobilization and passivity, with very strong needs for love, for self-esteem, and for commitment being forcibly suppressed through fear and denial. In this case, it seems sensible to do what we can to induce labor, relieve the pressure, and get the student's life off dead center.

These two situations call for Personal Inquiry, as discussed in Chapter 6. The distinctive element of educational method in these two situations of independent research and situational therapy is the diagnosis of individual need; and this calls for considerable ability to "put ourselves in the individual's place." Our power, as adults and professional educators, is used on behalf of the student to persuade other adults to work with us to find or set up situations which will offer the needed challenge or opportunity, and in which the student may safely explore ways of behaving and speculate about them.

Group investigation, as a second self-consistent educational method, is also concerned with getting the student to have planned experiences, reflect on them, and extend their meaning and usefulness through knowledge obtained from the experiences of other people. But group investigation faces what appears to be the fact: that there are a lot of things many students do not, presently, have a need to know. The unique function of group investigation is to stimulate new needs for education.

The method of group investigation follows from certain facts and principles, explained in Chapter 5. The broadest orienting principle is that when people live together in classroom, neighborhood, or nation, they develop a social order and a culture; and the more decisions and activities they carry out together the more detailed and "filled out" the culture becomes and the more explicit the expectations through which the social order is established, maintained, and modified. The expectations through which the social order is maintained and changed are anticipations of ways to behave and of responsibilities to be taken. These expectations are represented in "group standards" that set boundaries, limits, and challenges to behavior. The expectations we seek in the classroom stem from the discipline of the knowledge domain, and they translate belief into performance. Not only do we believe that ideas can be developed through individual reflection on experience; we also expect to engage in just such reflections. Not only do we understand that ideas are subject to test, and that there are accepted ways to so test ideas; we also expect actually to discover and use these ways to test our ideas. The social role of the student, then, is that of the inquirer. This is his way of life in the class.

ᛣThe culture and way of life of a group are emergent, not given. They are created by the students as they undertake activity. The source of the motivation for activity is that each student has a very real stake in the standards and expectations that became established, especially in the balance between psyche and socio operations. He cares very much what way of life will be possible in the class. He is driven by very profound and pervasive psyche needs for the kind of classroom in which he can survive as a person and find a place for himself in the organization. Algebra may mean less than nothing to him, but self-esteem, freedoms of sorts, feelings of growing adequacy, and stimulation that provoke him into rewarding activity are important. The heart of the method of group investigation is to arrange things in such a way that the students have the experience of creating a group dedicated to the furtherance of inquiry in the appropriate domain of knowledge. It will be through the processes of moving closer to such a culture over a period of time that they will come to learn what the discipline of the "subject" means, and make commitment to this growing discipline central in group memberships, and, by extension, in their own way of life with respect to the realm of phenomena being studied.

If you feel that such talk is just silly with regard to a subject like chemistry, I shall sympathize with you. But it depends a good deal on what you mean by chemistry as a school subject. If you mean an organization of facts and principles, like the table of contents of a book, then clearly I am talking nonsense; but if you mean a disciplined approach to the phenomena of chemical change, then my comments are apropos. There is no sensible argument over known facts, and I, for one, don't think the formula for calcium phosphate should be a matter for debate. But when we think about the *discipline* of chemistry, then right away we get into attitudes, problems of jumping to conclusions, difficulties of distinguishing among facts, principles and theories, distinctions between trial-and-error versus systematic approaches, different degrees of rigor in the idea of proof.

And think of the whole fabulously exciting problem of explaining why anything happens the way it does; the attempted use of analogies, moral principles, personifications, and deductions. The discipline of science is the control of speculation, and in a group the choice between two different speculative explanations is likely also to be a choice between the adherents to the two notions, even as in the adult world of science. The development of scientific discipline of the group's way of life in chemistry is bound to bring temperaments into clashes, and it is this that we are counting on at the beginning, when chemical concepts are not well enough internalized to generate their own further questions for the student. All of this begins to make explicit what we were hinting at in Chapter 3.

It is unfortunately all too clear that to get group investigation in classrooms will require two revolutions in practice. The first is the shift from the idea of "subjects" as collections of predigested organizations of information; and the second is the shift from governance of the classroom by teacher edict to governance by decisions developed from, or at least validated by, the experience of the group—within boundaries and in relation to phenomena identified by the teacher as objects for study.

Have I been spelling out something that may sound fine in theory but can't be done in practice? Am I in the position of Sherlock Holmes, for whose story of the "giant rat of Sumatra" the "world is not yet prepared"? I think not, but the only way to find out is to produce the "giant rat" and let you see for yourself.

Here, then, is a case study.

ACCOUNT OF A GROUP INVESTIGATION

My account presents the trials and tribulations of a group that was quite consciously guided by the principles we are developing here. It was a group of adult women, and the investigation was into the skills, attitudes, knowledge, and orientation one must learn in order to be an effective elementary schoolteacher. I should have preferred a case drawn from high school materials, but I do not have one that illustrates the principles adequately; and anyway, I tell myself, a more or less general book on education that is as heavy as this one probably ought to pay its respects to teacher training somewhere along the line.

The place, then, is the University of Chicago; the time, 1954; the dramatis personae: Professors Kenneth Rehage, Jacob Getzels, and I; eleven housewives and, before we were through, forty-one additional professors, teachers, resource people, and assorted experts, along with about a thousand school children. The eleven housewives were recruited for an experimental program in which we agreed to turn them into elementary schoolteachers. The ladies all had bachelor's degrees in various fields—biology, music, home economics, premedical training, botany, and so on. Eight of the eleven were married, and most of these had children. One had five and she commuted every day from the other side of town—an hour and a half each way. None had ever taught school, unless you count sporadic Sunday-school work and giving piano lessons to the neighbor's kids. Most of them were scared to death of going back to school.

Preparation for the course included a certain amount of bridge burning. What went up in flames was all previous concepts of required education courses. Gone were all the tidy pigeonholed course lattices of Educational Psychology, Child Development, Philosophy of Education, the School in the Social Order, and the rest. In place of these, we had the Laboratory School, full of teaching and learning processes going on to use as we wished three hours a day every day, an arrangement with the State Accrediting moguls that they would accept test grades without insisting on the traditional training curriculum, and, finally, the belief that if we survived it would be a Good Thing.

We started off with the help of the brass section. The chairman of the department told us he was Counting on Us, that the Department would Watch the Program with Interest, and that Inquiry makes Sense as the Means of Education. In effect, he laid a charge on the students and instructors together: to work out the meaning of inquiry for teacher training; and this sense of mission played its part in developing the group. The director of the laboratory school gave us the run of the place and defined the rules for running.

The first activity was to look at some actual classrooms in operation. These ranged from kindergarten through sixth grade. No instruction was given about what to observe. The women did not have much reaction to three of the seven classes but they were full of ideas and opinions about the other four, and we therefore focused discussion on these. We organized the class into three small subgroups, so that each person could talk three times as much and so each could speak candidly and share her feelings with others. The "findings"—

the range of ideas and reactions of the three subgroups—were then reported to the total group.

The reports on three of the classes were tame enough, but the kindergarten really drew fire. Our ladies were soon quite heatedly arguing over their interpretations of the kindergarten teacher's behavior and a very hot issue soon emerged: Was the kindergarten teacher kindly and supportive of the children or was she sadistic and mean to them? This first important interaction within the group was a rousing fight, and pretty soon the students began, in effect, to choose up sides. In this process, they also began, each for herself, to locate (and make) friends and enemies; in other words, each began to identify with a few others and to find her "place" in the group. During the discussion—which certainly revealed a great many attitudes and ideas about the kindergarten—the women also projected a great many attitudes and ideas about the nature of motivation to learn, conflict in the classroom, and classroom control by the teacher. We felt that they were using the kindergarten experience to explore concerns important to them in the course: What will be *our* reasons for learning? Will we be getting into conflict with each other? Is that good or bad? and, How are our teachers going to deal with us?

We instructors sat there, saying just enough to show the ladies that we were not dismayed at the battle. We were delighted with the involvement and tension that was building up: It would be just so much steam in the group-inquiry boilers. When new ideas stopped coming and the process had settled down into straight argumentativeness, we broke in but we did not want to settle the argument and thus show up one side as "right" and the other as "wrong"—or, more accurately, both sides as "wrong." We wanted the group to accept the fact of a keenly felt difference of opinion and to see that their task now would be to resolve this difference. Accordingly, we proposed that the group proceed more systematically to examine the factors that influence classroom activities.

We then presented a film strip that showed, through time-lapse photography, short samples of activities in seven classrooms; these ranged from highly permissive and student-directed ("free time" in kindergarten) to highly restrictive and teacher-directed (meaningless workbook activity in a sixth grade first-aid class). The group listed all the factors they could think of that might account for the differences among these pictured samples.

Of these factors, the purposes of the teacher seemed central. Sober discussion brought out that the teacher has both public and private purposes, and we hoped that the members of our group would realize that they, too, had private as well as public purposes and that it was all right with us. The next task of our group was to relate observed behavior of children to what they thought were the teacher's motivations. This led to the development of a check list for studying the behavior and roles of students, and from this, to interpret the purposes of the teacher.

I doubt very much that the class at this point realized that they had now returned to the issue that started the inquiry in the first place: the conflicting judgments about the kindergarten teacher. The original problem was an emotional clash between two kinds of evaluative judgments of a teacher, and it had arisen at a time when the group was new and members were anxious about themselves and the treatment they would get from the staff. This had led to the collection of new information and to several hours of sober analysis; and finally, there emerged a practical device in the form of a check sheet for enabling them to make judgments objectively. In other words, the original emotional and intuitive processes of the claw and fang had given way to the processes of control through discipline—in this case the discipline of thinking and knowledge. This, I submit, is educative inquiry. And I remind you where it started: in a clash among group members.

With the check sheet worked out, the group now expressed concern over whether it really would enable them to make "objective" judgments. They expressed this perfectly good scientific question, however, in language that suggested that the initial conflict was not forgotten, even though it appeared to be buried: they wondered if all the members of the group would, on viewing the same class, make the same diagnosis. We took this concern to reflect either a desire to avoid the pain of another serious clash or a desire to continue to get the rewards they had been getting from the processes of sober and reflective inquiry.

The group visited two more classes, and each person checked and rated the behavior she saw. They could hardly wait to compare their check sheets among themselves. They found many points of agreement and were gratified by this; in addition—and this would occur also with "expert" observers—there were a number of disagreements.

These were discussed quite freely, with the instructors encouraging the group to think of everything that might account for the differences. The instructors then moved in, from permissively accepting any "bright" ideas, to focus discussion on what further information they would need to settle the differences (or to choose among the hypotheses). The questions were written on the board, and were directed to the two classroom teachers that had been observed. In my notes on that day, I wrote, "The interviews were wonderful. The teachers, sensing the tremendous attentiveness and interest of the group, responded with candid, sincere, and glowing revelations of how they operate, what they take into account in dealing with the class, and what is important to them in the classroom."

From the "academic" or "achievement" standpoint, one might dismiss these interviews as simply information-giving sessions. From the standpoint of inquiry, which also means from the standpoint of the "whole person" and of the developing group, a number of other processes of great importance occurred. Until now, the women had been identifying closely with the boys and girls whose behavior they had been watching, for were not both in the same boat? But through these interviews, the identification shifted—falteringly and incompletely, to be sure, but nevertheless significantly. For the ladies now began to identify with the role of *teacher,* and two sorts of feelings became apparent in the group: first, of commitment to the purpose of becoming a teacher as a personally meaningful goal; and second, some anxieties as to how well they would be able to measure up to the kind of teacher they now felt they wanted to be.

These feelings give rise to personal problems, different from one person to the next. We tended, therefore, to encourage some personal inquiry in addition to the investigations by the group. Accordingly, we gathered together about thirty books and brought them to the laboratory. We commented on each, said that each student could select whichever interested her, and that the only pressure would be simply an expectation that each person would read *something*. That night all but one member of the group read all or parts of one or two volumes, and the reading of the group covered a very wide range: satire, principles of learning, the nature of elementary school purposes and curricula, and how to judge a school program. Reading from then on was completely voluntary, except for a few assignments at times when the members had to train themselves for special skills like interviewing and testing. And the amount of reading actually done was far greater than in the "regular" teacher-training program.

But even reading motivated by strong personal curiosity growing out of generalized anxiety and commitment needs to be assimilated. You can, I think, guess at our next step: talking privately and at length with each person in the class. In these conferences, our task was to listen, comment, suggest, reassure, and point to further goals and experiences that might be appropriate.

Two weeks had now gone by. The group had reached a kind of emotional "closure" or settlement of its own initial problem of becoming a group. They had done this through activities pointed directly at the social purpose of teacher preparation and indirectly at the group purpose of dealing with its own problems. And each woman was now launched on some personal inquiries of her own.

What, then, should be the next activities and investigations of the group as a group? What agenda should be planned for the next meeting? We instructors spent the weekend tussling with this problem. Had the group been a little further developed we would, of course, have done what we sometimes in fact did later: throw the question to the group. But in our judgment (right or wrong) the group was not yet ready to take this much responsibility for its own direction; they were still depending on us, and we felt that thwarting this need for confidence in our ability to guide them would cost us a great deal more time than the possible advantages were worth.

Our job, then, was to make a diagnosis of what the group was ready to become involved with. On the basis of the evidence of the interviews and discussions so far, could we locate some broad question that would immediately be recognized as crucial and important? Gradually we realized that a whole pattern of difficulties revolved around one major question: What can the teacher expect of children at different ages? We recalled that over and over again the group had been unable to interpret its own observations because they had no clear image of what children are like at various ages. Thus, for example, they were unable to tell whether observed performnace represented high or low achievement, whether learning was taking place, and whether the demands made by the observed teachers were likely to be too difficult on the one hand or too unprovocative on the other.

You will note that our question at this point, calling for description and comparison of the skills, attitudes, and orientations of children of different ages, is more specific and focused than the preceding one: to list the factors that influence the behavior of children in class. Moreover, the method for studying children would be primarily that of observation and generalization as distinguished from introspection and insight. And the study of children could be far more consciously self-directed by the student. Therefore, along with proposing the new question, we also proposed that our study of it should be planned as an illustration of inquiry; that we would be concerned not only with discovering facts about children but also with discovering how to conduct an inquiry and something about the roles needed in a group if inquiry were to proceed.

As it turned out, the work on child development represented three kinds of inquiry going on simultaneously. The first was personal inquiry, which centered around the "meaning" for each student of the facts about children. The quest for information is never solely for information; in social areas especially, it is also a quest for self-knowledge. Most of our women, during the child study, were almost consciously aware of a personal question: What age of youngster do I like? What sort of child will I be able to get along with? How important is intelligence, for instance, as compared with social skill? What sorts of problems of children are likely to crop up in the classroom? What makes a child popular with his classmates? As you can readily imagine, these questions, although consciously focused on boys and girls, were also self-concerns of our students; at some level of awareness they were asking these questions about themselves, too.

The second kind of inquiry had to do with the group as a social organization with a goal to achieve. The problems here had to do with organizing themselves for inquiry, with coordinating individual effort within group effort, with making the group a milieu for stimulating work and creative thought rather than for stifling ideas and substituting the goal of conformity and harmony for the goal of inquiry. The kind of group they needed was a kind few of them had experienced, and a great many attitudes, especially with regard to intermember relations, cropped up and had to be "worked through." Judging by the volume of conversation and the swapping of scuttlebutt that went on outside of class, that should have been a banner month for Illinois Bell Telephone Co.

The third kind of inquiry was directed ostensibly to getting facts about the cognitive, social, emotional, and physical development of children. This inquiry was rational, and was guided by "scientific method" as usually understood.

I trust that the teachers' awareness of the three "levels" of task, group process, and personal concern is discernible. As you read the case study, you see how the classrom teachers, called in as resource people for the conscious inquiry, also gave each student a great boost in her personal commitment to become a teacher. This was the beginning, really, of the development of "professional" attitudes and identifications by these ladies. But a new or strengthened commitment also increases the demands one makes on himself, and this stirs up new anxieties about one's adequacy. And you can see further that the instructors recognized these personal goings on and adapted their roles to these new individual needs.

I should like also to call attention to three further notions that the case study illustrates. The first is that the group grows in competence as time goes on. The members take over more and more of the supervisory responsibilities initially assumed by the teacher. They become increasingly aware not only of the "subject matter" but of themselves as inquirers consciously and deliberately plotting a strategy to guide their own efforts to learn the subject matter. In short, they develop the kind of educated schizophrenic "consciousness of self as actor while acting" that man ushered into the world when he became a tool user. And more and more, through increasing skills of diagnosis, they channel the impulse toward acting out into reality seeking and into testing of ideas through inquiry.

The second notion is that success or failure depends very much on the ability of the teacher to diagnose emerging concerns of the students. For these concerns, whether they be with aspects of tasks, group process, or personal self-concepts, provide the motivation for inquiry. Diagnosis is not done by instinct, supersensitivity, or blunt questioning. It is done by interpretation of data, and the data are perceptions of the students' own behavior. The teacher himself is continually engaged in inquiry about his class: what concerns are developing, or, more generally, what is the class at this point in time "ready" (e.g., motivated) for? Just as the student, in his inquiry, seeks situations from which he can get the data he needs, so the teacher likewise attempts to make the "situation" of the class as revealing as possible. In short, the teacher arranges or influences class activities in such a way that he can get the "feedback" he needs for continual diagnosis of the changing state of affairs in the class.

The third notion is that reflection does not go on during active give-and-take in a group. If one wants to engage in reflection during group discussion, he must withdraw psychologically; he must float off into a reverie or in some other way shut himself away from the barrage of stimulation and expectation of response by the group. Social interaction is terribly important in inquiry—and this whole chapter has been trying to explain how and why—but it is a necessary and not a sufficient condition. A good deal of "progressive" education can be commended for its grasp of the importance to motivation of social stimulation and activity, but at the same time it can be deplored for seldom getting the student off by himself to meditate. A good deal of "academic-traditional" education can be commended for at least getting the student alone with a book, but it can be deplored for its failure to provide him with any meaningful reason for being alone with the book.

As acting group members we do not engage in reflection—we are too busy being group members, necessarily concerned with the "welfare" of the group, with responding to ideas, with building plans and decisions, with maintaining and asserting social roles. To reflect, one must shuck off the demands of social roles; one must be himself, a whole person with a past history, a way of life, and a galaxy of aspirations and goals for his own future.

The intensely anxious person does not engage in reflection either. He is too wrought up to give himself the chance. He typically resists new insights because they are reinterpretations of reality and he has lost contact with reality. One of the very real hazards of "group work" is the arousal of undue anxiety about one's place and adequacy in the group; and this anxiety can be sufficiently preoccupying to block reflection long after the group has adjourned. It is for this reason that it seems quite irresponsible for the teacher to use group activities such as classroom "discussion" and subgroup committees unless he is willing to go the rest of the way to help students understand what is happening to them in the group interaction.

Reflection is encouraged by five conditions: first, keeping anxiety within bounds and translating it into issues to be resolved; second, noninterference and respect for the individual's privacy while he is trying to think; third, establishment of a generally nonthreatening "climate" through the habit of listening and responding with clarification, encouragement, and the objective definition of hard realities of all sorts; fourth, stimulation through challenge and confrontation by novel situations; and fifth, encouraging and utilizing suggestions and creative ideas ("contributions") which result from reflection. It is these that give the cues for defining the needs and interests for further steps of inquiry.

ADMINISTRATIVE MATTERS

Investigating groups of ten to fifteen students are to be carefully composed, and the whole population of students wanting a course may be drawn on for this purpose. In the preceding chapter, I have tried to show something of the nature of the problem of composing groups, but it is a bit too early to try at this point to lay down rules about it. It appears reasonable to me to suggest that what we probably shall want in groups will be: (a) enough communality of values so that communication is easy, that people will understand what they are saying to each other and will have similar expectations about ways of working; (b) enough difference in emotional response to stress so that there will be some clash among members about how to cope with the differences of opinion that arises; (c) enough similarity in level of sophistication and orientation toward the knowledge area to be investigated; and (d) avoidance of neurotic combinations of students that feed on each other. Beyond these specifications, we shall have to have specific knowledge of the sort of students the teacher can work with and the nature of the demands the course will make. Some of these demands are very much under the control of the teacher, and these are the ones whose strategic and sensitive modification by him will keep the investigation going in high gear.

The investigating groups will, we hope, be self-directing within their own planned investigations. During the actual conduct of the planned investigations, the students will be taking a good deal of initiative, and, for the most part, will be working independently or in ad hoc teams. The help they need will be mostly consultative, and they will be encouraged to get this help from whoever can give it, be he another student, student teacher, assistant teacher, regular teacher, or someone in the community. The teacher in charge will, of course, serve as consultant when needed, but it is possible that his biggest role will be to supervise the procedures the students need to act on their own behalf.

Two or three investigating groups could operate independently under the supervision of a team consisting of a teacher with three assistants. This team would meet together frequently, and the assistants would, through this participation, be receiving training for becoming "head teachers" themselves. One assistant would be assigned permanently to each investigating group, and during the diagnostic and planning periods the assistant would be part of the group. Each investigating group would need its own "home," and I can visualize a large room with three adjoining smaller rooms opening off it. The large room would have shop, library, and office facilities, as well as progress charts, files, and desk space for the teacher team. This large room would be strictly a workroom, and no student would be allowed out of his group room until he could define quite clearly exactly what he intended to do in the laboratory-library-workroom— or elsewhere in the school or community. The students would regard their group room as their seminar room: a place for planning, conferring, and arranging work. Individual students could work by themselves either in the group room or in the workroom; they would be guaranteed quiet in the workroom.

I think, however, that this last suggestion, referring to the larger class composed of three investigating groups might be put on ice for the time being. It will be enough for the next many months to concentrate on learning all we can about the composition of effective investigating groups and about the training and guidance of these groups in inquiry. This is a large task.

It is a large task not only for the schools but for every other functional organization in modern society. For what we have been struggling with in the microcosm of the classroom is part and parcel of the struggle for survival of the society of men on earth. We are, whether we like it or not, increasingly interdependent with all other men, and our survival is going to be decided by our ability, together, to develop a sense of common cause that expresses and reflects our common human aspirations. This sense of common cause will have to emerge from our experience in working together, and the quality of these experiences will in turn depend upon our ability to kindle and capture the flame of individual inspiration and insight. Life in these times *is* a social process of inquiry, of seeking to establish a way of life to which all can contribute, in which all can participate, and through which each may achieve self-realization simultaneously as a member of the emerging common society and of the human species. And the extent to which our boys and girls shall be effective in this quest is being decided right now by the quality of inquiry in the classroom.

9

Model 3:
Reflective Action

In which we consider that the school as a small community is maintained and improved through the more or less conscious effort of each citizen to become more effective in his own role; and that this striving, on the part of students, is consonant with the need of youth to develop a "place" for itself in the productive functioning of the community. We suggest Reflective Action as an educational model that can capitalize on these two conditions and, at the same time, make a unique and valuable contribution to the education of youth.

The development of the model of reflective action has a distinctive Aesopian flavor, for the theme is the conversion of a necessity into a virtue. The necessity is for the school to be concerned with many nonclassroom behaviors and actions of students; and the virtue is that the way of dealing with this concern can be turned to educative account.

The fact is that the student is not only someone who goes to classes, he is also a citizen in the school; and conversely, the school is not only a building in which classes are held, it is a social functional organization with all the characteristics of a small community—which, to complete the circle, therefore, must have citizens. Moreover, adolescents, seeking self-esteem through meaningful interdependence with others should, we suppose, be highly motivated to take the role of citizen. My impression from visiting high schools is that this is

160

generally true, and when it is not true, it is because what the administration calls a "citizen" is what the students would call a "subject" or "slave," thus leaving the generalization unscathed.

The function of the school is to educate; and the community of the school should therefore be an educative community, which means a community having a dominant orientation to the values and methods of educative experience. For a community to be united in common cause, its citizens must act not merely to maintain mechanical procedures and minimum individual rights. They must also act in an enlightened manner, which means thoughtfully and purposively; and when citizens act thoughtfully and purposively in common cause the consequence is that they continually change the community in the direction of the common goal. In practice this means that each person in the community seeks to act more effectively in his job and to do this he must get the cooperation of others to the extent that their own operation is contingent upon his. In short, in a community united in common cause, any citizen may initiate action; and the action involves others.

The school as a community is a place where different groups (students, teachers, officials, maintenance workers) must coexist; where these groups are interdependent in the maintenance of the physical plant, the creation of social norms and common values, the facilitation of adequate communications, and the generation and protection of the climate of inquiry. Within this interdependent way of life, however, each group is expected to initiate action to improve the conditions under which it functions. Teachers can do a better job of teaching if the students actively participate to maintain a lawful community; students can set up various services for their own group if the administration will permit; the engineer will be able to keep up with needed repairs if everybody reports things that do not work before rather than after they have been broken.

When this community is united in the common cause of education, every event, policy, attitude, and suggestion will be examined in the light of one paramount question: What is the immediate and long-range effect of this event, policy, etc., on the quality of education? The attitudes of janitors, the way the principal leads a faculty meeting, the leadership role of the teachers in the extracurricular program, the kind of deliberation going on in the student government, the manner of securing quiet in the cafeteria, the way the educational product is measured, the development of an elite group of students—all these things are not adequately comprehended until their probable effects on the child's education have been discerned.

In addition to demanding that action be enlightened, the school should demand that the way of participating to initiate, plan, and carry out the action should be educative. In other words, the aim is not only to improve the school as an educative community but also to learn something of significance that will enable the student to participate in a more enlightened way in *any* community. This "something" is likely to include information, applications of principles learned in courses, practice and insight into the methodology of action, and a greater sense of responsibility for the community of which he is a part.

We must therefore examine what we mean by enlightened action, the organizational conditions necessary for it to occur, and the steps or modifications required to make it educative.

THE COURSE OF ACTION IN THE SCHOOL: AN ILLUSTRATION

I think this would be a good place to call on Melvin, who is no longer sick of algebra.

Melvin had always had trouble with math, but he did well enough in other subjects, and was generally well thought of by teachers and students. Over the years various teachers had given Melvin extra hours of consultation and one even went to the length of giving him a diagnostic test to see why he couldn't learn algebra. I don't think it is necessary for me to make up a theory to explain why Melvin was unable to profit from the efforts of his teachers to help him; we'll just accept the fact. Melvin entered algebra with the bright determination to let bygones be bygones, and for a couple of weeks he got along fine; but then his deficiencies and lack of skills gradually began to overpower him, and by Thanksgiving he had little cause for celebration.

The start of action was a conversation among Melvin and four other boys who were engaged in some gastric rearrangements to make Joe's car run on stove oil instead of gasoline. The boys had been chatting about their different ideas, and gradually edged into their feelings about algebra. Melvin told of his troubles, and complained that somehow he got little help from the teacher, even though, he conceded, she seemed really to be trying to help. Two other boys told of having similar experiences. Then Charles said that he got the best help from Joanna, another student in the class. This led into a round of adolescent sniggering, and the subject was changed. But you will see that this conversation planted the seed. Melvin had expressed a concern, and it is important to note what sort of group he was able to express his concern to. Melvin had gotten reassurance that others had the same kind of problem—and this kind of reality-testing with friends is, so far as I can see, always necessary to begin action. Finally, we note that Charles planted a suggestion, which was, however, not picked up.

The next day during algebra there was a study period for the students to work on homework problems. Melvin struggled with the problems for a few minutes, and then fell to musing. Then he asked the teacher if he could study with Harry instead of by himself. She acquiesced, and the two boys worked together for the rest of the period. The following day Melvin turned in all the homework, and most of it was correct; he also recited three times, and one of his recitations was very good. The teacher learned later that Harry had helped Melvin for two hours after school and had rather enjoyed doing it.

The class droned on toward Christmas with mounting apprehension about the semester examination. The teacher selected eight students who seemed to her to stand in most deadly peril, and she suggested they come in for coaching after school. Then a thought struck her, and she asked Harry and Joanna if they would come in too and help the group. The coaching sessions worked well, and Harry and Joanna began to feel like professional consultants.

At the next meeting of the student council, there was a written proposal from Harry, Joanna, Melvin, and Charles and it carried a penciled approval from the algebra teacher. The proposal was that the student government through its representatives, and with the help of the teachers, identify a number of students who could serve as consultants to other students needing help in various subjects, and that means be found during the school day to set up the "consultations." The members of the council reacted variously. Some thought it was a fine idea and were all for setting it up right now, whereas others felt that it was the sort of thing that should be done informally, and therefore the council should not interest themselves in it. The group argued back and forth for awhile, and then Mr. Boone, their adviser, suggested that he thought they'd better get some facts to go on. How many students did the teachers feel could profit from such help if it were available? How many students would go to get such help? Could "consultants" be found and would they be willing to serve?

With Mr. Boone's encouragement, the council decided to appoint a committee consisting of Melvin and Joanna plus two of the councilors to formulate the questions and devise ways to get the information. The committee, at the next meeting of the representatives, laid the proposal before them and suggested that it be discussed in all the homerooms. In due time this occurred, and the response was overwhelmingly favorable. The council decided to go ahead. They wrote up a new proposal, incorporating data on the reaction of the students, and submitted this to the principal. He in turn, laid it before the faculty's Academic Committee, and this group decided to set the whole thing up. The principal, alarmed, met with them, and offered a counter-suggestion: that three of the committee plus three students, to be selected by the student council, work out a plan together. Two of the teachers grumbled at this, but the suggestion was adopted, and the joint committee went to work. I don't think the technical details add much to the picture of social action, so I'll summarize only the points that seem to me most important.

The teachers made lists of possible consultants and the students in each class were asked to turn in their private nominations for consultants. The committee put the two sorts of nominations together and selected students appearing on both lists. The principal, after talking with the study-hall teachers and librarian, decided that the most feasible arrangement would be to make several rooms, one for each subject, available for the consultations after school. It was decided that students would be encouraged to make their own decisions as to whether they needed help, but that it would be all right for teachers to nudge them a little. There was much debate in the committee as to the advisability of asking a teacher to supervise the consultations in each subject field, and it was decided not to; but it was also agreed to check up at the end of a month and see whether this decision was wise. There was also the question of whether to ask students to make appointments for consultation; but again, the provisional decision was to do the things requiring least in the way of special arrangements.

The consulting got under way, and was helpful and even enjoyable in some cases but not in others. The consultants took their roles seriously, and found themselves needing advice about how to deal with certain students who seemed resistant, stupid, time-wasting, etc. A training session was set up for the consultants with a psychologist from a nearby college to help. The consultants melded into a group, gave themselves a name, and by the end of the semester were being seen as a rather high prestige club. The group was also recognized by the student council, and a description of its activities was included in the student handbook. Two teachers were appointed as advisers to the consultant group. This experience with the student consultants led, two years later, to the development of the Skills Development Laboratory, described in Chapter 10. It also led to identification of several other ways students could help each other, and this expectation became part of the tradition of the school.

This illustration shows the genesis of social action:

1. An individual feels some concern. (Melvin.)

2. He tests this concern casually with persons he can trust, usually friends. (Charles, Joe, and two unidentified lads.)

3. If the concern is shared (legitimized), a nuclear action group can form (Melvin, Charles, Joanna, Teacher.)

4. Either just before or after forming the nuclear group, one or more of the concerned individuals typically takes exploratory action or looks up examples from the experience of others. (Melvin, with Harry.)

5. The nuclear group forms around the desire for action, not around the need to represent other organizations. (Important!)

6. The nuclear group looks for existing organizations within whose jurisdiction the action would fall; if it finds one, it makes a proposal or demand (as on the student council). If it finds no existing group to take over it has to decide whether to drop it or go ahead on its own.

7. A committee is formed to analyze the proposal and to collect data to ascertain need and interest in the larger clientele. (Council subcommittee.)

8. The persons contacted in the survey are those who would be affected by the contemplated action, and their reactions are sought.

(Student body, faculty, administration.)

9. A planning committee, usually drawn from the original nuclear group, organization executives, technical experts, and influential people draws up a plan. (Joint student and teacher committee.)

10. The plan is put into effect, which includes: announcing it, finding people for special roles, organizing their efforts, and making provisions for assessing the results of their efforts. (Joint committee plus student council.)

11. The persons taking special responsible roles need to be trained; and, through this experience they develop their identity as a special functional group. (Consultants plus advisers.)

12. This new group struggles for and is accorded a "place" in the formal and informal structure of the community. (By the student council.)

13. Other groups accommodate to the new group and develop expectations for what it does and how it does it. (Students, teachers, parents, etc.)

14. The various procedures become routinized and work smoothly. (With permanant faculty adviser.)

15. The new function gradually settles into ritual and apathy unless:

    a. the constant turnover of students maintains the sense of challenge. (Freshmen in, seniors out.)

    b. there is constant redefinition or expansion of function as new insights are gathered. (Add further services, develop new procedures.)

    c. a better way is found that makes the functional group unnecessary—or swallows it up. (Creation of the Skills Development Laboratory.)

ORGANIZATIONAL MATTERS

The development of action requires that there be open channels of communication. One cannot address the entire student body if there is no place where they can come together; one cannot get feedback and opinions from classes if there is not time allocated for this purpose; one cannot utilize resources and special contributions if there is no way to identify and locate them; one cannot propose things if nobody is listening. There is, in short, a minimum degree of organization required simply to provide communication channels.

This organization will change as the needs for communication and action change. Thus, in the Sophomore Project, we began by setting aside fifteen minutes each day during which the fifty students were divided into five ten-man "homeroom groups." Each such group could discuss anything it wished to about the conduct of the project, and, the next day, another fifteen minutes was available for the groups to report any concerns, raise any questions, or ask for any information they, as a group, wished. The teachers attempted to answer questions responsively. As time went on, however, the needs of the boys and girls went beyond requests for information. They wished to propose new ways to organize study periods, projects such as a parents' night and a party for the whole class, and better techniques for planning the daily schedule. (At one point they even wanted a Coke machine, but we won't go into that!) With the development of these proposals, they needed some kind of student government which could get data, consult with teachers, form action committees, and communicate with the administration. Accordingly a student council was formed for the project, and it worked in close relationship with the homeroom groups. But after several months of this, the community of fifty students had developed strong pressures for inquiry in the various subjects, and their desires for nonwork kinds of action pretty well disappeared. Moreover, many of the sorts of problems that had come before the student council were now being handled directly with the teacher or other students involved. Therefore the student council disbanded, and from then on government was through "town meetings," in which the whole community of students, teachers, assistant teachers, and research assistants pondered together on problems of mutual concern.

From this experience, I conclude that the form of the student government and the need for it may differ from place to place and from time to time, but there still must be *some* sort of student organization for action to be possible. In the same way, there is probably also need for some sort of organization of the faculty, and I would point out rather grumpily that it would be nice if the subcommittees, steering committees, departmental committees, welfare committees, grade committees, and committee on committees all had clear-cut, definable responsibilities and functions so that students (and teachers) would not always have to interview the principal to decide with whom to communicate. Further, there ought to be some organizational provision for communication, at the steering level, among students, faculty, and administrative officers. Finally, all organizational arrangements over and above the communications network should be developed only as needed and quickly dissolved as soon as decency allows. Ad hoc committees are very chic for action, as Melvin's case demonstrates.

Assuming there is enough organization, our basic situation for the start of action is informal voluntary conversation among students, and between students and teachers. From such conversations, any one of the participants may start action; and he does this by making a proposal to some appropriate officer or group. This officer or group tests with the initiator the seriousness of his intent or concern, and then either accepts the proposal or rejects it. If accepted, the proposal is routed to the proper agency for study; and if no such agency exists, one is set up (ad hoc). There then follow all the steps required for making decisions and plans, involving further people at appropriate times, training them, taking action, and so on.

The strategy of successful action, as extracted from a great deal of experience with citizen groups, consistently respects the following principles:[4]

1. During initial and problem-identifying stages, the movement develops among persons who already have prior relationships and who trust each other.

2. At each stage, plans are reality-tested, and the test is that the people about to be involved in action feel that the problem to be solved is important to them personally. If this amount of commitment hasn't developed after a reasonable amount of study of the problems plus give-and-take discussion which anticipates what might be done, the problem should be dropped.

3. Discussion of problems focuses on concrete specific cases, not on reality-avoiding stereotypes or generalities. Proposals and attitudes should be tested operationally with respect to efforts to visualize the action they call for.

4. Persons selected or grouped to study proposals and recommend plans of action should not necessarily be friends of the proposer or of his proposal. All that is required is that each can adopt an attitude of inquiry and that, preferably, among them they represent (un-

officially) most of the spectrum of relevant student attitudes. Membership in all action groups is based on willingness to work, not on ideology.

5. All decisions are subject to revision as a result of taking action. Procedures for getting and interpreting reactions and progress should be built into all plans for action.

6. Leadership is by teams, not individuals. This vastly increases the prospect that action will occur, and, if the team is carefully selected, it provides better leadership. The team mates use each other to discharge anxiety and hostility, help diagnose what was really going on, lay better plans for next meetings or supervisory contacts.

7. Action groups participate in discussions to clarify their own rules, functions, degree of autonomy, power and obligations with respect to the various other committees or groups involved in the action. It is especially important that groups set up by a central governmental agency, such as the student council, know exactly the boundaries of freedom and responsibility within which they work, and that this be determined by negotiation among the groups.

8. Voluntary participation in all groups depends on the rate of reward accruing to the members. If they are given a vague and frustrating task, a good deal of "goofing off" and socializing may be necessary to maintain reward through interpersonal gratifications; on the other hand, anything that can help the group gain satisfaction from work will reduce the need for nonwork activity.

TARGETS FOR ACTION

The student is a citizen in the school. He is also a member of the student body, which is a majority group. (Minority groups include teachers and other staff.) The student is a person in his own right, not merely a citizen and a group member. It is clear that he can act on behalf on himself, his group, or the larger community of the school, and that ideally his motivations of these three sorts would be compatible. Certainly the existence of these three sorts of motivations should be recognized and tapped in the action program.

The initiation of action comes from the sensitivities and drives of one or a few individuals, and therefore the actors in an action campaign or project must be volunteers. Reflective action, as an educational means, cannot be imposed across the board on all students. It is only for the particular students who are ready for it by virtue of personal commitments to causes or purposes. The amount of reflective action going on in a school will be a sensitive indicator of the freedom of thought and action possible within the school.

To say that the actors are volunteers does not, however, mean that others are not "involved." For these others are citizens, and citizens must assume responsibility. By responsibility I mean quite literally the ability to respond. The concept of initiation of action by volunteers is simply a mockery without the concept of response by those on whom the proposed action will impinge. And these others may be responding in their roles as individuals, group members, or citizens concerned with the broad purposes and policies of the community.

The list of possible targets for action is endless, and I would like to present a few samples, partly to stimulate your thinking and partly as a way of indirectly communicating some of the flavor of the school as a consistent educational milieu. In presenting these targets I hope that you will not attempt to *judge* the value of reflective action from these or other possible targets, for the educational value of reflective action is determined by the way the action is taken, not by the changes it produces; although these may and should be valuable for other reasons.

Here are some targets classified under the headings of individual interests, youth welfare, educational service, and steering.

Individual interests center around the creation of opportunities for new kinds of experience desired by individuals. Appropriate action requires finding enough other students with the same interest that the change seems legitimate and worth the trouble it will cause. Academic interests include such things as a special advanced course in mathematics, apprenticeship experience with science teachers, conversation and reading groups to study literature or foreign languages, e.g., special classes in Russian. Social interests include hobby clubs, social dancing, weekend work camps, three-day bus trips to the state capital, corresponding with students in other schools—possibly exchanging slides and tape recordings with them, serving as hosts to visiting students, possibly working out student "exchanges" during vacations or even during the school year. Managerial interests include setting up and operating a summer music and arts workshop, a school canteen, branch savings bank, lost-and-found bureau, labor union for student help in the cafeteria and office, Junior Achievement club.

Welfare interests express concern for one's fellows. Many students do have powerful altruistic leanings and there is very little opportunity for them to come to terms with such feelings. And the role of the "unfortunate" student is usually handled with a degree of callousness and with a display of cheap sentimentality that is downright debasing to all concerned. I therefore see merit in allowing students to set up a resource pool to give special academic help to those having trouble in the various subjects; possibly Melvin's adventure provides a prototype for this. Hospitalized, disabled, or bedridden convalescent students need special help. Some students simply need a friend or "big brother" to reinforce their superegos long enough to get their egos functioning again. Some students need economic aid and work experience; how about an employment service run by students? And what about the fact that half the brightest students do not go on to college? Is there a place here for a scholarship drive, and for persuasion by their colleagues, the college-bound?

By educational service I mean limited cooperative assistance in the teaching program. One thinks immediately of audio-visual service, of the manufacture by students of spelling tapes, foreign language tapes, and drill material of all sorts. I have been impressed, too, with the ability of students to work out new classroom procedures, such as card forms to aid in planning and scheduling study projects. The use of community resources in teaching is contingent on knowing what they are, and students are quite capable of casing field-trip possibilities, cataloguing curious collections, odd occupations, and strange specialities in the community.

Steering activities involve collaboration with adults, and participation in the consideration of policy. We seriously need joint student-teacher committees to conduct periodic evaluations of the educational program in the school. Heaven only knows what creative ideas—with useful germs of new insight—might be turned up by students through discussion of the pros and cons of an eleven-month school year, of special schools or curricula for "gifted" students, of the use of adult resources in classes and clubs.

The list is virtually endless. But remember that the educational value of these things—and I repeat this—is going to be in the way they are carried forward through reflective action.

MAKING ACTION EDUCATIVE

So far we have been considering conditions and methods of enlightened action whose purpose is to improve the community or the functioning of different members within the community. Now let us
consider what it would take to make the experience of participating
in action also contribute to one's education. I grant that one *learns*
from participation in action; but not all learning is *educative,* and for
the educational potential of action to be realized someone must
consciously supervise with the educational goal in mind.

I suggest the name "reflective action" for action carried out in an
educative manner. For action to be reflective action it must engage the
conscious mind; it must have an active intellectual component; it
must involve purposive goal-seeking, diagnosis, creating hypotheses,
rehearsing action in one's mind, connecting causes to effects, finding
commitments, seeing relationships between each step and long-range
aims, and so on. And these processes must be seen together as comprising a strategy of action. The student must *consciously* seek alternative possibilities at all times, collect data and knowledge sufficient
for wise selection among alternatives, attempt to explain and understand why the action he takes (carefully described) has the results it
is observed to have, and reflect on his experience of action to find
meanings of all sorts. Reflective action, with its concern for understanding and development of principles, sees the immediate act as
illustrative of human and social nature. It turns to political science
for ideas about control of power and decision processes; to the
Founding Fathers for affirmations of intentions and values; to sociology for insight into intergroup, communication, and organizational
problems; to cultural studies to reflect on and seek to make one's own
assumptions explicit; to government for models of coordinating structure and roles; and to law for principles to safeguard individual
rights. It assumes a historical perspective in the recognition that
problems being faced by a particular group at a particular time have
been encountered at other times and places—and will be again.

Reflective action, almost uniquely among educational methods,
fosters insight into the universals or the principles of human and
social behavior one is dealing with. Some of these principles are
articles of faith which can only be learned by reflection on experi-

ence—such as: that people, when given the facts objectively, tend to act intelligently; that situations made by man can be improved by man; that people generally act reasonably from their own point of view. Others of these principles are propositions about human behavior: that people are frustrated when they cannot discover what is expected of them or what the job demands; that the most painful condition for most people is to be torn between conflicting desires; that disagreements can be settled by getting down to concrete cases—and that disagreements are fostered by ideological debate; that the fact that different people react differently to the same situation is the basis for potentially wiser decisions by a group; that for a group to reach its goal every member must take responsibility for the welfare of the group.

In addition to propositions, there is always, in action, a host of personal meanings which are not unrelated to the evaluations one makes of himself and his motives, goals, roles and values. These meanings are extended and illuminated by learning of the experience of others, either at firsthand or through reading. Biographies, accounts of movements from revolutions to utopias, leadership manuals, movies like *Twelve Angry Men,* visits to settlement houses and community organizations, discussions with the alderman—all these can develop a vast amount of meaning and factual knowledge to connect with the student's personal involvement in action.

There are also skills of communication, report-writing, telephoning, oral presentation, record-keeping—yes, even filing and typing. And skills of group leadership and membership, of interviewing, of listening to others.

To make the action experience of students educative, the staff must be able to intervene in it or interrupt it at the most telling times; and to do this, the staff must keep enough contact with action that a telling time can be recognized. Staff members are, willy-nilly, silent partners in student action, and they must have and be seen as having legitimate and necessary relationships to it. Anyone who has ever sat as adviser to a student council will recognize that the staff role is difficult to discharge; at all times one is required to make the most delicate distinctions among advising, suggesting, commanding, interfering. Moreover, nearly all action groups, including adult groups, tend to be impatient with efforts to get them to be conscious of their assumptions at precisely the times when such consciousness would be most helpful.

Generally speaking, a great deal of difficulty can be avoided by taking the time to develop "house rules" which will make educative intervention legitimate in the minds of students. Such rules spell out the orderly series of steps (and alternative steps) through which action is to be developed. They do not try to spell out role-expectations because role-expectations cannot be legislated; these have to emerge from experiences of working together. They also do not spell out purposes, although the reasons for every step should be discussed and agreed to before the step is written down and accepted. My own preference would be to discuss and revise the series of steps each spring with a teacher-student steering committee for the action program. I would then train them (if necessary) to interpret this information to each action group they sanction.

The steps, to be developed in each school setting, are meant to safeguard orderly processes of action and the rights of others who will inevitably be affected. The stipulations most strategic for educational purposes seem to me to be these:

1. Every proposal to initiate action must be in writing, and must document several instances of the specific practices the proposer is concerned about. He must then tell, as well as he can, why these practices disturb him, either by reason of inconvenience or because of ethical objection to the principles he thinks are involved. If the proposal is not corrective but rather for installation of new practices, the proposer must explain the purpose and demonstrate that existing channels are in his mind inadequate. This document is to be countersigned by a member of the faculty (who hopefully has listened to him sympathetically and helped him formulate his case, whether or not the faculty member personally agrees with it.)

2. No decision for action is to be made on the basis of one suggested course of action. The process of decision is not merely to decide whether or not to give approval; it is to include formulation of at least two alternatives, collection of data providing a reasonable description of their pros and cons, and weighing of the respective merits of the proposals. The criteria used for weighing proposals must be formulated explicitly, and a clear report of the alternatives considered, the data, the criteria, and the decision must be included as

the preamble for all plans of action.

3. All plans for action must be approved by a faculty member. (I assume that the student steering committee would also want to approve, but that is up to them. I am here concentrating only on the educational safeguards.)

4. All plans for action after examination and possible modification by other committees that may have special responsibilities in the action program, must be presented orally to the clientele who are to be affected by the proposed action (e.g., the entire student body, one grade, volunteers). There will be two presentations. One is to be in the form of a critique, which discusses the policies, principles, and precedents involved. This critique is to be prepared with such help as may be needed from a faculty member, and it is to place the problem and the plan in a broad social, historical, economic, aesthetic (or other relevant) context. The other presentation will review the plan step by step, analyze its hoped-for consequences and implications, and candidly anticipate the kinds of difficulties likely to arise at different points of implementation.

The plan and critique are to be questioned by a committee containing a few students and one teacher selected for this purpose. If the cross-examination is judged satisfactory by the teacher, he will then signal his approval, and discussion will begin from the floor.

5. The method of collecting and interpreting data at different times during operations must be attested to in advance by a faculty member, who will also supervise the procedures.

6. Program reports, appraising action programs, are to be reviewed by a duly constituted committee, class, or other group at least once each semester, at termination of the action, or at the point of its incorporaion into routine procedures. Following the report, there will be discussion from the floor; and, after that, two faculty members will themselves lead a discussion on the central issues, conclusions, implications (for further action), and personal meanings of the action experience.

THE BROADER SETTING FOR REFLECTIVE ACTION

I have been attempting to tell a simple story. The nature of the school as a small community requires a machinery for action initiated by anyone in the organization; and the nature of the school's mission suggests that this action be supervised and made as educational as possible—and action under these circumstances I call reflective action.

The picture of the course of action, the organizational features and policies, and the supervision to make action reflective is just as appropriate to an enlightened factory, research laboratory, governmental agency, and church as it is to the school. With suitable modifications required by the factors of age of personnel, nature of the authority of leaders, and technical definition of major social functions, what I have been saying is not greatly different from what a modern management consultant might say to these other organizations. The common element in all these settings is the recognition of the inseparability of action and education.

The best test of the principles that I know of was in the reconstruction of my own neighborhood in Chicago. The organization was the Hyde Park Kenwood Community Conference, and I have referred to it several times already in this book. The Conference was an indigenous grass-roots group composed of citizen volunteers. The Conference undertook the social, psychological, and physical rehabilitation of an area one mile by one and a half miles, containing 72,000 citizens. The chief instrument of action was the block program, which gathered citizens together into semi-autonomous neighborhood associations, and each association was assisted to identify and deal with its own neighborhood problems. The immediate goal of block activity was to improve the neighborhood; but the ultimate and most important goal was adult education. For all the activities can be undersood most simply as a continuous inquiry into what it means to be a citizen. In trying to improve their community, citizens learned a great deal about its political, economic, and sociological workings; they learned skills of reaching decisions, and of searching for wisdom in dissent; they came to cherish the community and to value it; and they found new routes to self-esteem.[1] And the new buildings and shopping center being completed now, ten years after the first meeting of volunteers, have far less significance to me than the partial reconstruction of the way of life of the community.

I have brought my community into this discussion because the relationship between education—education as inquiry—and action is there, unclouded by the murky rhetoric that obscures what should be an equally clear relationship in the schools. Where did the idea come from that engagement in action is anti-intellectual? that it does not involve theorizing? that is has no generalizable outcome? No, these criticisms hold not for action, but only for unintelligent and nonreflective action. Laboratory research in physics is just as much a kind of action as planning, implementing, and continually improving on ways to help academically distressed students. Both are educative if disciplined by knowledge, conscious purpose, and a hard-boiled attitude toward assessed realities; neither are educative if conducted in a sentimental, wishful, impulsive, or self-aggrandizing manner.

People may choose to stay out of physics laboratories, but they cannot choose to stay out of organizational life. Beginning with the nursery school or kindergarten, every person lives a major part of his life in schools, offices, shops or bureaus; and every person is a citizen in a community. I believe that one has only to look around at our deteriorating cities and our emerging Organization Men to realize that development of the discipline of reflective action should be an important educational goal. And I further believe that the school, with its resources of knowledge and its control over itself as a miniature but real community, should be the place for learning this discipline.

Let me carry these suppositions further. I have presented Reflective Action as necessary to the student's way of life in the school and as preparation for his life as a citizen and as a functional member of society later. But what about his present way of life in the larger community, right now? For students, like teachers and other people, need a place in the larger community as well as in the school and family. Just as in the school, they will find this place in the larger community through active participation. And this action may be reflective and educative or it can be impulsive and willful.

I shall not insist that the school should supervise action of youth in the community. I do suggest that the induction of youth into the productive life of the community might well be the responsibility of a youth council composed of representatives elected from the student bodies of the high schools and advised by a group of responsible citizens.

One of the functions of this council will be to work with adult groups to develop new roles for youth, to give them a "place." The basic proposition is that the young do live in the community and must grow up to share in decisions and responsibilities governing the life of the communty. I don't think adults can "give" them a place; it's something they will have to work out with adults. And adults are not likely to move over and give up anything to them. The question is not which jobs can be done more cheaply with child labor than with adult labor. The question is rather which efforts of children will enrich the community and make it a better place for all. And I think the place to dig into this question is through an analysis of the community functions that impinge most directly on the lives of the young.

For example, Little Rock; Virginia; and Clinton, Tennessee. In these places, high school youth are simply pawns in the most devastating anti-educational connivings in the history of our country. I lie awake at night wondering what answer they would give, how they would work out the processes of integration, if they had a chance. They are the ones who must live with whatever decisions are made. Should they have no voice in the decisions? My own guess, supported by reports from these communities, is that a substantial percentage of the boys and girls would vote for keeping open a choice, letting each student make up his own mind, and that experimentally, over the years, with the help of each other, they would achieve integration to the extent they are able.

How about urban redevelopment? Several acres of housing have been cleared in my neighborhood to make room for parks. What philosophy should have been invoked? Should the youth have been canvassed, their needs diagnosed? What would happen if they were asked, through their own organization, to suggest the best use of some of the space? Could they—should they—help supervise the area after it is developed? Is there any kind of youth hangout that lies somewhere between the canteen or neighborhood center on the one hand and the parked car on the other? Is it needed? Are we adults likely to figure this one out for the kids?

And what about cars, anyway? Is the auto to continue to be an instrument of aggression and defiance in the hands of the young? Could they make and enforce a code of their own with respect to the use of cars? What would be our part in making such a plan work?

Are delinquent or near-delinquent gangs necessary? What would a city-wide youth convention come up with on this? Do you think they would have better ideas than we do about what these gangs are trying to accomplish, why they are needed, how their needs could be met more effectively within the law? What do you suppose would be the consequence of such a convention for the redefinition of parental roles?

These kinds of participation by youth could be interfering, time-wasting, and irresponsible. On the other hand, they have tremendous educational potential if undertaken responsibly, soberly, cooperatively. The youth leadership could meet one evening each week with carefully chosen adults in seminars to explore these problems areas and to plan strategies for extending the base of deliberation and action to all youth. I would like to see the adult education moguls involved in helping with such seminars.

The time is rapidly approaching when every community will have its local college. It is estimated that at the present time approximately 80 per cent of college students work part time. Do you suppose college students could, with training, become consultants and resource people for youth action groups in the school and community?

I have referred casually to training and supervision. My experience with educated adults engaged in action is that they all need training, if only to give them enough self-confidence that they will not be discombobulated by unexpected responses. I think it is quite possible that the teaching skills required may be more readily found among welfare workers, adult educators, industrial trainers, etc., than among teachers. Regardless of who supplies the training, or whether it is in the school or elsewhere in the community, there is a great deal that can be done through role-playing, examination of group process, feedback about the roles individuals take in a group, and so on.[2] There have been some experiments with Bethel-type workshops for adolescents,[3] and I believe they should be seriously considered by educators and schoolmen. Perhaps the place for such "off the job" training is in the leadership institutes that an increasing number of high schools now offer to all the student leaders during the week before school opens. My own inclination would be to provide it in a course in social psychology to be offered in lieu of one semester of biology in the tenth grade.

Let me close these speculations by reminding ourselves that a major function of education is to induct youth into the community and its way of life. But "inducting" youth is the process of helping them develop their place, as young adults actively participating in the total political, economic, cultural, and recreational aspects of life. The way to induction is through gradually increasing participation in the school and larger community, beginning with adolescence or earlier, and with respect to more and more facets and functions of society. And this is exactly what youth needs. I see this need as a strongly motivating force that can be connected through reflective action, to the enhancement of knowledge, attitudes, and skills developed through the entire educational program of the school.

NOTES

1. Julia Abrahamson, *A Neighborhood Finds Itself* (New York: Harper & Brothers, 1959), p. 370.
2. Matthew B. Miles, *Learning to Work in Groups* (New York: Bureau of Publications, Teachers College, Columbia University, 1959), p. 285.
3. National Training Laboratories, 1201 Sixteenth Street N.W., Washington 6, D.C.
4. Herbert A. Thelen, *Dynamics of Groups at Work* (Chicago: University of Chicago Press, 1954), p. 370. Chapter I, "Rebuilding the Community through Citizen Action," pp. 2-31.

10

Model 4:
Skill Development

In which we consider that the learning of skills is justified to increase one's competence to achieve his goals, and that routine practice without relationship to meaningful goals is mostly a waste of time. We suggest that a student engaged in genuine inquiry will acquire many skills in the course of that inquiry; but for those who need supervised practice, "remedial" help, or simply an opportunity to move at their own rate, the Skill Development Laboratory is proposed.

I don't think a child or an adult who "cannot spell" is therefore "cute" or touched with genius. I find nothing admirable about illegible handwriting. I enjoy reading a well-organized paper with some evidences of style—any style, almost; and I can't stand the meandering type of pointless narrative which, after a dramatic start, usually peters out along about the middle of the clothing advertisements. I have about concluded that most speeches aren't worth hearing, but I stay awake longer if they are at least grammatical, and a literate speech arouses my enthusiasm.

I also don't go for kids who chew with their mouths open, or for adults who hum loudly and tap their feet during a conversation. I like people to say "please" and "thank you," and to know better than to say anything but "fine" in reply to the question, "How are you?" I like drivers who stay on their own side of the road and who give definite interpretable signals when they are about to change course. I don't have feelings about whether a man should rise to greet me when I enter his office, but I do get annoyed if he doesn't even look up.

In both these paragraphs I am talking about the same subject: manners. The first paragraph deals with the manners of educated people; the second paragraph with those of socialized people. Both are the possessions of a civilized person. Both are learned primarily through imitation of other people whom one would like to be like. The first requirement for learning them, then, is that there be models of excellence available in daily contact with the child. Professor Harold Dunkel[2] makes the point very nicely in a recent discussion of foreign language teaching in the elementary school; he says, in effect, that the school should not try to teach the spoken language unless the teacher "speaks like a native."

Having a good model is, however, not enough—not by a long shot. The second requirement for learning manners is that the learner wants to be like the model person, and learning educational manners is seen by the learner as a way to achieve this feeling of "likeness." When this sort of identification is impossible or has gone wrong, the student appears to have "emotional blocks" to learning. This matter has been studied very extensively in connection with reading problems,[1] and emotional retreading is every bit as important as "skill practice" for such children. There are even people who believe that for the problem readers, skill practice activities, using tachistoscopes, eye pushers, and flash cards are useful only to the extent that going to that much trouble reassures and encourages the child.

Identification is, of course, helpful for all sorts of learning, because it means that energy will go into the relevant learning instead of being used to defend oneself. But identification is crucial in the learning of educational manners—the three R's—because a great deal of the three R's is quite literally nonsense. See for yourself:

Write out the letters of the alphabet on a sheet of paper. Do it twice, the first time illegibly and the second time legibly. Now just stare at your work and try to answer these two questions. First, why is "a" made that way? Whoever dreamed that up, anyway? Is there any body of experience or theory by means of which you could figure out why an "a" is made the way it is? Second, why is the one alphabet "legible" and the other "illegible?" Is there any reason on earth why the labels couldn't equally well be reversed—if you could persuade other people to agree to it? Our point, of course, is that handwriting is nonrational. There is no intellectual handle to get hold of it with. It's a purely arbitrary contrivance, and the only thing that makes a particular way of writing "right" is that the people who have the most say about such matters agree that it is "right." The same goes for spelling, grammar, style, pronunciation, word-meaning (of the stem words), computational procedures, and most of the rest of the three R's.

Unlike the learning of insights and generalizations, the learning of skills is usually a means to some other end, not an end in itself. This is tantamount to saying not that people want to learn skills but rather that they want to be able to do something else. I don't want to learn typing, if by that you mean holding my hands in some specified position, always pressing the @ key with my little finger, and using the shift-hold button when I type a string of caps. I do want to learn typing if by that you mean freeing my attention and energy for thinking as I write rather than having to squander it all on the machine. If, in attaining this goal, I happen to find your advice to use the little finger on the @ key helpful, I am perfectly willing to do it.

The same goes for other skills; computation, for example. I once watched a four-year-old girl figure out how many sausages each member of the family could have for dinner. There were seventeen sausages (little ones) frying in the skillet, and five persons in the family. Her answer was "three apiece and not quite a half more." When she got to school and learned that she couldn't do that in third grade because that is "division," sure enough, she couldn't, and when she got around to "division" in the fourth grade, she was baffled and frustrated. The moral obtrudes itself: she never set out to "learn division"; all she wanted was to know how many sausages she could count on.

This sort of thing is by no means unusual. The present methods of teaching skills get one so tied up in rules, conventions, specific procedures, and terminology—all of which appear as ends in themselves—that one is too self-conscious, fearful, and inhibited to put the effort in its only meaningful context: as a means to some genuine goal. I think it is very telling that one of the people who is helping to develop better methods of teaching mathematics was led to reject the traditional burden of claptrap through pondering over the fact that her favorite horse could add. Obviously the horse could not be expected to put figures in a straight column, one over the other, draw a line beneath the bottom figure, and then go down (or is it up?) the column!

THE SKILL DEVELOPMENT LABORATORY

In the normal course of personal inquiry, group investigation and reflective action, the student will need many skills. He will need to write reports, summarize numerical and experimental data, compose a speech, poem, story or news article, prepare an annotated bibliography or suvey of literature, participate in a panel discussion, conduct an interview, etc. These skills will not be ends in themselves. They are instrumental to the purposes of inquiry.[3]

I propose that a special facility, the Skill Development Laboratory, be developed to help students learn the skills they need at the times they need them. Let us imagine this Skill Development Laboratory as it might exist in a high school. It is on the top floor, away from noise and traffic, and it occupies a suite of its own. There is a large central space bounded by a dozen alcoves and four small offices. In the central space is an information booth and several rows of desks. At one end of the room are a dozen upholstered armchairs. There seem to be about fifty students and four adults.

We begin to notice details. The alcoves are all different. One of them is enclosed and through the glass door we can see a student standing on a little platform; he seems to be giving a speech. There is one other student sitting at the back of the room. He opens the door, and much to our surprise heads right for us; the speechmaker keeps on talking. Our visitor introduces himself: he is a senior student serving as a speech coach. His client is practicing a presentation for biology. If we have a few minutes to spare, could we come listen? We demur; what do we know about biology?—or speech techniques, for that matter? But this demurral makes us doubly attractive, we are told. A speech is supposed to be clear and intelligible—that's all; and this is not an elocution lesson.

We go in and sit down. The coach suggests that Jack begin in the middle, with that bit about the action of enzymes in the mouth. Jack nods, refers briefly to his notes, and fires away. After five minutes the coach stops him, beckons him to us and we chat. The coach asks us to tell Jack what information we just heard. We stumble a bit, and then repeat our lesson. The coach nods, and asks Jack if we got his points; Jack says we missed the main one. The question then is why? While Jack is thinking this over, the coach fills us in.

We are told that Jack can make a good outline, but that he has a lot of trouble getting across broad ideas. He tends to lose the audience in a wealth of details, he fails to tie these together into any larger principles. This is called a "speech lesson," and it is true that it will help Jack become more confident and overcome his tendency to mumble. But its more important purpose is to give Jack an opportunity to discover his own need to tie description to principle; he is a good observer but seldom draws generalizations from his observations. We were being used to give Jack feedback on this point. The coach also could give feedback in much the same way—just telling Jack what he understood from the speech. In addition, there is a recording machine with a microphone at the back of the space, and Jack can listen to his own talk. The record will be studied by Jack to see if he can identify places at which he could insert a comment or two in order to make the development of the fermentation principle more explicit.

Another boy goes to the alcove labeled "Recording." He speaks briefly to the student technician and then goes into a small sound-proofed booth. He dictates his own "spelling list." The technician then plays the record back to him, and he writes the words. He then goes to one of the desks, goes over his list, checks the words he suspects may be misspelled, and enters the number in a form in his diary. He then looks up the words he questions in the dictionary. Later, he goes to a coach who checks the spelling list rapidly and finds several words misspelled. The student and coach discuss the mis-spelled words, checking the student's pronunciation of them. The coach fills out a new "prescription" for another practise session.

This concludes the lesson. The student leaves his tape and diary at the "materials" alcove. The coach enters some coded symbols on an IBM card; these cards will be analyzed to discover what sort of help was given and the coach's estimate of its effectiveness. From this will come suggestions for bettering the service of the Center and also information to be "fed back" to various teachers about the kinds of difficulties that are sufficiently widespread to justify spending class time on them.

Another "client" has picked up a packet of flash cards which show

German words, and we see him seated at one of the desks busily going through the pack, sorting out the ones he is uncertain about. Then he studies the correct answers which are given on the backs of the cards, shuffles the deck and goes through it again . . . and again. Next he gets out his German book and starts reading, making note of the words he has to look up. A bit later, the student goes to another alcove where the coach is waiting. They discuss the words the student had to look up, and the coach tries to help him distinguish between the words that are "new" and the ones that are derived from stems he already knows. This involves a review of noun cases as well as verb rules. Next time, the student will begin by making another set of flash cards for himself.

Another student is given four social studies reference books and a list of questions. He is busily seated at a desk trying to find the place in the appropriate book where each question is answered. His problem is a lack of proficiency in using a table of contents and an index. His coach will later check his answers against a key, and they will discuss the particular questions that baffled the student. The list of questions, incidentally, was prepared by the teacher. It is a long list, and the teacher has checked for this student the ones she thinks will be most profitable for him to practice with.

Still another student has shaken a dozen slips of paper out of an envelope. He is now concentrating on trying to piece them together, as if they were some sort of puzzle. Well, for him, they are! These slips of paper were prepared by his coach last time; each shows one step in the proof of a theorem in geometry, and the student's task is to assemble them in the proper order. Having done that, he will write down the reason for each step. He will then check his work against the book, enter his score in the diary, and study his mistakes. At this point he will be ready for the coach.

We note that these students are imperiled to different degrees. Some of them are severely handicapped—they are "remedial cases." Others are getting along all right, but want to do better—for example, to develop a foreign language vocabulary or to improve their skill in writing. The chances are good that the remedial cases were referred to the Center by a counselor, who in turn had been alerted by a teacher. The student may have been the subject of a case conference, participated in by his teachers, his counselor, and one of the Center's supervisors. He may be at the laboratory during class time, if his peril is great enough.

Four faculty members supervise the operation of the center. The supervisors have somewhat different responsibilities, and they work as a team. One of them is responsible for maintaining communication between the Center, student government, counselors, teachers, and the administration. He is also responsible for staff self-training within the laboratory. A second supervisor is highly trained for remedial work in all phases of the language arts. A third one is the science-math specialist. A fourth one may have special ingenuity at devising new procedures, involving the use of recorders, learning machines, games, puzzles, and apparatus of all sorts. All the supervisors must be highly competent counselors. I can see real advantages in having three of the supervisors be regular teachers who do a tour of duty in the Center every five years or so.

I have one closing point. While writing this little fantasy, I have been trying in my mind to distinguish "remedial" students from the others, and I find this almost impossible. All the students need diagnostic help, individual attention, and the rest. If "remedial" means anything, it is an arbitrary thing given by comparing test scores of the individual with some arbitrary "norm." But the laboratory is not concerned with arbitrary definitions. It will work with anyone, no matter what his level of initial competence, who feels a need—for whatever reason—to improve his productions or his proficiency.

NOTES

1. Helen Robinson, "Personality and Reading," Chapter in Arthur Traxler (ed.), *Modern Educational Problems* (Washington, D.C.: American Council on Education, 1953), pp. 87-97.
2. Harold Dunkel, "A Few Facts about Foreign Language Study," *Elementary School Journal,* LIX, No. 1 (October 1958), 31-34.
3. John Dewey, *School and Society* (Chicago: University of Chicago Press, 1899), p. 125.

11

Do-It-Yourself:
The Greatest Project

In which we squarely face the fact that schools cannot improve very much by themselves; and that any significant improvement of education is going to require joint action by the school and community. We here spell out what this means, the policies to guide action, the kind of organization required, and the strategy of action-inquiry which develops its targets as it operates. We suggest several major educational changes that are needed and offer them as beginning problems to initiate action and to usher in the cooperative way of school-community life.

The most fascinating question in the world is, How does one thing lead to another? Here we are, standing in the present but this is merely one tiny event in a long series that began with time and will end in the unforeseeable future. Time is a mountain whose peak is the present. The past slopes off one side and the future off the other. Looking in one direction we make explanations; looking in the other, predictions. People then, now, and in time to come will always be on the peak, midway between explanations and predictions; caught in both, both overlapping and each giving its unique flavor to the quest that is life. In looking backward we start with facts and then build an image; in looking forward we build an image and then, through action, make the facts. To the extent that we do both we are able to be wise.

A sequence of events is not reversible. What has happened has happened, and there is no way to undo it. Because actions and men are interdependent, a small change anywhere may lead to a staggering array of changes, only a few of which were foreseen. Actions always seem more reasonable when only their immediate goals are considered. Many things that look immediately attractive as the way out of a difficulty only land us deeper in the mire, a fear which haunts me with respect to the efforts to patch up the schools.

I don't suppose a wife would run off with the chauffeur if she knew that this would cause her husband's favorite huntin' dawg to die. After all, whatever she may feel about her husband, she has nothing against the dog. But little did she know in taking that first little step that the shock would kill her mother-in-law; that the candles around the coffin would set the house on fire; that the sparks would ignite the stable and roast the master's horse; and that his dog would die from eating burnt horse meat.[2] On the other hand, I am not sure she should have called for a conference with her chauffeur, her mother-in-law, her husband, his horse, and Rover. There must be some middle ground between thinking only of the immediate present and thinking of everything imaginable. And, however action is planned, it seems only prudent to have fire extinguishers around, just in case.

In this book I have taken the position that changes, through education and action, are actually brought about by somebody doing something different; that is, acting differently, changing his own functional role, participating in a new way in processes that are already in motion. He may be guiding his new behavior by some new insight about purpose, or some new perception of limitations or opportunities discerned among the conditions. I have made process central because it *is* central; that's what life is. We know the world through participating in it, e.g., experiencing it either directly or vicariously. We change the world by acting differently and encouraging others to act differently; this is what we mean by change. A new organization or a new building are both by-products of processes of change; they did not just spontaneously generate themselves. And the purposes of activity are simply the tendencies inhering in them and translated into statements of where we will be at some future time if our intervention in these processes accords with stated policies.

The second major position of the book is that interrelationships exist among persons, groups, activities, and functions. This is why a change anywhere may lead to further changes in other parts of a system. It is why to make a change in a classroom you may have to change the school; and to change the school you may have to educate the community. Moreover, it is this insight that makes us see that the educational effort of the school is, by itself, simply uninterpretable as anything more than a hurdle race over achievement tests unless relationships are perceived between the experiences of the student in and out of school.

I think it would be useful at this point to read into the record an explicit statement of what we are going to have to deal with in the effort to improve education. Getzels and I pulled this summary out of our reflections on discussions of education by eight social scientists.[5] As you read it, think about some school you know well and try to describe each of the characteristics as it is found in that particular school. This summary will serve its purpose if you finish it with the feeling that there are many angles, many ports of entry into the problem of improving the school.

The school is a social institution.

Like other institutions, it is embedded in a historical, physical, and social environment, which stipulates certain resources and limitations.

It can be conceived as a social system with specific structure and function.

As a social system, it interlocks with other social systems—political, economic, familial—and its structure and function cannot be fully understood without reference to the other systems.

It may, however, also be seen as an entity in its own right, and, as such, it may be conceived as a "society in miniature" with functions that must be carried out, roles that must be filled, regulations that must be followed, and so on.

As a society in miniature, it is inhabited by human beings who have characteristic needs and drives, capacities and interests, aspirations and emotions.

It has an internal structure, with formal and informal organizations, channels of communication, hierarchies of influence, prestige, and authority.

It has a culture, with manifest and latent values, traditions, symbols, and ways of approaching problems; it has, as the anthropologist might say, "a way of life."

It is continually in flux through the maturation and learning of its members, changes in policy and in external demands, variations in inductees, and variations in the nature of the relationship to the other systems.

A change in one part of the system is ultimately reflected in changes in all other parts of the system, and a change in one system is reflected, however tenuously, in all other systems in the society.

It follows that in order to improve itself the school must work with other parts of the community; as a matter of fact the whole definition of education—what is possible, what it is for, and what assumptions are to guide it—is implicit in the way of life of the entire society. If the present Organization Man and Procedures-Their-Own-Justification type of society is maladaptive and headed for nonsurvival, then it behooves all of us to be aware of the trends, and educate ourselves to emphasize better purposes and to discover better ways to achieve them. Education must to some extent stand outside of its own culture and society: it must be able to see what is going on. And, citizens at all levels of age, status, and "background," must debate the issues and, in so doing, both adapt the society to its times and set up the provisions for the education to be given to children. The two cannot be separated.

With regard to the present state of affairs in education, it is a fad to blame everyone and everything for the deficiencies of our educational system. But, if this gives you comfort, then you must also pay the price for that comfort by accepting the implication that if everyone is to blame then everyone must help to improve education. Hence the title for this chapter.

THE BASIC QUESTIONS

I think three questions must be answered during any effort to bring about educational change in any organization. These questions derive from our concepts of what an educational institution is and what its purposes are. The purpose of the questions will be to help us get data to describe the state of affairs in language in such a way that we can begin to identify targets for change. It seems to me that there are three such basic questions which will have to be answered or faced up to sooner or later in any sober effort to improve on educational agency. (You will see that these same questions, with very slight change, could apply equally well to *any* organization, whatever its purpose.)

1. Each person, student or teacher, must somehow adapt his way of life to that of the school or agency. He adapts in his own way by being inspired to work hard, by going passive, by hiding in a clique, by attacking, etc. In the process, if he is a student, he seeks, avoids, resists, or acquiesces in the efforts to educate him. The first question is: What sort of adaptation is each student making to the school? Is it educationally facilitative or destructive? Which of our students are making the most out of their opportunities for learning, which are doing only what has to be done, which are doing little or nothing except under compulsion? Put another way, what I am asking is: To what extent is the school reaching each child, and with what result?

2. Each class begins as a collection of boys and girls and teacher. Each class develops into some sort of group, and the group may be oriented primarily to comfort, pleasing the teacher, engaging in inquiry, covering the ground, passing examinations, having a good time, swapping opinions, being polite and mannerly, and so on. The second question, then, is what is the basic orientation of each class? What purpose seems best to account for its particular set of rules and regulations? What goal of education would best account for the particular ways in which children participate in the classroom? What sort of values seem to govern the classroom as a small society?

3. The school itself, as well as its various parts, exists within a community which makes demands upon it. Different people expect different things from the school and from the various parts of its academic and extracurricular programs. Moreover, the school makes demands on the community for reinforcement of its goals, money, understanding, and so on. Each school, then, must somehow adapt itself to the community, and vice versa. The way it does this is through making decisions about *policies*. These policies attempt to reconcile the demands on teachers and staff that emerge from within the school with the demands on the school from the outside. The question is: How adequate and satisfactory is the means by which the school arrives at its decisions? And, even more simple and fundamental, to what extent and with respect to what things does the faculty engage in truly professional discussion about educational problems they are actually confronted with in their own present operation?

ACTION STRATEGY: SYSTEMS AND GROUPS

These questions have a curious special value: they sum everything up. The fact that we ask them implies our goals quite clearly: We want processes through which students adapt themselves in an educationally facilitative way; we want classes in which inquiry is going on; we want policies of a kind whereby the school maintains an integral and realistic two-way professional relationship to the community.

The nature of a question tells us something about the method of action: that we need data simply to describe the things about the situation that are relevant. Having such a description, along with clear purposes, we may now reflect on the data to see what they "mean" to us; out of such reflections will come the specific goals for immediate action as well as the general image of a long-range program. And with these things defined and on a firm footing, we can now proceed to act, making use of an appropriate combination of personal inquiry, group investigation, and action research.

All this is, I suppose, rather obvious. It is also incomplete. The missing dimension is people. Who is to do what, how are they to be selected and involved, who besides the workers most immediately concerned must be informed about what? We have been continually emphasizing the concept that the school cannot improve itself by itself, that the functioning of the educational *system* rather than the school is the target of change. The practical meaning of these words lies in their influence on the strategy of action. Many action strategies have failed because they did not know what to do about people. The resistance to the idea of the educational system is, I suspect, the result of fear, anxiety, and apprehensions about developing and maintaining relationships with all sorts of people and groups. I do not know any school persons who welcome such an idea, and I attempted in Chapter 4 to describe their predicament, if not sympathize with it outright.

I think the first thing that strikes me about the idea of the educational system is that some systems are manageable and others are not. The most manageable system is a small (in population) school district with one high school, whose geographic borders coincide with the borders of political, cultural, religious and other systems, and which is attended only by youth from within the town. The reason for this is that there is so much interaction among all the systems (educational, political, economic, etc.) that matters get extraordinarily complicated if each system involves an entirely different set of people.

This thinking leads to the concept of the regional school. Within a large city, for example, ideally the boundaries of the high school district would enclose a complete neighborhood, with commercial, political, health, park, and other facilities; and possibly, even, with physical boundaries (such as highways, hills, rivers). Educational control of the high schools in the city as a whole would be decentralized, with a considerably larger number of certain kinds of decisions being made locally. There would be the possibility of setting up a local citizens' education committee, and in all ways organizational life and communication would be vastly easier than in many large cities at present. Moreover, the high school would tend to be a unifying organization within the community, and could contribute to its cohesiveness and stability. The teachers would be expected to live in the community too, and to be citizens as well as instructors.

There are several educational systems that nest within each other. The school is the smallest, and some actions such as scheduling classes, can be considered as internal to the school. For these actions this system is large enough. We could think of the school plus the families of the students as comprising the next larger system, and for some actions, such as reporting progress to parents, this is adequate. Then there might next be the region just described, with all the functions of a modern society going on within its boundaries; and this would be the system involved in actually providing the bulk of the school-directed educational experiences (e.g., Personal Inquiry) to boys and girls. If the school is part of a city system, the entire city comprises the next system, for the entire city will be involved in policy making and support for the school and as the territory in which the students have many experiences. Beyond this, especially for certain legal and support purposes, there is the county, state, and nation.

Thus each of these systems is appropriate and must be considered for some purposes but not for others. And within each of these systems as geographically defined, there are certain people and groups involved directly, and others involved only indirectly or peripherally in each of the functions. By "directly" and "indirectly" I mean also formally and informally; this is also the distinction between delegated and undelegated responsibility and expectations of influence. Having identified the system appropriate for the function we are interested in, we next have to ferret out: (1) the people or groups who carry out the function; (2) those who incidentally affect the function by the way they carry out their business; (3) those whose opinion and informally exerted influence determines what can and cannot be done, and (4) those whose attitudes determine the general climate of optimism or apathy within the system as a whole. Each such category of persons will be involved at different times, for different specific purposes, in different organizational structures, with different means of communication, and with different demands and rewards for participation.

For the most part, one never knows in advance what groups will need to be involved at what time. For this reason, part of the planning of strategy includes "building in" the kinds of procedures that will enable one to get the data he needs to make wise judgments on this score.

We note that action may be within a system or between two systems. Thus the improvement of processes, such as the activity of doing homework, will mostly be within one system composed of the school (teachers and students) plus the parents of the students. The teachers, students, and parents will look at the same data about homework, will contribute their ideas and interpretations, and will share in the same purpose, namely, to arrive at better policies about the use and guidance of homework. These people are involved together because they participate in the same enterprise (getting homework done). The attitudes and behaviors of each affect the success of the other. They are functionally interdependent.

It would be relatively easy to get action, to arrive at new policies (question 3) on the basis of information about how the students adapt to the present demands of homework activities (question 1) and about the influence or contribution homework currently makes to the development of inquiry by the class (question 2). The strategy outlined above could be put into effect rather simply.

Action to change the *conditions* under which processes occur is usually action between two systems. Thus the state of the school budget is an important condition with considerable influence on the several educational processes within the school. To increase the budget requires action between the educational and economic systems (at least). We see that this gets complicated. Thus, consider raising the tax rate, and, for the sake of simplicity, let's imagine that there is an organized group of realtors strongly opposed. We may further assume that the educators (board and administrators) are strongly for the raise. In this situation there is no functional interdependence, no legitimate, inevitable, existing, or necessary contact or relationship between the two groups. There are no channels of communication, no rationale for cooperation, no common cause.

In this situation two kinds of strategies are possible. The first is engagement in a struggle for power, exemplified in a tug of war over the potential tax dollar. Victory is to the group that can muster the most beef at the polls.

The second strategy is to develop a larger system in such a way that some new functional interdependence is perceived to exist between the two groups. This more inclusive system might center around the *common* interest and function of providing the best possible education for the children. I believe that action to improve conditions through one system making demands in terms of its *vested* interests on another system is likely to be unsuccessful. For success, action must shift to the development of common *purpose* shared within a larger system and then voluntarily implemented by each system (economic, educational, etc.) in whatever ways are legitimately comprehended within its basic function. In simple English, the only sound way for a school to solve its financial problems is by working with other groups to develop a long-range set of community goals for education; then, through some kind of community council, the school system helps each group to discover how to participate with its own special skills and activities in the movement toward the goals. Conditions cannot be successfully changed by one system making demands upon or threats against another; but conditions are changed as a by-product of the way a system is operated as it adapts its legitimate functions to new purposes.

I have referred to the common goal in the community as "to develop the best possible education for our children." This is at least an improvement over the vested interest of the educator "to maintain our schools," for this goal is barely distinguishable from the strictly bureaucratic goal "to maintain our group of educators." My own experience in the reconstruction of my community suggests that even the broad educational goal may well be too narrow. An even better goal is "to improve our community," for such a goal legitimizes a wider range of possible meanings invested in improving education. The outstanding illustration of this point is that our businessmen have learned that the reason we must have the best possible schools is to hold families in the neighborhood. They believe that bad schools create a strong pressure to drive families elsewhere. Through this perception, they connect good schools to stable communities; and they connect this to the maintenance of real values, which in turn is of central importance to their conduct of business. The value of the stable community was made explicit in relation to the flight to the suburbs; once explicit in this connection, the real estate men were able to realize the effect on the community of certain off-beat panic-inspiring practices, and to take steps to discipline the functioning of their own group. Thus the goal of better education was transmuted to the larger goal of the better community; and this larger goal enabled a variety of groups both to accept the educational goal and at the same time voluntarily improve some of their own practices within the domain of their traditional functions. The Superintendent of Schools in our great city could hardly believe his eyes and ears the day a delegation of our community's most prominent businessmen came to his office to request the floating of a bond issue to improve the city's schools![1]

It seems to me the inference is quite unmistakable: the improvement and maintenance of education is one aspect of the improvement and maintenance of a decent community, and a great deal of effort from otherwise "difficult" groups can be released into educational improvement if they can see the connection to the broader community goal with which their own functions are obviously connected. This is the reason for proposing a citizens' advisory council in each educational "region"; we may now add that this committee will function best to improve the schools if it concerns itself with all aspects of the community's welfare.

POTENTIALS FOR ACTION

It is easier to get action in some organizations and communities than in others. With respect to citizen action in block groups, Sarchet[4] found the one important condition is the degree of homogeneity of social position, class, and housing. Even before they have started to flock together, we tend to identify most readily with people whose upbringing and way of life are most like ours; we trust these people more, and are more open to communication and response. It doesn't take much of an incident to enable such people to strike up a conversation with each other. The similarity is social—manners, morals, language patterns, common experiences; it is not temperamental. They have shared enough of the same things in life to be able to understand each other, but they do not necessarily react to these shared things in the same way. The overlap, as Rapaport[3] puts it, is linguistic (same words for same objects) and semantic (enough common experience that meanings can be communicated); but persons holding these things in common may vary in their likes and dislikes, their tendencies toward optimism or pessimism, the things they have faith in or distrust, their ways of reacting to stress, and so on. The fact that they do react differently is the source of much of a group's drive and, eventually, its wisdom.

People may be quite similar socially and have a stake in the community and yet not realize it. Since we behave in terms of what we think the world is like, and since we are more confident of our thoughts if we know that others see things the same way, the extent to which perceptions are known to be shared clearly makes a difference. Perceptions are more likely to be shared if people already are in communication with each other, and this has led some community organizers to place stress on the prior existence of organized groups. Our own experience suggests that the existence of organized groups may or not make much difference in the potential for action. In the first place, organized groups do not necessarily talk about things that are important to share, such as perceptions of newcomers, problems, and bad conditions in the neighborhood. In the second place, even if they share perceptions that matter, they may also develop and share a common attitude of apathy or discouragement. Any school administrator who starts action by organizing the faculty into committees will know what I am talking about.

One of the important problems for action people is simply to know what kind of sociological information they need to have at each point; another problem is how to get it. There are four ways to get the information, and I commend them all to a principal or superintendent. First, he can accumulate it as he talks with people and as they reveal their friendships, biases, values, and perceptions; second, he can seek people who know, such as health nurses, credit organizations, social workers, politicians; third, he can consult members of various groups, either in a board or informally; fourth, he can look within his own school for teachers and parents who may have firsthand acquaintance with parts of the community, or who, failing this, can give him entree to others who do. I think a very good tip would be to jot down on a map of the community the names of persons one discovers, over time, to be able and willing informants.

Information getting is a big job. It is also a job that can be divided up. The principal or superintendent who tries to do it all himself either does not trust anyone else or is a glutton for work. If he doesn't trust anyone else, any action whose success depends on voluntary cooperation will fail. If he is a glutton for work, that's his business—I suppose—and I will only point out that he is passing up the opportunity to further the training and development of competence in his own staff and of potential citizen leaders. Yet if he doesn't get out in the field himself, how is he going to be able to know what he is talking about?

What we see, then, is that a certain amount of personal inquiry by the principal is probably desirable. On the basis of this, he then forms and trains an information-getting group, in this case probably composed of teachers, parents identified in the PTA, and if necessary, particular informants from other parts of the community not well known by the others. With this group, he conducts a group investigation (Chapter 8) to get the facts and at the same time to test the possibilities of several different courses of action. The data thus obtained can then be used to justify proposals or to confront others and thus stimulate them to come up with proposals. The proposals can be to do something or to get additional data of another sort or from additional people.

The principal who has got the message about dividing the work may be tempted to go the whole way and unload the entire job on someone else. One typical pattern is to go before the faculty, present a somewhat rambling statement ending with the need to have a committee look into "this." I will lower the veil on the various ways by which the committee gets appointed, and will merely point out that several months later there may or may not be another report to tuck away and forget. There is a principle governing these things: Work cannot be delegated until its purposes and first steps have been explored together, and then it should be delegated to the persons who, at this juncture, are competent and motivated to do it. If there are no such persons, then the action will fail; what is needed is further information, more discussion, and, possibly, expert assistance to help the group formulate the problem in terms that have meaning for itself.

THE SKELETON NETWORK

We must seek some sort of organizational framework that lies somewhere between ad hoc committees surrounded by disorganization, on the one hand, and a rigidly structured bureaucratic "official" table of organization on the other. The desired network would always be standing by, would be well enough defined that every individual in the community and school would know where to go with suggestions and complaints, would be self-maintaining, and would be able in an orderly way to get action started, supervised, and assessed. I shall call this the skeleton framework for action. The skeleton organization in times of quiescence is a communications network. It serves as an information clearinghouse and switchboard for routing messages to the appropriate quarters. It plans and conducts occasional meetings for reporting, two-way conversation, and assessment of operations by those concerned in them. An example of a skeleton organization is a PTA, run by a permanent steering committee with the help of a couple of parents chosen from each grade level; a school faculty in which a program committee assesses faculty interests and plans a half-day workshop each semester; a citizen organization whose board of directors stages annual area-wide mass meetings to initiate or continue discussion of operations and issues. This communication function is necessitated by two considerations: first, that many people not directly involved in operations are nevertheless affected by them, and some minimum level of cooperation, enablement, and feedback is required to keep operations responsive to its larger clientele; and second, in any far-flung operation, the workers tend to be specialists who do not really see the "whole picture" and who therefore fail to understand the full significance of their work. They are also deprived of the possibility of contributing valuable perceptions and "angles" of their own to the improvement of operations.

For educational action, limited skeleton networks are needed within the student body, within the faculty, among the parents (possibly in each grade), and within each of the functional systems (religious, economic, political, etc.) in the community. In these larger systems, the stand-by steering committee might well be a subcommittee within a professional association. Although not involved directly as teachers or students, the religious, business, trades, scientific and other systems are interdependent with education for training, interpretation, and recruitment of their own future functionaries.

Moving another step beyond the separate system-based skeletons, we see a need for an over-all community Citizens Education Council, composed of broad-gauge individuals whose concern is for the whole state of education throughout the community, and who see education not merely as what goes on in schools but as the function through which society maintains itself and, ultimately, the human species. In this council the Superintendent of Schools is present as a member or, possibly, consultant. The other members, being wise and clear-headed citizens, will also probably be prominent in their own spheres; which in turn means they will probably be members of the steering committee within their respective systems. That being the case, the Education Council will have among its membership full knowledge of the education-relevant thinking in each system, plus the positions and skills needed to insure good communication with the outlying steering committees.

You may wonder why I describe these members of the Council in such a devious way. Wouldn't it be easier to say that each member *represents* the system he comes from? The answer is that it would indeed be easier, and maybe that is why most such councils are in fact composed of official representatives. But that is also the reason why many councils are do-nothing ineffective groups: the official representative is trapped in a conflict of loyalty between the Council and the group he represents. He is not free to think about the Council's problems directly; he always has the hidden motive of protecting his own group, appearing to support its policies, and so on.

The Council of "concerned citizens" takes responsibility when needed for communication across systems. I say "when needed" because the group of parents, for example, lives in all the systems and no group of living people exists that does not cut across at least social, political, and economic systems. The role needed from the Council in cross-system communication will, I think, be rather formal.

The Council will have no periods of quiescence. It will be an investigating group and a steering committee for action; and its primary method of action will be through stirring up and coordinating efforts within the various systems. The Council will need funds of its own and possibly an executive secretary; and it will call in consultants and experts from time to time. It will be the body responsible, through subcommittees and other means, for formulating, revising, and disseminating the community's long-range plans for educational improvement.

PROGRAMS FOR SCHOOL IMPROVEMENT

Inquiry in classrooms

You have probably noticed that I think very well of inquiry, so let us speculate about how a school might go about having some. We note, first, that to achieve inquiry will mean changing the way teachers teach, and this, then, is the target for change. Moreover, teachers do not change their way of teaching unless they want to, have the opportunity, and are helped to find the necessary resources to maintain the new methods. The process required will be that of self-training, and it will go on within the group of teachers. The steering committee will be composed of teachers.

This committee will need to act on behalf of the teachers, and to do this it will have to have a means of easy communication with them. I shall assume faculty meetings run by the steering committee are possible. Through open discussion in the faculty, a beginning analysis can be made of problems to be solved. They will need to develop some tentative definition of inquiry, and the means to arrive at this will be through (a) demonstrating and analyzing classroom teaching methods to isolate and identify the components of inquiry; (b) reading books and consulting reports; (c) talking with scholars in their various fields to get guidance in formulating the theme of inquiry in each knowledge discipline (e.g., in history, inquiry is the "cross-examination of testimony by doubt"; in chemistry it is the "discovery and application of the processes of material change through the control of energy"; in social studies it is "the analysis of functional interdependence and the control of expectation through agreement," and so on).

The committee will keep track of the various investigations being conducted by voluntary groups of faculty members, and will provide the forum for presentation, discussion, and deliberation on the experiences and tentative formulations of these groups. The committee will also attempt to analyze the obstacles to inquiry that are uncovered by the studies of the teachers—and will discuss with the principal how action can be taken to reduce the barriers.[6]

They will discover that present examinations do not measure growth in ability to inquire, and this will call for the invention of new tests. Then it will be necessary to work with the PTA or other organization of parents to acquaint them with the new methods of evaluating achievement. If the faculty decides that present textbooks are unsuitable and that they need a shelf of reference books instead, this will involve the economic system and will require help from the school budget; or it might be the occasion for enlisting the interest of nearby universities who could lend some materials; or of any one of a number of foundations, associations, and state or federal offices that would provide the funds.

The school board could attempt to find practice teachers and professors who could team up with selected teachers to experiment with methods of inquiring in particular subjects. Hiring policies could be altered to strengthen the faculty's own resources and aptitudes.

The basic image of action is in this case simple, however elaborated or proliferated it may become: direction by a coordinating and steering group of teachers, backed to the hilt by the administration, and encouraged to identify manageable investigations of all sorts that teachers can undertake in the school, in the community, and in summer workshops. Further, there would be the periodic exchange of information among the faculty, and the administration would be alert to make such changes as would reinforce new methods as they were developed. The principal, with proper high-level clearance, would feel free to involve any other group in the project, always exploring with such groups the common interest that would legitimize his demands. The Citizens Education Council would be informed of progress from time to time, and would interpret to the community the significance of the investigation in whatever way it felt was appropriate.

Broadening the curriculum

The notion that the entire community could be a laboratory for study and action has cropped up in our discussions of personal inquiry, group investigation, and action research. Unlike the development of inquiry which is after all a professional matter for the present teaching staff, the extension of learning situations into the community will call for the help, as adjunct teachers, of many citizens. Citizens serving as on-location supervisors and experts must modify their own functional roles in order to make room for the students, and this means that plans will have to be worrked out cooperatively with groups in the various functional systems. Thus I can visualize a subgroup of the regional businessmen's association exploring the sorts opportunities that could be opened up in businesses. I can imagine the planning of the first experience jointly by a class, the manager of a firm, and the teacher; followed by the experience of the class in the firm; reading and study by the class to assist them in interpreting and finding universals in their experience; and reporting of findings at a session attended by several businessmen. And I can see a meeting of the business association in which the experience is discussed, and in which the members begin to imagine all sorts of roles students could take in the businesses to the mutual educational and economic advantage of all.

On a somewhat grander scale, one might imagine the Educational Council sponsoring mass meetings in order to begin public discussion of the possibility of supervised educational experience in the community; recruiting from such meetings a number of adults to become a seminar for the purpose of clarifying what they conceive to be the possible educational contribution to be made by business houses, churches, and other functional agencies; presenting their ideas to professional associations; and finally setting up joint teacher-citizen study committees to make plans in each course for the extension of the curriculum.

Teachable classes

The idea that each teacher would do a better job if he had a congenial and manageable class seems rather obvious. And the notion that a teachable class for one teacher might not be the same as a teachable class for another teacher using somewhat different methods seems reasonable, too. The notion that the teachers themselves, with suitable help, may be able to define the kinds of students with whom they are most and least successful could provide the basis for an action program that might very much improve education.

The ubiquitous teacher steering committee might, after discussion with the faculty, organize the following plan:

1. Each teacher will pay special attention to his classes during March, and, primarily through observations, will attempt to identify the students who seem to be getting most and least out of his class—regardless of marks on "achievement" tests.

2. Each teacher will discuss his selections with other teachers who also have the same students in their classes, and this group will attempt to describe what qualities, aptitudes, or traits seem to distinguish between the two sorts of students. On the basis of a series of "diagnostic conferences," the teachers will write a description of the "kind of student to give to Mr. Brown," and to each of the other teachers of the subject.

3. These descriptions will be given to the teachers in the grade below, and they will attempt to select from their knowledge of their classes the students best fitting the specifications for each teacher.

4. The students thus selected for the next year's classes will be checked by the counselors and advisers to see if there are any combinations that ought to be separated, or friends who ought to be placed together, or other special circumstances that ought to be taken into account.

5. The administration will make every effort to schedule the classes according to the selections made by the teachers.[7]

Over time, the faculty will, I expect, find that the experience of studying their own students is indeed useful; and the discussions of the students who should be assigned to each teacher will be rather revealing. This sort of discussion could lead into the problem of how best to teach given "types" of students, the swapping of experiences, and, ultimately, the setting up of classes in which different methods had been developed to be most suitable for defined categories of students.

Community reinforcement

The community that values and celebrates education will have an easier time improving the schools. I would like to see the Citizens' Education Council set up an academic festival committee to plan a Saturday afternoon of mathematics. The public would be invited, and there would be demonstrations and contests of mathematical skills by mathematics classes from third grade through high school. Businesses, laboratories, and bureaus could show some of the ways (preferably dramatic) they use mathematics for forecasting, stock-taking, operations control, etc. A prominent mathematician could be invited to discuss the present developments and opportunities in the field. There could be exhibits of puzzles, perspective drawings, and other products of the children.

This sort of thing would work best on a regional basis, and I should think that three festivals a year, each built around one area of study, could gradually have a significant influence on the academic climate of the community.

Also on a regional basis, I think it would be rather interesting to see what could be done with a variety of avocational groups composed of selected adults and youth. Possibilities include drama, painting, sculpture, dance, photography, TV, theater, cabinetmaking, fly-tying, boatbuilding, orchestra, movie-making, city planning, gardening, reading circles, and even "adult education" classes. Each group would be run by a committee of adults and high school students. Students eligible for such participation would be selected by teachers, who would also give special coaching. Adults would also have to prove their eligibility.

One page per week in the local newspaper could be planned and written by the students. It should have pictures, and keep the public informed of exciting inquiries conducted by the students in the school and community.

Reference has already been made to annual mass meetings to enable the community to review progress and consider next steps. Such discussion will be most meaningful when projected against a long-range developmental program for school improvement. The attitude toward money at such meetings should not be that the schools need and want some large amount to cover a hodge-podge of expense but rather that to carry the program forward through its logical steps will require a specified amount of money. It is the program that requires the money, not the schools. I would even push this point further: I'd like the school budget to be incorporated in the budget of the Citizens' Education Council, which would present the budget for the educational efforts throughout the community (including family and adult education). The school budget would be simply a part of the total and its purpose would be to enable the school to carry out its part of the agreed-upon educational development.

Mention has also been made in passing of the notion of maintaining in the school a file of useful citizens. I would now generalize this point by saying that the human resources of communities are very badly utilized for education. In the community there are experts in all branches of knowledge dealt with in schools, and the more of these people help, the higher the community's regard will be for the educational program. Specially qualified citizens can help with curriculum, advice and consultation to students, semiskilled manpower in classes, etc.

I would also like to see teachers being utilized in inquiries going on in business, scientific planning, and other functions of the community. The major reason, of course, is to help them learn more about the use of their knowledge in inquiry. But this could also be a highly desirable way to give them working relationships with adults within the productive activities of the community. Further, as a practical matter, many teachers do need part-time and summer jobs and are going to seek them. As long as this is true, the community might as well make a virtue of the necessity, and help them find work that will contribute to their teaching competence. I also think that a good many teachers have skills and wisdom to contribute to many enterprises outside the school, and there would be mutual advantage to some of them serving as consultants to local enterprises.

The society of youth

Anything to improve the sense of belongingness and place of youth in the community will lighten the task of the schools as well as enable youth to get more out of experience in schools.

I therefore propose that an adult council be formed to assist youth to organize their own society, and to make readily available to youth a large number of consultant-experts from all the functional systems of the community. These adults would have three responsibilities: (a) to assist the students to think maturely, wisely, and constructively about their own projects and organization; (b) to develop with them adult cooperation in community projects and interests, such as maintenance of civic services, community surveys of traffic, housing, street lighting, sidewalks, recreational facilities, etc.; and (c) to help particular boys and girls find work and service experience which may be especially meaningful at a particular stage of their development. This latter proposal has already been discussed as Personal

Inquiry sponsored by the schools. But there is really no reason why the schools are necessarily the best agents to run that program, and the joint responsibility could be divided between school and community council in any way that seems realistic.

THE SPIRIT OF ACTION

The point of action is partly in "what" it achieves and partly in "how" it goes about achieving it. The "what" is conceptualized as models or images of the long-range desirable and the short-range possible. The "how" is the way one participates or intervenes in the affairs to be changed, and one is already making changes as soon as he intervenes in some new way.

Books like this can help one become clearer in his own mind about models he has or can construct to work toward. Books can indicate some of the kinds of acts that one will probably have to contend with. Books can swap experiences from other situations both to demonstrate that action is possible and to stimulate someone else's interest or commitment to do something himself.

Books cannot tell anyone what to do. All the advice in the world —even good advice—can represent only half or less of the thoughts that the practitioner must consider. The other half arises from the actual local scene, and many of the local facts cannot be discovered except as action is started. The best action will be continually guided by the effort to see relationships—past, present, and possible—between local descriptive information and conceptual dynamic models. In trying to ferret out or develop these relationships, one will inevitably change his models and become aware of hitherto unnoticed facts. The process of seeking these relationships is itself the process of inquiry.

Action is the operational aspect of inquiry. Inquiry is what an inquiring mind does, and right action is action which furthers, widens, and deepens the inquiry. Action inquiry cannot fail because its success is determined by its mode, not its by-products. The only sense in which failure is possible is that specific expectations may not materialize on schedule. In this case the failure is in the prediction which is seen to be inaccurate, rather than in the action. The tension and anxiety in action programs come from equating success to specific anticipated by-products, and many a man who would draw back in horror at the principle that "the end justifies the means" will, in his own life, judge that action was good if the desired ends arrive punctually. This is just as wrong as its converse, that action is bad if the desired ends take longer to achieve—or are impossible to achieve.

The criterion of good, effective, proper, and appropriate action is that the motivating spirit is the spirit of inquiry. In this spirit, conflicting ideas can be tolerated and turned into a source of strength; doubts and resistances can be diagnosed to throw light on new factors and new perceptions of what the "real" problems are; "personal" concerns and "ulterior" motives can be re-interpreted with the individual in such a way that he can satisfy his needs better by working with the program he is helping to define. The enemy or target of action is, to the inquirer, the objectively defined circumstances and conditions to be changed. The target of change is the way things are done and the way the action roles are organized and coordinated. Action is best when it is guided by purposes, and this means it is most effective when each actor, each person in the situation understands his specific purposes and legitimizes them by open discussion throughout the organization. Under these conditions the effort of each person to achieve his own purposes becomes identical with the taking of action by the organization. The organizational legitimization of individual striving makes individual striving possible in the first place and provides the *modus vivendi* of social action. It is the key concept in "democracy," is a fundamental requirement for autonomy, and it shifts the organizational climate and concern from bureaucratic maintenance to professionally oriented inquiry.

NOTES

1. Julia Abrahamson, *op. cit.*
2. Columbia Phonograph Record entitled "No News," *circa* 1923.
3. Anatol Rapaport, *Operational Philosophy* (New York: Harper & Brothers, 1954), p. 158.
4. Bettie B. Sarchet, *Block Groups and Community Change.* (University of Chicago: Human Dynamics Laboratory. July 1955, p. 126 (planographed).
5. Herbert A. Thelen and J. W. Getzels, "The Social Sciences: Conceptual Framework for Education," *School Review*, LXV, No. 3 (Autumn 1957), 339-355.
6. Herbert A. Thelen, *Dynamics of Groups at Work* (Chicago: University of

Chicago Press, 1954). Chapter 3 spells out in detail the design and principles for faculty self-training.

7. Proposal emerging from Grouping Research, U.S. Office of Education, Co-operative Research Project: "Development of Educational Methods for Different Types of Students." University of Chicago, Herbert A. Thelen. *Op. cit.*, Chapter 8.

Epilogue:
Destiny

The writing of this book has been a challenging engagement in inquiry. The inquiry has sought meaning in the domain where private personal experience interacts with social public problems, and, in trying to bring these two elements together, my understanding of both has been considerably enriched. This book is my attempt to share with you some of these understandings, communicated as the record of thoughts, facts, fantasies, and purposes I have become aware of in my quest.

This book has been one long test of the assertion I began with, that "As judged by what could be done if we were to understand and apply modern knowledge to educational problems, all our schools are obsolescent." We accept rather too readily, I think, the existence of "the fifty-year lag of education behind the social sciences." I hope that my effort to delineate the lag at all levels from quasi-philosophical theory to specific classroom procedures will make the lag a little harder to live with. In short, I'd like to see some action.

THE TRAP

The times when action is most difficult are probably the times when it is most needed, for the hardest times are times of doubt, ambivalence, and conflict. These characteristics are greatest when opposing forces are strongest, when one is caught in a powerful squeeze and no longer has any room in which to maneuver. In a society whose state of affairs is probably best symbolized by the cold war, all parts of life lose some of their degrees of freedom. There is no new idea, no bold stroke, no creative insight, no purpose that can lead us out of bondage. So we pour our energy into defending and maintaining what we have; and when what we have as a nation is a formula for raising the standard of living to unimaginable heights, it is easy to drift along, uneasily perhaps, but sleepily in our fools' paradise.

Education is in shackles. It is caught in a squeeze of incredible strength. The explosion of population creates such pressure that some schools consider themselves lucky to be able merely to house the boys and girls. The mobility of the population, in search of better living, means that some schools have a 300 per cent turnover of pupils within a single school year. These two factors alone—to say nothing of the shortage of teachers, would be sufficient to account for the present desperate search for short cuts, for processing machinery, for factory methods. And the easiest short cut is to return to a simpler concept of an education with cut-and-dried lessons, packaged and inviolable subject matter, routines of all sorts, centralized authority and restriction to the most routine objective of assimilating "subject matter." Institutionalization of procedures, with the help of all the gimmicks we can find, has come a long way, and I see little indication that it won't go further. The quest is for "practices that work," for the devices that "have proven to be successful." And we know what we mean by success: getting good marks in courses of study appropriate to mental ability. Our institutionalized system is complete: we even think we know what place each individual should have in society; we know to what he should aspire, and we feel outraged when a fair percentage of the students somehow don't have enough sense to act that way. But we manfully shoulder the blame because boys and girls are our responsibility, and then we make our diagnosis: All that's wrong with the educational machine is that it is *inefficient;* the problem is one of means, not ends. And the more efficient the means become, the tighter the bonds are woven; there is no longer to be room for error; and when, finally, there is no room for error there is also no room for insight and discovery.

But the quest for efficiency is itself inefficient, for something human and intuitive cannot allow us to give wholehearted commitment to such a goal. We may seem to act one way, but we call our action by other names. Thus the completely prepackaged set of lessons prepared by national experts for one particular high school subject, and designed to be as teacher-proof as possible, is represented as an aid to "critical thinking." The development of teaching machines in which the only possible way of differentiating among pupils is to let some take longer than others, prevents "failure" and therefore maintains and builds "motivation," thus "strengthening the student's educational purposes." Our nation-wide examination system for college entrance, whose effect may well be to stamp out practically every dimension of freedom for teachers, is labeled an effort to salvage and "develop talented boys and girls."

The way out of this sort of confusion and uneasiness is to return to a sense of high purpose. In the old days this could be done through a comparatively simple process of rededication and inspiration; and it worked because we had faith in the instrumental dynamics of redemption and retribution. These processes, enveloped in a religious and ethical mystique, had a kind of validity that could not be questioned. They provided the operational definition of justice, and they brought forgiveness, and set things right. They had the sanction of divine authority, and the highest purpose of Man was to approach the state of godliness.

These processes no longer have the old magic. We have observed too much, experienced too much, analyzed too much. We have cursed too often and not been struck by lightning; nations have laid each other waste and a few years later found themselves allies; the old ways of sinning have been found excusable and they therefore no longer have the expected consequences. We no longer know what to expect, and we have therefore lost the capability of action. We have, through science, almost lost our faith-giving "superstitious" processes that gave life coherence and a rationale for striving. In short, our old purposes have all but disappeared and we have not found new ones. And so we have fallen back on whatever rituals and procedures are clear cut and accomplishable.

ORGANIZATION

The thing that makes procedures clear cut and accomplishable is their anchorage in a fractionated social organization. The two are part and parcel of the same thing.

Society and with it the power of the organization was undoubtedly the first most important of all Man's inventions. Aside from the fact that it made survival of the species possible, it also opened the door to the development of civilization, with its arts of commerce, science and technology, all of which required concerted and coordinated effort. The burning question for men confronted with a problem is "How shall we organize?" and men had to be organized before even that question could be raised and discussed.

Organization is a product of groups of men; but action is always something individuals do. They act within organizational expectations, of course, yet each man must find his own way of acting to carry out these expectations. Action and process, because they are part of life, always reserve to themselves a private corner, a unique energy system, a human response. Organization, however, is explicit and public, defined, perceived in common, and for the common good. Maintenance of the social order through organization is a goal which is necessary, has face validity, is explicit, and can, in all its parts, be legislated and modified. The individual survives, then, through membership in the group. But the sense of redemption and retribution meaningful to the person, loses its meaning when applied to the member of a group. If the group shares ideas and experiences, it also shares guilt and anxiety, and through this sharing removes it from the individual. The argument of *mea culpa,* as worked out in organizational life, practically finished off the Protestant ethic.

The idea of organization, which is public and explicable, has replaced the idea of process, which is private and to some extent hidden in the wellsprings of the human mystery. But this is also the replacement of the fact by its symbol; it is the grand synecdoche. We seek the symbols of success rather than successful action; the pattern of traits of an educated man (critical thinking, social attitudes, broad interests, health habits, etc.) rather than the capability of acting like an educated man; the organized findings of science rather than the process of inquiry which is its essence. Our high standard of living and immense industrial productivity do not bespeak a primary interest in the productive goal, but rather in the maintenance of an organization that has to produce in order to survive. The meaning of action is to maintain the organization; and the justification of organization is the procedures it maintains. The meaning of action to achieve purposes held to be valuable as ends has well-nigh disappeared. The watchword at international, national, community, and even personal levels has become "maintenance."

If science has destroyed the old superstitions it has also entrenched the concept of organization. Organization did not just take over by default when the moral ethic was weakened. The same processes of science produced both results simultaneously. Through science organization suddenly assumed its full power and stature, for with scientific specialization and coordination all things appeared possible. And organization changed from a necessity (to be minimized) to a virtue (to be dominant).

THE HIDDEN PURPOSE

Organizational life requires division of effort. We have divided science into basic science and technology; pure science gets the facts and technology uses them. Management sets up the plant, and workers operate it. Education teaches children the facts and then, as adults, they use the facts. The scientist sets up hypotheses and his assistants test them. The individual has fantasies, speculations, and opinions, but the group decides whether they are "objective." The practitioner, genius, and intuitive pre-scientist find out what the world is like, but the theorist makes the ideas respectable—by organizing them. We also have, I may add, the people who know and lead and decide and the rest who follow.

We have made hard and fast divisions between thinking and doing, creating and applying, planning and acting, preparing and fulfilling. The age of reason, the development of science, the domination of organization, and the simple increase in density of the human population have interacted among each other to create these divisions. But these divisions have made modern life purposeless. For as long as we maintain the division we shall never have to find an organizing principle to integrate the parts. The organizing principle we have thus succeeded in avoiding is *purpose*. Thus, by one of those odd paradoxes that frequently represent the highest wisdom, the hidden purpose of modern society is to avoid the necessity for purposes. Since the practical importance of purpose is to enable us to see how to recognize and choose among alternatives, the practical consequence of avoiding purposes is avoidance of the necessity for choosing, and with this, of course, the flight from freedom, for freedom without choice is impossible.

We are caught at all levels, the person, the group, the society, in a trap all of whose expectations and procedures are tightly bound up with all other expectations and procedures. We find it hard to recognize the trap because it is not static; it is more like a machine that witlessly churns. The input to the machine is people and resources, and its output is more possessions and realignments of groups at all levels depending on who has the technological upper hand at the moment (like the game of Monopoly), and ever fewer degrees of freedom for everybody. In our commendable effort to reduce material inequalities among men we are also reducing the right to be unequal in other ways: attitudinal, intellectual, expressive. We don't want to rock the societal boat with internal conflict and dissension, not realizing that stability in society is a dynamic thing, a moving "steady state" based on continuously facing up to conflict and resolving it in the directions of consciously held values. Our effort to avoid dissension has kept us from developing the processes through which dissension can be handled intelligently, and, since in fact dissension cannot be avoided, the net result is that, once started, it runs wild. People get sucked in, and sooner or later, what started out as a routine struggle by the leaders of the steelworkers' union (let us say) to maintain their power within their own organization, becomes a symbolic and actual struggle over rights of industry, labor, and government; and, as this goes on there finally emerges the problem of national economic survival in the face of competition from across the seas. Or, if you want another example, consider the consequences of our avoidance of being involved in dissension with Japan when she invaded Manchukuo, and with Italy when she took Ethiopia.

Thus the weakening of a social dynamic guided by purpose and thus able to deal with inevitable dissensions is moving us to a sort of thermodynamic societal suicide, with no potentials for the generation and flow of insights, and with uncontrolled material processes rapidly getting the upper hand and, ultimately, extinguishing the species.

THE HUMAN QEST

There is, however, a counterdynamic, however shaky its condition at the moment, and possible salvation will be through the strengthening of it.

This counterdynamic is the process of inquiry: inquiry in all affairs of men and in the development of the capacity for inquiry throughout all educational experiences. Oddly enough, the idea of inquiry is strongly associated with modern science, even though the actual significance of science has been to reduce the freedom of inquiry. The period of history that seems to have been most oriented to inquiry (within a particular group of citizens) was the so-called Golden Age of Greece—which is not generally thought of as "scientific," even though historians of science usually find some ideas from this period which seem to anticipate many important scientific concepts. I should say that inquiry can go on without what we call science, but science cannot succeed without inquiry.

The way in which science has contributed to our present bondage is through our misinterpretation of the meaning of science. We have seized and exploited its findings, very much like a glutton with a credit card in a super-delicatessen. Like the glutton, we gorge ourselves on scientific findings and reify them as *the* goal of science.

Scientists themselves have been dazzled by findings, and have more often than not (especially before Hiroshima) thought that finding out things is the purpose rather than merely the by-product of science. The usefulness of findings for raising the standard of living—the pragmatic test of validity—has blinded us to the far more significant fact of the scientific quest, of the development of the method of inquiry. Findings are science's short-range benefits, but the method of inquiry is its long-range value. I have said that the invention of organization was Man's first most important achievement; I now add that the development of inquiry will be his second. Both of these inventions change the species and are necessary for its survival. But both must become a part of the nature of Man himself, not just given house room in certain groups. Organization is by now a part of every man, but inquiry is not. The significant product of science and education will be the incorporation within the human animal of the capability and habit of inquiry.

To bring this about requires an understanding of the universal existence of the human quest in all parts of life. It requires the recognition that science is a product of men, and that what we can understand and learn from the personal experience of scientists may be science's grandest contribution. What we call science is only the situation in which inquiry is easiest to demonstrate, explicate, and study. The engagement in scientific pursuits is only a role that some people play; but the assimilation of the discipline of inquiry in all areas of life is the integration of the scientific function, through education, within the whole society. Just as theological study and interpretation constructed the moral and ethical code on which we used to depend, so scientific and educational study is needed to construct the disciplines of interdependent living and of the individual pursuit of freedom. The specialized and technical study of the theologian was assimilated as the religious way of life of the people. In the same way, the engagement in specialized and technical inquiry by the scientist must be assimilated in the civilized and inquiring way of life of man.

The condition of assimilation is interdependence, which is the ultimate *raison d'être* for organization. The process of assimilation is the quest of the individual for integration among his formal and informal roles. The dynamic of assimilation is open, deliberative discussion. The system within which assimilation occurs may be the individual, group, organization, community, nation, or world. The guidance of assimilation is through the purposes and rules of a social order oriented to inquiry. The nature of assimilation is the emergent awareness of conflict, the purposive examination of individual perceptions, the planning of investigative action, the study of reactions and consequences of action, and so on. These processes go on within every system and among all systems.

The job of education as the maintainer of society and the developer of individuals is to discover values and experiences that need to be assimilated from all parts of community life, and to seek, create, and intervene in the processes of interdependence among all the people in the community. The process of discovery is not something apart from the processes of intervention. Education is an aspect of life, and in the largest sense, every man with a purpose is to some extent both a teacher and a student.

The highly organized society seeks to break life down into functions which can be delegated to specially trained or competent people. In this process it loses its control over the functions, and that part of each function which is everybody's business falls by the wayside. Society or the community cannot properly get out from under its responsibility for each function; it can, however, within the framework of broad purposes established by the whole community, delegate most of the responsibility for instrumentation. What we have done in most areas of living is to delegate the instrumental functions and ignore our purpose-formulating and broad policy-making responsibilities. Since each functional group must have boundaries within which to operate, it has had to take to itself the undelegated and unexercised communal responsibility and then to engage, through pressure tactics, in the effort to make its conceptions of policies and purposes stick.

It is thus that education has become equated to running schools. It is also thus that the objectives of education have tended in practice, at least, to be determined by the pressures of legislative, professional, and academic groups rather than by communal conception of purpose.

It seems very clear to me that the unshackling of education is closely intertwined with the reconstruction of a way of life in which each community seeks to establish and reinterpret broad and enduring purposes as it tries, in all its functional systems, to live in accordance with its purposes. Education is simply the name for that part or aspect of all community life which is responsive to the demands of human nature, social interdependence, and societal goals; which seeks to relate these meaningfully to a sense of larger purpose and thus find significance in the great adventure of Man on Earth.

Index

Ability grouping, 132
   See Grouping, Teachable classes
Abrahamson, Julia, 180, 209
Academic festivals, 205-206
Acting out, 22-23; in conversation, 138-139; vs inquiry in group, 126-129
Action
   conditions and potentials, 197-198; educative, 83-85, 174-175; in school, example, 162-166; participants needed for, 195; skeleton framework for, 200-201; spirit of, 208-209; strategies in systems, 195-198; targets for, in school, 169-171
Activities, teacher training, 150-157; vs. inquiry, 144
Administrator, pressures from community, 58-60
Adolescents, commercial exploitation of, 66; needs, 65
Adult and youth cooperation, 177-179; joint council, 207
Anderson, Harold A., 28
Animal nature, 22-23
Assessment of schools, questions for, 191-193
Attention, in inquiry, 19, 51
Autonomous person, image of, 89-90
Autonomy, development, 27; seeking, 75

Behavior, natural, 18-25
Bettelheim, Bruno, 132, 137
Biological domain, 39-43
Bion, W.R., 28
Black box, 42

Campbell, Roald, 2
Cause and effect, behavior, 42
Change, of group members, 136; in physical world, 36; resistance to, 45; social, 189; social systems, 57
Character, from experience, 26
Chase, Francis S., 2, 27-28
Citizen action, example, 176-177; principles for, 168-169; resource file, 207
Classroom as social science laboratory, 47
Commitment, in four countries, 125-126
Community, contributions to education, 10; Educational Council, 196, 197, 201-203, 205, 206; educational impact, 54-55; educative, 160-162; mores, 117; reinforcement of education, 205-207; relations with schools, Chapter 11; values, 68-71; youth participation in, 177-179
Communications network, community, 200-201; school, 167-168
Composition of group, experiments on, 126-131; effect on inquiry, 145
Conflict, animal vs. social, 74; avoidance, 215-216; dramatic nature of, 22; group anarchy, 64; in inquiry groups, 150; psyche vs. social group, 115-121; social, 59-60
Cornog, William H., 27
Creativity, in problem formulation, 26; vs. fight in groups, 129-130
Culture, adolescent, 67; agreements in, 44; discipline, 147-148; educative development, 80; factors in deci-

sions, 125-126; limitations by, 33; traditional, 44

DeHaan, Robert, 78, 88
Democracy, pseudo, in schools, 68
Deprived children, 78
Deviates, biological, 41
Dewey, John, 34, 187
Diagnosis, 107; in groups, 150-157
Diagnostic conference, 117-119
Discipline, biological domain, 43; chemistry, 148; in group investigation, 147-148; humanities, 50; knowledge domains, 35; physical science, 36-39; social domain, 46-48; stress, 23
Domains of knowledge, 35-51
Drill, skills, 184-187
Dunkel, Harold, 2, 187
Dynamics, action, 172-174; group, 114-121; survival, 215-216

Education, aspect of life, 218-219; failure of, 25-27; in re. social change, 9-10; shackled, 212-213; approaches to understanding, 17
Educational issues, 10-12
Educational systems, manageable, 193-194; thinking about, 12-14
Educative action, 172-175; legitimacy of, 177; dynamic in group, 145-148; learning from, 136
Eggan, Fred, 44
Eight Year Study, 7
Emergent awareness, 52
Emotionality in groups, 126-131
Equality of opportunity, 11
Expectations, in social systems, 56-57
Experience, dramatic, 22; personal meaning, 49-50; reflection on, 35
Experimentation, school improvement, 7, 62

Factors, psyche-needs, 122-124
Failure, crucial, of education, 25-27
Family, place of adolescent in, 66
Faust, Clarence H., 27
Financial improvement, schools, 196-197
Force, social, 58-61
Friends vs. non-friends, 129-131

Getzels, Jacob, 2, 45, 53, 73, 87, 149, 190, 209
Gifted students, six case studies, 91-95
Gilchrist, Robert S., 27
Goals, community, 191, 196-197; for education, 11
Goldblatt, Irene, 73
Goodlad, John, 2
Gowin, Robert, 2
Gradolph, Ida and Phil, 128, 137
Group, as action instrument, 82-84; dynamics of, Chapter 7; emergent culture, 14; growth, 155; Investigation, Chapter 8; administration of, 157-159; case illustration, 148-152; dynamics of, 82; overview of, 79-80; rationale for, 145-148
Grouping, bases for, 132-133; faculty participation in, 204-205; theoretical criteria for, 133-134
Group work, hazard, 156
Growth, models and norms, 41

Havighurst, Robert, 78, 88
Hess, Robert, 66, 73
Human beings, natural processes, 21; nature of, 74; Quest of, 216-219; tendencies of, 13
Humanities, 48-50
Hyde Park-Kenwood Citizen Action, 2, 176

Ideas, six aspects, 32-33
Identifications, in skill learning, 182; of adolescents, 66
Imitation, skill learning, 182
Improvement of schools, four approaches, 6-8; *see also* School improvement
Individual differences, 40; *See* Factors
Inquiry, 21-22, 75; common to four models, 85; creative element, 26; development in schools, 202-203; educative, 24-25, 139; examples in schools, 140-145; in conversations, 138-139; incorporation in human nature, 216-219; joint, school and community, Chapter 11; spirit of, in action, 208-209; steps, 51-53; types in groups, 154-155
Inservice training, teachers, 202-205

Interdependence, of changes, 189-190; in society, 43-44, 75
Interests, common vs. vested, 196
Interpretation, of knowledge, 49-50
Issues in Education, 10-12; community role, 10; equal opportunity, 11; goal conflict, 11; nature of knowledge, 11

Jennings, Helen Hall, 116, 120, 137

Knowledge, 50-51; absolute vs. provisional, 11; Domains and disciplines, 35-51; how viewed in schools, 29-30; nature and educational implications of, Chapter 3; seeking, by organism, 41; social domain, 43-48; subjective domain, 28, 48-50

LaBarre, Weston, 22, 28, 42, 53
Laboratory, community as a, 203-204; method in social studies, 48; Skill Development, 184-187
Latta, Howard A., 27
Learning, not "needed", 113-114; psyche factors in, 122-124; skills, case examples, 184-187; teacher preparation, 202-205; types of, 136
Lewin, Kurt, 73
Lippitt, Ronald, 2
Lockstep, 25
Lund, Kenneth W., 27

Maintenance, as social goal, 214
Manners, 181-182
Mass meetings, 206
Meaning, reorganization of thoughts, 31; values invested in, 20
Michael, Lloyd S., 27
Miles, Mathew B., 180
Milieu, educative, 160-162
Models for education, overview, four types, 77-85
Morin, Alexander, 2
Mother-child relationship, 19-20

National Training Laboratories, 180
New York Activity Study, 8
Nylen, Donald, 2

Objectives, educational, biological domain, 43; humanities or subjective domain, 50; physical science, 38; social science, 47-48
Obstacles, to school improvement, 8
Oeser, Oscar, 2
Organism, biological, 40-41
Organization, changes, questions, 191-193; for personal inquiry, 109-112; invention of, 213-215; human, 22, 70
Ossification, institutional, 6

Parsons, Talcott, 73
Part-whole relations, biology, 40
Personal inquiry, Chapter 6; five conditions for success, 106-109; six episodes, 96-105; overview, 77
Physical domain, 36-39
Physiology, 39-40
Predictability, 37
Prejudice, learning of, 55
Problem-solving, reasonableness, 26
Progressivism, post War I, 9
Psyche group, 116-121; needs, 121-125
Public relations, 61-64; cooperation in, 196-198
Purposes, social and educational, 213-216

Quasi-stationary equilibrium, 58

Rapaport, Anatol, 198, 209
Rationality, vs. intelligence, 24
Readiness, for un-needed learning, 114
Reflection, conditions for, 156-157; need for, 52-53; on experience, 35
Reflective Action, Chapter 9; overview, 82-85
Regional school, advantages, 193-194
Rehage, Kenneth J., 149
Remedial students, 187
Riesman, David, 44, 53, 73
Robinson, Helen, 187
Roles, development of, 76; need for, 66-68
Rudolph, 4-5

Sarchet, Bettie, 197, 209
School, and community improvement, 197-198; as educative milieu, 160-161; child society in, 67-68; -community cooperation, Chapter 11;

-community relations, 13, 54-62, 71-73; educative, character, 29; improvement of, superintendent in, 199-200; obsolescence, 1; part of all social systems, 56-57; societal characteristics, 190-191
Science, misunderstanding of, 217
Self-acceptance, 43; -direction, 91-95; esteem, 65; regulation, 41
Shils, Edward, 73
Skeleton action organization, 200-201
Skills, arbitrary nature of, 182-184; development of, 86, Chapter 10
Social action, genesis, 165-166; principles, 168-169
Social domain, 43-47
Social order, development, 14; necessity, 44; referent of inquiry, 52
Social science, perspective on schools, 190-191; summary of, 45-46
Society, and Education, Chapter 4; cold war squeeze, 211-213; development of, 43-44; meaning for education, 13
Socio group, 116-121
Sophomore Project, 2, 90-95, 134-136, 167
Speech practice, 184-185
Spelling, drill, 185
Spindler, G.D., 73
Sputnik, 60
Steering committee, faculty, 203
Stock, Dorothy, 28
Strategy, action power vs. cooperation, 196
Stress, dealing with, 22-24
Student, learning conditions for, 134-136; government, 167
Subjective domain, 48-50
Superintendent, action role, 199-200
Survival and inquiry, 158-159
Systems, educational, 13, 193-197

Talented children, 78
Task, in socio group, 118
Teachable groups, 81-82, 131-137, 157; how to form, 204-205
Teacher, cultural guidance by, 81; jobs for, 207; of skills, 187; task of, 136
Teaching-Learning process, factors in, 134-136
Teacher training, model for, 148-157
Technology, self-justifying, 9, Epilogue
Testing, by educators, 42
Theory, School Burning, 4
Thelen, H.A., 28, 53, 137, 180, 209
Tinkering in schools, 7
Tolman, Edward, 34
Tyler, Ralph W., 27

Understanding, resistance to, 33
University of Chicago, 2, 121, 148
U.S. Office of Education, 2, 8, 121, 209

Values, change in, 68-71
Vital principle, yielding, 39
Vocabulary drill, 185-186

White, Leonard D., 28
Whorf, Benjamin Lee, 32
Whyte, William H., Jr., 73
Work experience, see Personal Inquiry; community participation in, 203-204; vs. emotionality in group, 126-129

Youth, action targets for, 177-179; adult efforts with, 207; classes with citizens, 206; place in community, 14, 64-68, 180; seeking roles, 76-77

Set in Times Roman
Format by Anne Hertz
Manufactured by The Haddon Craftsmen, Inc.
Published by HARPER & BROTHERS, *New York*